DATE DUE

SCHOLARSHIP IN WOMEN'S HISTORY: REDISCOVERED AND NEW

Editor

GERDA LERNER

A CARLSON PUBLISHING SERIES

For a complete listing of the titles in this series,
please see the back of this book.

The British and American Women's Trade Union Leagues, 1890-1925

A CASE STUDY OF FEMINISM AND CLASS

Robin Miller Jacoby

CARLSON
Publishing Inc

BROOKLYN, NEW YORK, 1994

Please see the end of this volume for a listing of all the titles in the Carlson Publishing Series *Scholarship in Women's History: Rediscovered and New*, edited by Gerda Lerner, of which this is Volume 7.

Library of Congress Cataloging-in-Publication Data

Jacoby, Robin Miller
     The British and American women's trade union leagues, 1890-1925 /
  by Robin Miller Jacoby
       p.   cm. — (Scholarship in women's history ; 7)
     Includes bibliographical references and index.
     ISBN 0-926019-68-6
     1. Women's Trade Union League (Great Britain)—History. 2. Women's
  Trade Union League of America—History. 3. National Women's Trade
  Union League of America—History. 4. Women in trade-unions—Great
  Britain—History. 5. Women in trade-unions—United States—History.
  6. Feminism—Great Britain—History. 7. Feminism—United States—History.
  8. Social classes—Great Britain—History. 9. Social classes—United
  States—History. I. Title. II. Series.
   HD6079.2.G7J33   1994
   331.4'78'0941—dc20   94-19126

Typographic design: Julian Waters

Typeface: Bitstream ITC Galliard

Jacket and Case design: Alison Lew

Index prepared by Scholars Editorial Services, Inc., Madison, Wisconsin.

Printed on acid-free, 250-year-life paper.

Manufactured in the United States of America.

Contents

For my parents, Robert and Gertrude Miller, with gratitude and respect.
For my children, Peter and Leah Jacoby, with love and hope for the future.

Editor's Introduction
to the Series

An important aspect of the development of modern scholarship in Women's History has been the recovery of lost, forgotten or neglected sources. In the 1960s, when the practitioners of Women's History were so few as to be virtually invisible to the general profession, one of the commonly heard answers to the question, why is there nothing about women in your text? was that, unfortunately, women until the most recent past, had to be counted among the illiterate and had therefore not left many sources. It was common then to refer to women as among the "anonymous"—a group that included members of minority racial and ethnic groups of both sexes, most working-class people, colonials, Native Americans and women. In short, most of the populations of the past. These ignorant and erroneous answers satisfied only those who wished to stifle discussion, but they did make the issue of "sources" an urgent concern to practitioners of Women's History.

To historians who had done work in primary sources regarding women, it was obvious that the alleged dearth of sources did not exist, but it was true that the sources were not readily available. In archives and finding guides, women disappeared under the names of male family members. The voluminous records of their organizational work were disorganized, uncatalogued, and not infrequently rotting in file boxes in basement storage rooms. Since few if any researchers were interested in them, there seemed to be little purpose in making them accessible or even maintaining them. There were no archival projects to preserve the primary sources of American women comparable to the well-supported archival projects concerning Presidents and male political leaders. There were only a few and quite partial bibliographies of American women, while the encyclopedic reference works, such as the *DAB* (*Dictionary of American Biography*) or similar sources traditionally neglected to include all but a small number of women notables.

When the three-volume *Notable American Women: 1607—1950: A Biographical Dictionary* appeared in 1971, (to be followed by a fourth volume in 1980), it marked an important contribution to sources on women.[1] This comprehensive scholarly work consisted of 1,801 entries, with a biographical essay and a bibliography of works by and about each woman under discussion. It readily became obvious to even the casual user of these volumes how few modern biographies of these notable women existed, despite the availability of sources.

The real breakthrough regarding "sources" was made by a "grand manuscript search," begun in 1971, which aimed to survey historical archives in every state and identify their holdings pertaining to women. This project was started by a small committee—Clarke Chambers, Carl Degler, Janet James, Anne Firor Scott and myself. After a mail questionnaire survey of 11,000 repositories in every state, to which more than 7,000 repositories responded, it was clear that the sources on women were far wider and deeper than anyone had suspected. Ultimately, the survey resulted in a two-volume reference tool, Andrea Hinding, ed., *Women's History Sources: A Guide to Archives and Manuscript Collections in the United States*.[2]

The project proved that there were unused and neglected sources of Women's History to be found literally in every archive in the country. Participation in the survey convinced many archivists to reorganize and reclassify their holdings, so that materials about women could be more readily identified.

The arguments about "illiterate women" and absence of sources are no longer heard, but the problem of having accessible sources for Women's History continued. Even after archives and libraries reorganized and reclassified their source holding on the subject, most of the pertinent materials were not available in print. Many of the early developers of Women's History worked on source collections, reprint edition projects and, of course, bibliographies. The rapid and quite spectacular expansion of the field brought with it such great demand for sources that publishers at last responded. The past twenty years have seen a virtual flood of publications in Women's History, so that the previous dearth of material seems almost inconceivable to today's students.

For myself, having put a good many years of my professional life into the development of "source books" and bibliographies, it did not seem particularly urgent to continue the effort under the present conditions. But I was awakened to the fact that there might still be a problem of neglected and forgotten sources in Women's History as a result of a conference, which Kathryn Sklar and I organized in 1988. The Wingspread Conference "Graduate Training in U.S. Women's History" brought together 63 representatives of 57 institutions of higher education who each represented a graduate program in Women's History. As part of our preparation for the conference, we asked each person invited to list all the dissertations in Women's History she had directed or was then directing. The result was staggering: it appeared that there were 99 completed dissertations and 236 then underway. This was by no means the entire national output, since we surveyed only the 63 participants at the conference and did not survey the many faculty persons not represented, who had directed such dissertations. The questions arose—What happened to all these dissertations? Why did so many of them not get published?

When Ralph Carlson approached me at about that time with the idea of publishing "lost sources" in Women's History, I was more ready than I would have been without benefit of the Wingspread survey to believe that, indeed, there still were some such neglected sources out there, and to undertake such a project.

We used the dissertation list from the Wingspread Conference as a starting point. A researcher then went through all the reference works listing dissertations in history and other fields in the English language from 1870 to the present. Among these she identified 1,235 titles in what we now call Women's History. We then cross-checked these titles against the electronic catalog of the Library of Congress, which represents every book owned by the LC (or to define it differently, every book copyrighted and published in the U.S.). This cross-check revealed that of the 1,235 dissertations, 314 had been published, which is more than 25 percent. That represents an unusually high publication ratio, which may be a reflection of the growth and quality of the field.

A further selection based on abstracts of the 921 unpublished dissertations narrowed the field to 101. Of these we could not locate 33 authors or the authors were not interested in publication. Out of the 68 remaining dissertations we selected the eleven we considered best in both scholarship and writing. These are first-rate books that should have been published earlier and that for one reason or another fell between the cracks.

Why did they not get published earlier? In the case of the Boatwright manuscript, an unusually brilliant Master's thesis done in 1939, undoubtedly the neglect of Women's History at that time made the topic seem unsuitable for publication. Similar considerations may have worked against publication of several other earlier dissertations. In other cases, lack of mentorship and inexperience discouraged the writers from pursuing publication in the face of one or two rejections of their manuscripts. Several of the most valuable books in the series required considerable rewriting under editorial supervision, which, apparently, had not earlier been available to the authors. There are also several authors who became members of what we call "the lost generation," historians getting their degrees in the 1980s when there were few jobs available. This group of historians, which disproportionately consisted of women, retooled and went into different fields. Three of the books in this series are the work of these historians, who needed considerable persuasion to do the necessary revisions and editing. We are pleased to have found their works and to have persisted in the effort of making them available to a wider readership, since they have a distinct contribution to make.

The books in this series cover a wide range of topics. Two of them are detailed studies in the status of women, one in Georgia, 1783-1860, the other in Russia in the early 1900s. Two are valuable additions to the literature on the anti-woman's suffrage campaigns in the U.S. Of the four books dealing with the history of women's organizations, three are detailed regional studies and one is a comparative history of the British and American Women's Trade Union League. Finally, the three biographical studies of eighteenth- and nineteenth-century women offer either new information or new interpretations of their subjects.

Eleanor Miot Boatwright, *Status of Women in Georgia, 1783—1860*, was discovered by Professor Anne Firor Scott in the Duke University archives and represents, in her words "a buried treasure." An M.A. thesis written by a high school teacher in Augusta, Georgia, its level of scholarship and the depth of its research are of the quality expected of a dissertation. The author has drawn on a vast range of primary sources, including legal sources that were then commonly used for social history, to document and analyze the social customs, class differences, work and religion of white women in Georgia. While her treatment of race relations reflects the limitations of scholarship on that subject in the 1930s, she gives careful attention to the impact of race relations on white women. Her analysis of the linkage made by Southern male apologists for slavery between the subordination ("protection") of women and the subordination of slaves (also rationalized as their "protection") is particularly insightful. The work has much information to offer the contemporary scholar and can be compared in its scholarship and its general approach to the work of Julia Spruill and Elizabeth Massey. When it is evaluated in comparison with other social histories of its period, its research methodology and interpretative focus on women are truly remarkable.

Anne Bobroff-Hajal's, *Working Women in Russia Under the Hunger Tsar: Political Activism and Daily Life*, is a fascinating, excellently researched study of a topic on which there is virtually no material available in the English language. Focusing on women industrial workers in Russia's Central Industrial Region, most of them employed in textile production, Bobroff studied their daily lives and family patterns, their gender socialization, their working and living conditions and their political activism during the Revolution: in political organizations, in food riots and in street fighting. The fact that these women and their families lived mostly in factory barracks will be of added interest to labor historians, who may wish to compare their lives and activities with other similarly situated groups in the U.S. and England. Drawing on a rich mixture of folkloric sources, local newspapers, oral histories, workers' memoirs and ethnographic material, Bobroff presents a convincing and intimate picture of working-class life before the Russian Revolution. Bobroff finds that the particularly strong mother-child bonding of Russian women workers, to which they were indoctrinated from childhood on, undermined their ability to form coherent political groups capable of maintaining their identity over a long period of time. Her thesis, excellently supported and well argued, may undermine some commonly held beliefs on this subject. It should prove of interest to all scholars working on gender socialization and to others working on labor culture, working-class activism, and class consciousness.

Rosemary Keller, *Patriotism and the Female Sex: Abigail Adams and the American Revolution*, is a sophisticated, well-documented interpretation of Abigail Adams's intellectual and political development, set firmly within the historical context. Compared with other Abigail Adams biographies, this work is outstanding in treating her seriously as an agent in history and as an independent intellectual. Abigail Adams emerges from this study as a woman going as far as it was possible to go within the limits of the gender conventions of her time and struggling valiantly, through influencing her husband, to extend these gender conventions. This is an accomplishment quite sufficient for one woman's life time. Professor Keller's sensitive biography makes a real contribution to colonial and women's history.

Elizabeth Ann Bartlett, *Liberty, Equality, Sorority: The Origins and Integrity of Feminist Thought: Frances Wright, Sarah Grimké and Margaret Fuller*, is another work of intellectual history. It attempts to define a common "feminism" emerging from the thought of these important nineteenth-century thinkers and concludes that feminism, in order to sustain itself, must balance the tensions between the concepts of liberty, equality, and sorority. The lucid, well-researched discussions of each woman's life and work should appeal to the general reader and make this book a valuable addition to courses in intellectual history and women's history and literature.

Mary Grant, *Private Woman, Public Person: An Account of the Life of Julia Ward Howe from 1819 to 1868*, is a sensitive, feminist study of Howe's life and thought up to the turning point in 1868, when she decided to dedicate her life to public activism in behalf of women. By carefully analyzing Howe's private letters and journals, the author uncovers a freer, more powerful and creative writer beneath the formal *persona* of the author of "The Battle Hymn of the Republic" than we have hitherto known. She also discusses in detail Howe's fascinating, never published, unfinished novel, "Eva and Raphael," which features a number of then taboo subjects, such as rape, madness and an androgynous character. This well-written biography reveals new aspects and dimensions of Julia Ward Howe's life and work.

Jane Jerome Camhi, *Women Against Women: American Anti-Suffragism, 1880-1920*, and Thomas J. Jablonsky, *The Home, Heaven, and Mother Party: Female Anti-Suffragists in America, 1868-1920*, are complementary studies that should be indispensable for any serious student or scholar of woman suffrage. They are, in fact, the only extant book-length studies of anti-suffragism. This important movement has until now been accessible to modern readers only through the somewhat biased lens of contemporary suffragists' observations. They consistently underestimated its scope and significance and did not engage with its basic paradox, that it was a movement by women against women.

Jane Camhi's comprehensive study of nationwide anti-woman's suffrage movements makes this paradox a central theme. Camhi analyses the "antis'" ideas and ideology and offers some thought-provoking theories about the competing and contradictory positions women took in regard to formal political power. Her insightful profile of a noted anti-suffragist, Ida Tarbell, is an additional contribution this fine book makes to the historical literature.

Thomas Jablonsky's study is focused more narrowly on the organizational history of the rise and fall of the movement. The book is based on extensive research in the organizational records of the anti-suffragists on a state and national level, the records of Congressional hearings, biographical works and the manuscripts of leaders. Jablonsky takes the "antis" seriously and disproves the suffragists' argument that they were merely pawns of male interest groups. He offers a sympathetic, but critical evaluation of their ideas. His detailed attention to organizational efforts in states other than the major battle-grounds—Massachusetts, New York and Illinois—make this book a valuable resource for scholars in history, political science and Women's History.

The four remaining books in the series all focus on aspects of women's organizational activities. Taken together, they reveal the amazing energy, creativity, and persistence of women's institution building on the community and local level. They sustain and highlight the thesis that women built the infrastructures of community life, while men held the positions of visible power. Based on research in four distinctly different regions, these studies should prove useful not only for the intrinsic worth of each, but for comparative purposes.

Darlene Roth, *Matronage: Patterns in Women's Organizations, Atlanta, Georgia, 1890-1940*, is a thoroughly researched, gracefully written study of the networks of women's organizations in that city. The author's focus on conservative women's organizations, such as the Daughters of the American Revolution, the Colonial Dames, and the African-American Chatauqua Circle, adds to the significance of the book. The author defines "matronage" as the functions and institutionalization of the networks of social association among women. By focusing on a Southern city in the Progressive era, Roth provides rich comparative material for the study of women's voluntarism. She challenges notions of the lack of organizational involvement by Southern women. She traces the development of women's activities from communal service orientation—the building of war memorials—to advocacy of the claims of women and children and, finally, to advocacy of women's rights. Her comparative approach, based on the study of the records of white and African-American women's organizations and leadership—she studied 508 white and 150 black women—is illuminating and offers new insights. The book should be of interest to readers in Urban and Community History, Southern History, and Women's History.

Robin Miller Jacoby, *The British and American Women's Trade Union Leagues, 1890-1925: A Case Study of Feminism and Class*, is a comparative study of working-class women in Britain and America in the Progressive period. Although parts of this work have appeared as articles in scholarly journals, the work has never before been accessible in its entirety. Jacoby traces the development of Women's Trade Union Leagues in Britain and America, exploring their different trajectories and settings. By focusing on the interaction of women's and labor movements, the author provides rich empirical material. Her analysis of the tensions and overlapping interests of feminism and class consciousness is important to feminist theory. Her discussion of protective labor legislation, as it was debated and acted upon in two different contexts, makes an important contribution to the existing literature. It also addressees issues still topical and hotly debated in the present day. The book will be of interest to labor historians, Women's History specialists, and the general public.

Janice Steinschneider, *An Improved Woman: The Wisconsin Federation of Women's Clubs, 1895-1920*, is a richly documented study based on a multitude of primary sources, which reveals the amazing range of women's activities as community builders and agents of change. Wisconsin clubwomen founded libraries, fostered changes in school curricula and worked to start kindergartens and playgrounds. They helped preserve historic and natural landmarks and organized to improve public health services. They built a sound political base—long before they had the right of suffrage—from which they trained women leaders for whom they then helped to secure public appointments. They worked to gain access for women to university education and employment and, in addition to many other good causes, they worked for world peace. Steinschneider's description and analysis of "women's public sphere" is highly sophisticated. Hers is one of the best studies on the subject and should prove indispensable to all concerned with understanding women's political activities, their construction of a public sphere for women, and their efforts and successes as builders of large coalitions.

Margit Misangyi Watts, *High Tea at Halekulani: Feminist Theory and American Clubwomen*, is a more narrowly focused study of clubwomen's work than are the other three, yet its significance ranges far above that of its subject matter. Watts tells the story of the Outdoor Circle, an upper-class white women's club in Hawaii, from its founding in 1911 on. Its main activities were to make Hawaii beautiful: to plant trees, clean up eyesores, preserve nature and rid the islands of billboards. To achieve these modest goals, the women had to become consummate politicians and lobbyists and learn how to run grassroots boycotts and publicity and educational campaigns, and how to form long-lasting coalitions. Above all, as Watts's fine theoretical analysis shows, they insisted that their female vision, their woman-centered view, become an accepted part of the public discourse. This case study is rich in theoretical implications. Together with the other three studies of women's club activities it offers not only a wealth of practical examples of women's work for social change, but it also shows that such work both resists patriarchal views and practices and redefines them in the interests of women.

Gerda Lerner
Madison, Wisconsin

Acknowledgments

Work on this book was fundamentally completed many years ago when I was a young faculty member at the University of Michigan, and I remain deeply grateful for the support, encouragement, and patience extended to me during those years by my students, colleagues, friends, and family.

My special thanks to Miriam Cohen, Margaret Lourie, and Marilyn Young for reading several chapters of the manuscript in draft form and for their unfailing willingness and ability to offer criticism and encouragement at just the right times and in just the right words.

Conversations with David Bien, Peggy Bien, Henry Binford, Shirley Blum, Maurine Greenwald, Daphne Grew, Leonard Radinsky, Elinor Rosenberg, William Rosenberg, and John Shy contributed far more than they may know to the completion of the initial version of this work.

This book began as a doctoral dissertation at Harvard University, and David Landes, my advisor, provided important encouragement at the inception of the study. I was grateful for the faith he consistently showed in me, and I especially appreciated his support and cooperation at critical moments in the last stages of the project.

My deepest debt of gratitude is to my friend and former colleague, Raymond Grew. He gave unstintingly of his time, insights, and acute critical judgment. The conversations with him made working on this manuscript an especially stimulating and rewarding experience.

My husband, Jonathan Jacoby, played an essential role in this project; his sense of humor and unwavering faith in me were crucial contributions. His extraordinary willingness to make adjustments in his own life to give me the space necessary to teach and to write during those early years of my career and our marriage was a reflection of his deep commitment to feminist ideals.

Much has changed in my life, in the scholarly world of women's history, and in the social, economic, and political worlds of women's work and status since this study was originally undertaken. Nonetheless, the issues it addresses are still interesting, important, and relevant—historically and currently. I am grateful to Gerda Lerner, an historian whose work and values I have long admired, for selecting this manuscript for publication, and I am honored to have my work included in this series.

Cambridge, Massachusetts
June 1994

Introduction

Questions about how concepts of feminism intersect with the ideology and actuality of class differences provided the impetus for this comparative study of the British and American Women's Trade Union Leagues in the period from 1890 to 1925.[1] The leagues were autonomous, but related, reform organizations composed of women from the upper classes, as well as the working class, who were drawn together out of a common concern for the problems of women in the industrial labor force. Both leagues were founded by coalitions of trade unionists and social reformers, and they pursued similar sets of goals, although with varying degrees of emphasis and success. They attempted to improve the position of women workers by organizing them into trade unions; lobbying for legislation controlling hours, wages, and working conditions; and educating women workers, trade union men, and middle-class women regarding the special problems of women workers and the value of organization and legislation on their behalf.

As mixed-class women's labor organizations, flanked in each country by a male-dominated labor movement and a middle-class-dominated feminist movement, the leagues contained in their very structure the contradictions inherent in the concepts of class and female solidarity. Although neither league concerned itself with extensive theoretical discussions of the relationship between feminism and class, their dual identity as women's labor organizations meant that these issues were intrinsically involved in the functioning of both organizations. Thus, a comparative history of the British and American Women's Trade Union Leagues provides a case study of the response of two groups of women who confronted this problem in the early twentieth century. By comparing these two organizations from societies that were similar in many respects but were also marked by clear social and political differences, the factors of class and sex can be more clearly discerned.

The leagues are gradually gaining recognition for their pioneering efforts to improve the work life of women in the industrial labor force.[2] Although the American WTUL is discussed in several works, these accounts are either not based on extensive use of primary sources or they deal with only limited periods or aspects of the WTUL's history.[3] In addition, none of these studies deals in a sustained way with the implications of the WTUL's role as a woman's labor organization.[4] The British WTUL has never been the subject of a thorough investigation. The only analysis is a cursory but nonetheless astute discussion by William O'Neill in an introductory section of his documentary anthology, *The Woman Movement: Feminism in the United States and England*. These pages in O'Neill and the one chapter on the British WTUL in Gladys Boone's, *The Women's Trade Union Leagues of Great Britain and the United States of America* represent the only attempts to approach the two leagues in a comparative perspective.

This study analyzes and compares the history of the British WTUL and the American at the national level and uses the issues of feminism and class as a central analytic framework. More broadly, it examines the relationship among three intersecting comparative topics: the different but interrelated experiences of men and women in the industrial labor force of each country; the orientation of the British and American labor movements; and the composition and concerns of the feminist movement in each country. Ultimately it is the similarities and differences in these aspects of British and American history that account for many of the similarities and differences in the histories of the two leagues. Although these aspects of British and American history are discussed only as they relate to the histories of the Women's Trade Union Leagues, this comparative history of the leagues extends our understanding of these broader areas of British and American social history.

Although the framework of feminism and class could be used to study either league in isolation, a comparative approach illuminates certain aspects of the history of the leagues and of British and American society in this period that might not otherwise stand out so clearly. By examining the leagues' organizing policies, their relationship with their respective labor movements, their stance as feminist organizations, and their political roles, certain fundamental similarities emerge concerning the problems of women and, more specifically, the position of women workers in industrial societies in the late nineteenth and early twentieth centuries. In the context of these similarities, the comparison highlights basic differences in the social history and political systems of the two countries and at the same time identifies the ways these differences affected the history of the Women's Trade Union Leagues.

This study of the leagues is organized topically, although the first chapter establishes the social and theoretical background against which the leagues developed and the last chapter discusses the International Federation of Working Women, an organization formed under the impetus of the leagues in 1919. Chapters Two through Five examine the three major areas of WTUL activity: organizing women workers into trade unions; educating middle- and working-class men and women regarding the position of women workers; and lobbying for legislation to improve the situation of women workers.

Since the primary goal of both leagues was to organize women, this aspect of their work is discussed first, with greater attention paid to their approach to the unionization of women than to general organizational history. The British were considerably more successful than the Americans in increasing female membership in trade unions during the period under consideration, but both groups realized that unionizing women workers was highly problematic and not to be accomplished easily or quickly. To facilitate the unionization of women and the raising of their status within the labor movement, the leagues, especially the American one, turned to educational activities to supplement their organizing efforts; these activities are discussed in Chapter Three. However, even these two avenues of approach proved insufficient for solving the problems of women workers; progress in both areas was very slow, and the mass of women workers in each country remained untouched by the leagues' efforts. Thus, the leagues put considerable energy into lobbying for labor legislation, which they viewed as a third and complementary approach to achieving improved conditions for women workers. It was in this area that the differences in the two countries' social and political structures had the greatest effect on the leagues, and for this reason, their legislative efforts are treated in separate chapters. Although these various approaches are discussed sequentially, it is important to keep in mind that they occurred more or less simultaneously.

As a culmination of their domestic efforts, the leagues were moved to establish an international organization concerned with unionization, education, and legislation. The International Federation of Working Women, which is the subject of Chapter Six, lasted only a few years, dissolving over conflicts between the British and the Americans concerning the issues of feminism and class. This discussion of the IFWW extends and highlights the comparative history of the British and American Women's Trade Union Leagues and serves as a concluding comment on their achievements and failures.

The British and American
Women's Trade Union
Leagues, 1890-1925

ONE

The Problems of Women and Workers: Social and Theoretical Background

Two fundamental similarities between Britain and the United States shaped the social context in which the Women's Trade Union Leagues developed. By the late nineteenth century both countries were significantly industrialized and had come to accept a common ideology as to the social roles appropriate for women. However, within this context several important differences affected the histories of the leagues.

One critical difference was the broader orientation of the British labor movement. Influenced by advocates of "the new unionism," Britain began to incorporate unskilled workers into trade unions in the 1890s, whereas comparable concern for the unskilled and commitment to organizing along industrial rather than craft lines did not develop as a powerful force within the American labor movement until the 1930s. Since most women workers were unskilled, the greater receptivity of the British labor movement was a significant factor in the operation of the British WTUL. A further problem facing the American WTUL was the heterogeneity of the American labor force. Language barriers and ethnic differences impeded the development of feelings of solidarity among women workers, and employers often consciously exploited these differences to keep their work force divided. These differences accounted in large part for the considerably greater success of the British in increasing the number of women in trade unions, even though women workers were clustered in the same sectors of the labor force in both countries.[1]

Feminist movements attacking the legal restrictions on and the limited economic, political, and educational opportunities available to women had developed in both countries in the mid-nineteenth century. By the 1890s the struggle to obtain voting rights for women had become dominant in both the British and American feminist movements. However, limited suffrage (based on property qualifications) still existed in Britain, and the British women's suffrage movement was asking that suffrage be extended to women who met the property qualifications required of men. Thus, although working-class women had something to gain by establishing the principle of women's suffrage, they would not necessarily obtain the right to vote so long as property qualifications remained. Since universal suffrage for men already existed in the United States, all women there would gain the right to vote once women's suffrage was granted. This difference contributed to the closer identification of the American than the British WTUL with the suffrage movement.

Although often overlooked because of its very obviousness, the vast difference in physical size (and population) between Britain and the United States also had a notable effect on the development of both leagues. The British WTUL was able to operate out of a central London office, whereas the American WTUL had a national headquarters (in Chicago) and branch offices in various cities.[2] Maintaining local leagues was crucial to the vitality and effectiveness of the American WTUL, but sustaining this network of offices and personnel was a drain on the finances and energies of leading activists.

This difference in the organizational structure of the two leagues produced an unanticipated methodological problem in carrying out this study. Primary sources on the American WTUL proved to be much richer in quantity and quality than those for the British: personal letters and organizational documents were significantly more detailed and complete. British activists, all based in London, could simply talk to one another in person or over the telephone. The Americans, because of physical distance, had to handle much of their communication by letter. This may have been more burdensome for them, but it was a boon to historians of the league.

The history of the Women's Trade Union Leagues must be seen in the broader context of the impact of industrialization on women. Although historical scholarship has begun to question and refine the widely accepted view that industrialization caused the separation of work from the home, the fact remains that industrialization did increasingly lead to the transfer from the home to the factory of many productive processes.[3] Among the processes that underwent this transformation were those related to food and clothing, areas of production that had traditionally fallen within the sphere of women's work. As a result, many working-class women simply moved their work from the home to the factory; many women of the upper classes, however, experienced the loss of an economically productive role.

Although the British labor force between 1890 and 1920 contained a much higher percentage of women than the American, women employed in the industrial sector in both countries were characteristically unskilled, clustered in the lowest paying jobs, and unorganized.[4] These conditions and prevailing attitudes as to the roles appropriate for women all interrelated, and they combined to produce a significantly different industrial experience for women than for men.

Organizing women workers into trade unions was a difficult and discouraging process because of the age of women workers, the length of their employment, the types of jobs they held, their wage scale, the structure of the labor movement, and the prevailing concept of femininity. The typical woman worker in both countries was a young (sixteen to twenty-six) single woman who expected to work for a few years prior to her marriage. Thus, women considered themselves and were regarded by male workers and employers as only temporary members of the labor force, and they were treated as a labor pool to fill an expanding industrial economy's needs for unskilled workers.

In most factories the different processes were rigidly defined as men's jobs or women's jobs; the men's jobs consistently called for more skill and commanded higher wages. For example, in the garment industry, cutting the cloth was invariably done by men, while the basic sewing of seams or finishing work, such as sewing buttons, was done by women.[5] Full-time male workers earned on the average twice as much as full-time female workers.

This disparity in wages was a major obstacle to the development of feelings of solidarity among male and female workers, especially when job processes were simplified so that unskilled women could be substituted for skilled men or when women were actually given the same jobs as men. An anonymous Chicago garment worker, who had begun working at the age of twelve to help support her family, wrote an account of her work experiences in 1911, which illustrates this problem. At the age of eighteen, after having worked in the same factory for three years, she was offered the position of assistant foreman. She happily accepted, since the promotion would raise her wages from an average of $7.00 per week to a guaranteed salary of $10.00. However, she was surprised to find that "suddenly all the men seemed to be getting ugly to me, and I didn't know why." She soon learned the reason for their behavior:

> The assistant foreman who was there before me was a man, and he got $22, and then you see they thought I knew just about as much, and they offered me the job and they only gave me $10, and I did not know I was working for less than the man; so all the other men hated me and tried to take it out on me.

The men quickly showed their resentment:

> One day the foreman wanted me to carry a bundle of 350 pairs of sleeves to another room. The bundle was on the floor, and I said it was too heavy for me to lift, and he told me to ask the men to carry it for me, saying that he would not do it. Then the men jeered at me, and said why did I want them to help me when I had taken their job for less; so I had to lift that bundle, and as I lifted it, it hurt me and I dropped it, and then the men jeered, and I was bound to carry it, and so I did, and I hurt myself and I have had to have the doctors look after me ever since, and that was over two years ago.

Because she was a woman, she was not only paid less, but the foreman treated her differently from a male assistant.

> . . . he made me do all his errands for him—running downstairs to buy his cigars or matches, or to get him a glass of water or anything else—and he said many things to me which no nice girl wants to hear, and no nice girl wants to run and buy cigars and things for a man.[6]

Her promotion, which provided money she desperately needed, had come at a high psychological and physical cost.

This woman's wages of approximately $7.00 per week before her promotion were somewhat higher than those of most American women workers, which tended to average closer to $6.00 a week.[7] In Britain women's wages in the early twentieth century averaged 7s. 6d. a week (about $1.80).[8] An indication of the difference unionization and the chance to work at a skilled job could make is revealed in the fact that in Lancashire, the one place where women were not denied access to skilled jobs and to union membership, it was not exceptional for women textile workers to earn 24s. a week.[9] Women's wages in both countries were low partly because of the unskilled nature of their jobs, but also because it was assumed that their earnings were a supplementary, rather than a primary, income for a family.

Since the labor movement in both countries was more interested in skilled workers, locals covering women's jobs often simply did not exist. Women were therefore forced to create an organization to encompass their job categories and then were faced with the task of convincing an existing union to extend its definition of the craft to include unskilled and semiskilled workers. This process involved going to meetings, often at night, and pushing forcefully for recognition from male workers and employers. Since such behavior was contrary to notions internalized by both men and women about proper behavior for women, it was difficult for women to initiate and sustain such activity.

Even when individual women workers were able to overcome this cultural conditioning, they often encountered resistance from their families. Rose Schneiderman, an early member of the American WTUL who became a well-known labor activist, mentioned her mother's opposition to her involvement in the labor movement, which began in 1903. "It was such an exciting time. A new life opened up for me. . . . The only cloud in the picture was Mother's attitude toward my becoming a trade unionist. She kept saying I'd never get married . . . a prophecy which came true." Her mother was also concerned about her daughter "being out of the house almost every evening."[10] Another woman worker wrote of her father's and boyfriend's opposition to her participation in union and strike activities. Both men were trade unionists, but her father spoke for both of them when he said, "I don't think it's a woman's place to be hangin' around street corners. . . . Union is all good and well by itself, but it was never meant for the women."[11]

A further obstacle to the organization of women workers was the lack of places where they could meet; union meetings were often held in pubs or social halls where women felt neither comfortable nor welcome. A major activity of both the British and American Women's Trade Union Leagues was finding and renting places where women could meet with other women workers or with male coworkers or employers.

Finally, language barriers and ethnic differences impeded the development of feelings of solidarity among American workers, and employers often exploited these differences to keep their work force divided. It was not uncommon for an employer to arrange his workers so that people of dissimilar backgrounds were clustered together in a factory; for example, a group of workers could include a Russian Jew, an Italian, a Bohemian, and a Slav.[12]

5

During the major strikes in the garment industry in this period, there were sometimes as many as nineteen groups of workers meeting simultaneously to discuss strike issues and tactics in their own language with their own people.

Intrinsically related to the economic changes involved in industrialization was the codification of what has become known as the Cult of Domesticity—the ideology that women belonged demurely and submissively in the home and that their primary function was to be the moral guardians of society through their maternal and wifely roles.[13] Some version of this ideology permeated all classes of British and American society, even though all classes could obviously not afford to live out its implications.

The women's movement that developed primarily among middle-class women in Britain and America in the mid-nineteenth century reflected both an attack on the restricted definition of what was considered women's sphere and an internalization of prevailing notions on the nature of women. The former led to the women's rights movement—the demand for legal, political, educational, and economic equality; the latter was expressed through what has been termed social feminism.[14] Social feminists expanded the scope of their role as moral guardians to include society at large as well as their individual families, and then focused their reform energies on problems that particularly affected the women they viewed as "their less fortunate sisters."

The process of industrialization defined more sharply class differences between women;[15] while it created an oppressive work life for most women in the industrial labor force, it also created an oppressive leisure life for many middle-class women. These two forms of segregation account for the existence and development of organizations like the British and American Women's Trade Union Leagues.

* * *

It is precisely because the leagues were created in response to the needs of both middle- and working-class women that they serve as an appropriate vehicle for examining the relationship between feminism and class consciousness. Feminism and class consciousness are obviously complex notions in themselves, and very little serious theoretical attention has been paid to the relationship between them.[16] Broadly defined, feminism is the belief that women have the right to social, political, economic, and legal equality with men. Feminists have been concerned with describing the ways women are an oppressed group, with analyzing the reasons why this is so, and with rectifying

6

this situation. In the interest of establishing the common bonds between all women, feminist theoreticians and activists have tended to ignore the impact of class (and racial) divisions among women.

Since most Western feminist movements have been dominated by white, middle-class women, whose only source of oppression has been their gender, feminist thought and activity have implicitly reflected a middle-class bias. Middle-class feminists have either tended to assume that they were speaking for all women, or they have recognized class (and racial) divisions to the extent of pointing out (quite validly) that within each of these groupings, women do not have rights or opportunities equal to those of men. In other words, the basic premise of feminism has been that all women suffer social disabilities simply because they are women.

A more socially aware and politically sophisticated version of this premise is that when factors of race and class are taken into account, some women are doubly or triply oppressed; they share the problems of all women regardless of class or race, and in addition they must deal with the psychological, social, and economic problems of being poor and/or nonwhite. White, middle-class feminists, on the other hand, have tended to be impatient with women of other classes or races hesitant to identify wholeheartedly with feminist causes because of their commitment to class or racial solidarity.

Marxist theoreticians have subsumed "the woman question" under "the social question" and thereby ignored its cross-class dimensions. Marx and his nineteenth-century followers assumed that industrialization set the stage for the solution of the woman question. As Engles wrote:

> The first premise for the emancipation of women is the reintroduction of the entire female sex into public industry. . . . And this has become possible only as a result of modern large-scale industry, which not only permits of the participation of women in production in large numbers, but actually calls for it and, moreover, strives to convert private domestic work also into a public industry.[17]

However, as Juliet Mitchell has astutely pointed out, "the liberation of women remains a normative ideal, an adjunct to socialist theory, not structurally integrated into it."[18] Marxists have been unwilling to consider the special nature of women as an oppressed social group just as feminists have disregarded the importance of class divisions among women.

Nor have Marxists dealt in sufficient depth with the impact of women's reproductive and social roles within the family on their relationship to the labor force. Mitchell posits that the condition of women is based on "production, reproduction, socialization, and sexuality." She analyzes these components and their interconnection, maintaining that:

> The variations of woman's condition throughout history will be the result of the different combinations of these elements. . . . The concrete combination of these produce the "complex unity" of her [woman's] position; but each separate structure may have reached a different "moment" at any given historical time.[19]

In other words, strategies for fundamental social change regarding the condition of women must be based on an understanding of each of these structures and the connections among them. As things change within each structure, the total synthesis shifts, and feminists must be aware of this dialectical process as they work toward their goal.

In short, feminism simultaneously complements and conflicts with the ideologies of class. It is complementary in that it implies equal rights and opportunities for women within sexually mixed, class-based settings, such as labor unions; it is in conflict in that it also implies that gender identification creates a solidarity transcending class divisions.

Moreover, feminism and class consciousness are both broad conceptual umbrellas that can be used by reformers ranging from liberals who would offer specific rights and opportunities to those previously denied them to radicals who are working for fundamental changes in the social structure. Historically, feminist and labor movements have included people with diverse visions, which has been a cause of considerable conflict over strategies, tactics, and goals. In addition, since feminism can in some ways be perceived as conflicting with rather than complementing the notion of class solidarity, working-class feminists can find themselves caught between their allegiance to the struggles of their class and to those of their sex. Throughout their history, the British and American Women's Trade Union Leagues responded in various ways to their dual commitment to ideals of feminism and unionism, but both leagues, in different ways and for different reasons, ultimately failed to achieve in theory and practice a solid synthesis of feminism and class solidarity.

During the period under discussion, the dominant strains of feminist thinking, which were accepted by WTUL members, encompassed two somewhat contradictory premises. First, women should have the same political, legal, educational, and economic rights as men; second, owing to women's reproductive and maternal roles, they were physically, psychologically, and

8

intellectually different from men in certain fundamental ways. Feminists held that the assumptions underlying these premises—that all women were oppressed and that all women were potential or actual mothers—created a bond of sisterhood among all women that theoretically transcended class, racial, and national differences. It was precisely these assumptions of sisterhood and oppression that underlay the formation and subsequent histories of the leagues and provided the rationale for their mixed class membership.

Although by the late nineteenth and early twentieth centuries the lines between working-class and middle-class women were beginning to blur because of the expansion of the service sector of the economy and the significant growth in the number of women in white-collar jobs, class differences within the leagues were clearly defined. Since the leagues were primarily concerned with the problems of women in the industrial sector of the labor force, WTUL activists tended to be either women in blue-collar jobs or non-wage-earning middle-class women, who were called "allies" or "ally members" in the American WTUL. Thus, although the issue of class identity is complicated, within the leagues class distinctions among the members were obvious to all concerned.

* * *

Independent of each other, the British and American leagues were linked through personal contact among their leaders and a common focus on the problems of women workers. The journal of each organization often carried news of the activities of the other, and on occasion representatives of the British WTUL attended the American league's biennial conventions.

The British WTUL was established first, as the result of a visit to the United States in 1873 by Emma Smith Paterson. The daughter of a headmaster of a London school for the sons of servants, Emma Smith was "a quietly determined young woman, at ease in any company, and particularly sensitive to the needs of the working people."[20] She was apprenticed to a bookbinder in her early teens, and although she did not work in this trade beyond her apprenticeship, she proudly considered herself a working woman. Her father died in 1864 when she was sixteen, leaving the family in poverty; at that point she took a job as a governess but left her post to become the assistant secretary of the London Working Men's Club and Institute Union in 1867. In 1873 she married Thomas Paterson, a cabinet maker and honorary secretary of the union, and they pooled their savings to finance a honeymoon trip to the United States. Thomas Paterson was eager to learn about the labor movement in America, and Emma, a feminist who had come to feel that the woman suffrage movement represented a very limited approach to the problems of women, was interested in the position of women workers in the United States.

Finding the condition of American women workers considerably worse than she had anticipated, she was, however, impressed by what she later described as "some successful unions consisting of and managed by working women," which she had encountered in New York.[21] Not much is known about any of these unions; they were apparently part of the group of short-lived, independent organizations, more like benefit societies, that characterized the history of most labor unions in the United States until the late nineteenth century.

Emma Paterson had been peripherally involved in similar groups in England in the 1860s, and her contact with these New York unions intensified her interest in the possibility of British women workers forming unions "to help themselves, as men had done, by combination."[22] On her return to London, she published an article entitled "The Position of Women and How to Improve It," in which she discussed the sweated conditions and low pay of most women workers and the need for organization among them.[23] She encouraged the unionization of women workers because, in addition to the increased wages and improved working conditions they could gain through collective action, they would also benefit from the financial assistance unions provided their members in times of illness or economic depression. Claiming that "women have suffered deeply for want of such assistance," she contrasted the situations of male and female bookbinders in 1871, when a delay in passing the revised prayer book through the House of Commons caused severe unemployment in that trade.[24] While the men were able to collect relief funds during this period, the women, not being union members, were left without any form of assistance.

Paterson pointed out that even when men were made aware of the problems of women workers, they were not inclined to help them. She cited as evidence discussions at the past three Trade Union Congresses, where the dominant view had been that although women might benefit from unions, they were incapable of forming them. Paterson took issue with this point of view, arguing, "The only ground for this assertion appears to be that women *have not* yet formed unions. Probably they have not done so, because they have not quite seen how to set about it."[25]

To meet this problem, she proposed the formation of "a general organization of working women" encompassing women workers "in any trade all over the country." She outlined a suggested structure for such an organization and invited reactions to her proposal from "all persons interested in improving the social condition of women . . . especially . . . from women engaged in trades."[26]

Very few working women responded to Paterson's proposal, and the group that met in July 1874 to establish the Women's Protective and Provident League consisted primarily of middle-class feminists and male social reformers, such as Jessie Boucherett, Emily Faithfull, Canon Kingsley, the Reverend Stewart Headlam, and Hodgson Pratt. The only trade unionists were Henry King, secretary of the London Society of Journeymen Bookbinders, and George Shipton, a housepainter by trade who was the secretary of the London Trades Council; both men strongly believed that the labor movement would be incomplete until it included women, an attitude not shared by most male labor leaders. Although the main object of the Women's Protective and Provident League was to encourage the spread of trade unionism among women, the words "trade union" were deliberately not included in the new organization's name. This was done in part to placate male unionists, who tended to view trade unions as a masculine domain. It also reflected the league's desire to win the support of people outside the working class, many of whom were still relatively hostile to the idea of trade unions for men or for women.[27]

While the idea of organizing women into trade unions was regarded by many as a radical notion, the league's initial approach was in fact quite conservative politically. The league's executive board was "anxious to disclaim any views of antagonism towards the employers of female labour as a class," and one of the organization's stated objects was "to promote an *entente cordiale* between the labourer, the employers, and the consumer." The league deprecated strikes as "rash and mistaken" actions and emphasized unionization as a means of preventing decreases in wage rates, rather than as a tool for gaining higher wages.[28]

Paterson's initial proposal had envisioned a national general union of women workers, which might ultimately be divided into separate trade societies. She thought that beginning with a general union would allow "those who are tolerably well paid to help those who are very badly paid."[29] Such a union was established in Bristol, but on reflection the league decided that "it would not be advisable, in the first instance, to endeavour to form a national union

11

managed from a centre." It decided instead "to promote the formation of separate societies in the various trades in which women are employed, keeping in view, however, the desirability of ultimately promoting some kind of federation of the various societies."[30]

In the interest of obviating "the special difficulties which have hitherto prevented working women from combining for mutual protection and benefit," the league was prepared to undertake "the work of organization and the preliminary expenses of printing bills, advertising, and hiring rooms for meetings." It would also "include persons, who have leisure, to act as Provisional Honorary Secretaries" and would provide newly formed groups with "office accomodation [sic] at a very moderate charge." Since the league's goal was to create independent and self-supporting women's unions, its criterion for the type of assistance it offered was that it be "of such a character as to develop self-reliance and encourage the independent growth and management of the societies." The league prided itself on not giving "direct pecuniary help" and insisted that a union's benefit payments be paid only from funds contributed by its members.[31]

Following these guidelines, the league organized approximately forty women's unions in England and Scotland between 1874 and the time of Emma Paterson's premature death at the age of thirty-eight in 1886. Few of the groups, however, had more than a few hundred members, and about half of these organizations disintegrated within a year of their establishment. In some cases the members became discouraged and left the union; others did not survive the loss of a popular leader or could not sustain themselves financially. The strongest groups, such as the Dewsbury Woolen Weavers or the Leicester Seamers and Stitchers, amalgamated with the men's unions in their trade and thus were lost to the women's labor movement. According to Barbara Drake, "In 1886 the combined membership of women's societies was probably less than 2,500 women, of whom at least one-half belonged to the London district."[32] Under the league's influence, these organizations were more oriented toward benefit society activities than militant trade union struggles, but even as benefit societies they failed to acknowledge the special pattern of women workers' lives. They did not pay benefits to women who left work owing to pregnancy or childbirth, and they did not return any portion of a member's dues if she left the labor force to marry.

Discouraged by its lack of success in creating stable, independent women's unions, the league in the mid-1880s began to reevaluate its policies. Indicative of this reevaluation was the resolution passed at the 1886 annual meeting, stating, "the best way to extend the work of the League is to lay stress on its *protective* as distinct from its *provident* element."[33] By the late 1880s the league had come to question its initial feminist orientation on the creation of independent women's unions and had begun to seek closer ties to the male labor movement and to move away from its conciliatory attitudes toward employers. Further influenced by the success of the London matchgirls' strike in 1888 and some of the theories and practices of "the new unionism," the league renamed itself the Women's Trade Union League in 1890 and began the second phase of its history committed to a more aggressive and class-conscious approach to the problems of women workers.

* * *

The American WTUL was established in 1903 as the result of a visit to England by William English Walling, a wealthy young socialist. After graduating from the University of Chicago, Walling worked briefly as a factory inspector in Illinois and then moved to New York, where he became active in the settlement house movement as a resident of the University Settlement on New York's Lower East Side. His experiences as a factory inspector and settlement resident had sparked his interest in the problems of women workers and made him a strong supporter of the labor movement.[34] On a trip to England in 1902 and 1903 he sought out the leaders of the British WTUL, and, impressed by the philosophy and work of the league, he began talking with various people on his return to the United States about the possibility of creating an American version of this organization.

One of the most enthusiastic supporters of Walling's idea was Mary Kenney O'Sullivan, a bookbinder who had been briefly employed as an AFL organizer in 1892. She had begun her career as a labor activist in Chicago in the late 1880s, when she organized a union of women bookbinders. When she was appointed as the AFL's first woman organizer, she moved east and began to organize garment workers in New York City, shirtwaist makers in Troy, New York, and printers, bookbinders, shoe workers, and carpet weavers in Massachusetts. However, five months after hiring her, the AFL executive committee decided it was no longer interested in supporting a general women's organizer and terminated her appointment. She moved back to Chicago, where she spent the following year organizing garment workers and lobbying in Springfield for the state's first factory law regulating the employment of women and children. In October 1894 she married John O'Sullivan, a Boston streetcar workers' organizer, who encouraged her to keep up her labor work. The couple lived in Boston, and over the years Mary Kenney O'Sullivan remained active in both the labor and settlement house movements, maintaining her special interest in the problems of women workers.[35]

O'Sullivan's early experiences with Jane Addams had convinced her that women outside the working class were capable of caring deeply about and working effectively for the unionization of women. In the late 1880s, when O'Sullivan became involved in labor activities in Chicago, Addams invited her to Hull House for dinner. Writing about that evening years later, she recalled:

> I went with much suspicion as I thought the people at Hull House belonged to the "rich and the great" and I hadn't any reason to feel they were friends of the Trade Union cause and I went wholly to defend the Trade U. movement if anyone said a word against it, and to my great surprise Miss Addams asked if there was anything she could do to forward and help the cause; that was one of the greatest moments of my life when I discovered that there were really people outside of the workers who cared. I said, yes, you could let us meet here, also help distribute circulars in factories, all of which Miss Addams personally did with me; nothing too much can be said for the hard work done at that time because the workers and the employers did not believe in the cause.[36]

O'Sullivan had had similar positive experiences with women social reformers in Boston and immediately responded to Walling's proposal that they create an organization that would combine the principles of the labor movement and the goals of social feminism. O'Sullivan suggested that a special meeting be called to discuss plans for an American WTUL in conjunction with the AFL convention then being held in Boston. O'Sullivan and Walling made the necessary arrangements and invited members of the AFL executive council, convention delegates from trades employing large numbers of women, and a number of Boston-area social reformers and settlement residents.

Not many AFL officers or delegates attended the three meetings held on November 14, 17, and 19, 1903. Of those few, the most prominent were John O'Brien, president of the Buffalo Retail Clerks' Association, and Max Morris, an officer of the Retail Clerks' Protective Association and a member of the AFL executive council. With the exception of Nellie Parker, who represented a Boston women's union and was one of the four women delegates (out of a total of 496) attending the AFL convention, all the labor representatives were men. By contrast, almost all the social reformers and settlement residents were women. Included in this group were Vida Scudder, a Wellesley College professor and a resident of Boston's College Settlement; Belva Herron, an economist at the University of Nebraska who was temporarily living in Boston at the College Settlement; and Mary Morton Kehew, a prominent Boston social reformer who was known for "her sincere friendship to the trade union movement."[37]

By the end of the third session, the Women's Trade Union League of America had been officially formed, officers had been elected, and a constitution adopted. The founders had decided that it would be in the best interests of the new organization to have nationally known women among the first slate of officers.[38] Mary Morton Kehew was elected president; Jane Addams, who was not at the Boston meetings, accepted the post of vice president; Mary Kenney O'Sullivan was chosen as secretary; and Mary Donovan, secretary of the Lynn, Massachusetts, Central Labor Union, was elected treasurer. The executive board consisted of two social reformers and three trade unionists: Mary McDowell of the University of Chicago Settlement, who had been active in organizing women in the Chicago meat packing industry; Lillian Wald, head of the Henry St. Nurses' Settlement in New York, who, with her colleague Lavinia Dock, had organized some small women's unions of New York garment finishers and buttonhole makers in the 1890s; Mary Freitas, a textile worker from Lowell, Massachusetts; Leonora O'Reilly, a member of the New York Garment Workers' Union; and Ellen Lindstrom, a garment workers' organizer from Chicago.[39]

The WTUL's constitution succinctly stated the purpose of the organization: "to assist in the organization of women wage-earners into trade unions." It also indicated that membership was open "to any person . . . who will declare himself or herself willing to assist those trade unions already existing which have women members and to aid in the formation of new unions of women wage earners."[40] Although the WTUL was not the first American venture in cross-class female cooperation in the unionization of women, it did represent the first organizational attempt to create an egalitarian alliance among women of different classes.[41] To indicate its seriousness of purpose as a women's labor organization, the constitution stipulated that the executive board, which was composed of the four officers and five other elected members, must consist of a majority of women "who are or have been trade unionists in good standing." The others were to be women who were "well known to be earnest sympathizers and workers for the cause of trade unionism."[42]

By early 1905 local branches of the WTUL had been established in Chicago, New York, and Boston, and although other leagues were formed later, these three remained the strongest and most important throughout the WTUL's history. One of the founding members of the New York league was Margaret Dreier, who became a central figure in the national WTUL. The daughter of a wealthy German immigrant, Margaret and her sister Mary (who joined the New York league shortly after it was formed and remained active in it until its dissolution in 1950) grew up in Brooklyn Heights. Aside from the fact that she was still single at the age of thirty-five when she joined the New York WTUL, Margaret Dreier's life had followed a conventional pattern for a young woman of her social background. She had traveled abroad, studied with private tutors, and spent her days "seeing friends, going to luncheons, receptions, dinners and a round of parties, concerts and opera." Like many other young women of her social status, she "grew weary, after several years, of having nothing but social activities" and became involved in various volunteer charity activities as a way of feeling socially useful. She became an officer of the Brooklyn Hospital Women's Auxiliary, a member of the City Visiting Committee for the state institutions for the insane, and head of the Legislative Committee of the Women's Municipal League of New York.[43]

She gradually realized, however, that these traditional charity activities were palliatives and did little to attack the root causes of poverty and illness. Her interest in industrial conditions was initially aroused by her hospital work, where she saw children crippled with rheumatism from standing in water while working in rubber factories. It was stimulated by her participation in a Women's Municipal League study of employment agencies, and it was this experience that channeled her growing interest in industrial problems into a specific concern for women workers. Thus, when at the suggestion of Leonora O'Reilly, a friend of both Margaret and Mary Dreier, William English Walling invited Margaret to be one of the charter members of the New York WTUL, she was immediately and deeply interested in the goals of this organization. She served as one of the New York league's first presidents and became president of the Chicago league shortly after she moved to that city upon her marriage to Raymond Robins in June 1905. Margaret Dreier Robins was elected president of the national WTUL in 1907, and from then until her retirement in 1922, she essentially devoted her life to the WTUL and the cause of women workers.

Reflecting the backgrounds of its founding members, the American WTUL was committed from its inception to unionization, education, and legislation as complementary approaches to improving the situation of women workers.[44] It began its work in 1903 with a vision of cross-class sisterhood operating in the interests of women workers, and seeing itself as representing the fusion of the labor movement and the women's movement, it set out to gain the good will and cooperation of each.

* * *

Beginning with similar long-term goals, both the British and American Women's Trade Union Leagues quickly found themselves preoccupied with the problems of organization, strengthening their own organizations and organizing trade unions of women workers. Despite these similar goals, however, the differences in their origins and social composition increasingly affected their approaches to unionization, education, and legislation.

TWO

The Power of Unionization

"Please send the organiser immediately, for our Amalgamated Society has decided that if the women of this town cannot be organised, they must be exterminated."[1] Presumably the men of this Midlands Amalgamated Society did not literally intend to exterminate the women workers in their town, but this dramatic concluding sentence in a letter sent to the British WTUL in the early 1900s indirectly indicates several problems shared by both the British and the American Women's Trade Union Leagues. The statement brings out the critical issue of the response of existing unions to the inclusion of women; it reveals that organizing women workers was not an easy task; and it hints at the complex interconnection of social and economic factors that underlay the position of women in the industrial labor force.

Both the British and American leagues defined organizing women workers into trade unions as their primary objective, for they believed that this was ultimately the only effective way to change the long hours, low pay, and miserable working conditions that characterized the jobs of most women. League members assumed that once women were unionized, they could then act collectively to improve their working conditions and could also become respected and involved members of the labor movement. The non-working-class members of both leagues talked extensively of being committed to organizing work as a way of helping women workers to help themselves; they prided themselves on being involved in activities that attacked what they perceived to be the root of the problems of women workers, rather than occupying themselves with more socially conventional charitable palliatives.[2]

Members of both leagues, however, discovered that organizing women into strong and stable trade unions and increasing their involvement in the labor movement were far more difficult to achieve than they anticipated. Although the organizing, educational, and legislative activities of both leagues had significant positive impact on the position of women workers, neither league was able to bring about significant changes in the sexual composition of the leadership of their respective labor movements. The British WTUL, however,

19

was considerably more successful than the American in effecting a massive increase in the number of unionized women workers. Unfortunately, neither league kept consistent records of the number of women it organized; nevertheless, since the leagues were virtually the only group in either country promoting the unionization of women, it is reasonable to assume that they were directly or indirectly responsible for most of the increases in female trade union membership in Britain between 1890 and 1920 and in the United States between 1903 and 1925.

Statistics on female trade union membership are meaningful only when they can be correlated with information on the size of the total female labor force, and the earliest available statistics that can be matched with such census data are for 1901 in Britain and 1910 in the United States.[3] In fact, the only available data on female trade union membership in the United States for the period under consideration is for 1910 and 1920.[4] While for comparative purposes it would be useful to have American data for 1900, literary evidence indicates that the most significant growth in trade union membership among women prior to 1910 came in a spurt resulting from strikes in the garment industry in the winter of 1909-1910. In other words, if statistical data were available for the 1900-1910 period, they would show the 1910 figure to be based on major changes just prior to 1910, rather than the result of a steady increase over those ten years.

In both Britain and the United States women workers were clustered in the agricultural, clerical, manufacturing, and service sectors of the labor force in the first two decades of the twentieth century.[5] They comprised 29.1 percent of the total British labor force in 1901, 29.5 percent in 1911, and 29.4 percent in 1921.[6] In the United States women accounted for 18.3 percent of the labor force in 1900, 19.9 percent in 1910, and 20.4 percent in 1920.[7] In calculating the percentage of unionized women relative to the total number of females in the labor force, those in agriculture and domestic service were excluded since there were no attempts to organize these workers. Thus, based on a raw figure of women in potentially organizable job categories, the 152,000 women in British trade unions in 1901 represented 5.7 percent of the female labor force. By 1911 the number of organized women had increased to 335,000 or 10.6 percent of the female labor force, and by 1921 there were 1,005,000 women in trade unions, accounting for 26.8 percent of the female labor force.[8] In the United States only 2.2 percent or 76,748 women were in trade unions in 1910, and that number had increased to only 396,000, or 7.5 percent of the female labor force, by 1920.[9] Both the raw numbers and the percentages indicate that the British organized significantly more women workers than did the Americans.[10]

The greater success of the British league was due to a combination of factors. The British labor movement was considerably more receptive than the American to the inclusion of unskilled and semiskilled workers. Neither labor movement was particularly aggressive about or committed to improving the position of women per se, but the British movement's growing interest in the unionization of workers whose skill level had hitherto kept them out of craft-based trade unions made many leading male unionists more inclined to be sympathetic to the WTUL's concern for the position of women workers.

In addition, after 1903 the British league was led by Mary Macarthur, a trade unionist with close personal and political ties to the labor movement and the Labour Party.[11] The American WTUL, on the other hand, was dominated throughout this period by Margaret Dreier Robins, a well-meaning and intensely dedicated woman, but one whose social background and political and cultural orientation made her an ally rather than a member of the working class.[12]

The British WTUL's consistent focus was on organizing activities, whereas the American league tended to take a more diffuse and indirect approach to the problems involved in unionizing women. Finally, in 1906, the British WTUL created a bona fide general women's trade union, the National Federation of Women Workers, which was affiliated with the Trades Union Congress and served as an umbrella organization uniting women's unions from a variety of trades.

Although WTUL members prided themselves on being practically rather than theoretically oriented, their practical work was based on certain assumptions regarding the position of women workers and the changes necessary to improve their situation. Since there is some correlation between theory and practice, it is important to explore the content of those assumptions as a basis for understanding more clearly the leagues' interaction with both trade union men and women workers.

If strategies are to lead to significant radical (in the sense of deep-rooted) changes in the position of women in the labor force and within the labor movement, they must take into account the dual oppression of female workers as women and as workers and understand the connections between these two dimensions of such women's lives. In other words, to achieve their tactical goals of organizing women into unions and raising their status within the labor movement, the leagues had to develop strategies that reflected an

21

awareness that women workers were more than simply unskilled, low-paid workers who happened to be female. They had to understand that it was not accidental that females were clustered in those jobs and that their low level of trade union organization was related to their being female as well as to their being in a sector of the labor force that the labor movement had tended to ignore.

Dominant social attitudes regarding women's appropriate roles and behavior significantly influenced the types of jobs available to working-class women, their reasons for working, their sense of identity as workers, their personal style, and their interest in and knowledge of the potential benefits of trade union organization. The same set of sex role imperatives of course also affected men and formed the context out of which they responded to WTUL attempts to integrate women into the labor movement. Thus, the long-range effectiveness of WTUL organizing efforts was in part dependent on how clearly WTUL members understood the situation of women workers as reflecting the dual dynamics of class and sexual oppression and on how creative they were in developing tactics that would lead to changes in both aspects of women workers' lives.

* * *

The policies of the British league initially reflected a greater commitment to feminist ideals than to class solidarity. Under the leadership of Emma Paterson, the league advocated the creation of independent unions composed only of women. It was willing to accept the help of sympathetic male unionists in its organizing efforts, but it opposed organizing women into existing male-dominated unions, claiming that women's economic interests were different from men's and would suffer in mixed unions.[13] Although its early efforts among relatively skilled and well-paid workers, such as bookbinders, tailors, and upholsterers, resulted in the creation of a number of small but stable unions, the league soon realized that the vast majority of women workers were unskilled and very poorly paid and that it was much more difficult for them to sustain autonomous unions.

Paterson's death in 1886 provided the impetus for an assessment of league policies and programs, and the late 1880s were also marked by a new receptivity on the part of many men's unions, especially in the textile trades, to the inclusion of women. The league welcomed this new interest.[14]

The league revised its constitution in 1889 to allow unions as well as individual workers to be members of the league. It invited any union with women members to affiliate with the league, and in return for a small membership fee based on the number of women members in the union, the league offered the services of a woman organizer for a certain period of time each year. The league furthermore would "send a representative on occasions of serious trade disputes affecting the labour of women when affiliated unions desire such help," on the condition that the union receiving such assistance would pay half the expenses incurred by this representative.[15]

These changes in the league's approach to the unionization of women make for a clear demarcation between the period when the league existed as the Women's Protective and Provident League and its subsequent functioning as the Women's Trade Union League. Between 1890 and its dissolution in 1921, the WTUL continued to emphasize the integration of women into the male labor movement, and its organizing policies were based on its perceptions of why women workers needed to be unionized and of what obstacles impeded this process.

By the late 1880's members of the league had begun to stress the issue of class solidarity. They defined the low pay of women workers, which they assumed could be raised through collective action, as the primary problem because it affected the entire working class by acting as a depressant on male wages as well as being unfair to women. The league's *Annual Report* for 1888 forcefully argued for combination among women workers as the only way to break the vicious circle set in motion by "the undue cheapness of women's work." Emphasizing a class rather than a feminist perspective, the league reasoned that "as work of all sorts tends more and more to pass into the hands of women, not because they do it better, but because they do it more cheaply," men's jobs were being lost or their wages lowered, thus making it "more essential for women to support themselves and their families." This produced intense competition among women, "resulting in a despairing readiness to accept work at any price." Therefore, the WTUL contended, "the raising of women's wages . . . is the change which at this moment is most urgent, in the interests of men," and they noted that this interconnection of male and female wage scales illustrated "the solidarity of interests among the whole working class community."[16]

This point of view was echoed throughout the years in the writings and speeches of WTUL members. An editorial in the *Woman Worker* (a WTUL publication) that supported "the awakening" of women but decried the

23

attitudes of some middle-class feminists toward men further emphasized the essential identity of interests of men and women workers. Mary Macarthur concluded it by reminding her readers that trade union membership among women was important, not only because it gave them some power over their work situations, but because it also served "to buttress and safeguard the standard wages and conditions secured by men."[17]

The WTUL held that, in addition to the positive impact the organization of women would have on the wage scales of both women and men, only through organized collective action would women workers be able to change the long hours, the miserable working conditions, and the harsh and often arbitrarily imposed fines that characterized their work situations. Reforms in all these areas were essential to allow the healthy "physical, mental, and moral development" of female workers, especially since the majority of them were in their teens or early twenties.[18]

Because she considered some of the intangible benefits of trade union membership as important as the directly job-related ones, Macarthur often spoke of bread as food for the body and flowers as food for the soul and described herself as "fighting for the flowers as well as the bread."[19] She regarded trade unions as "schools of social and economic education—education in its widest and truest sense," for they developed their members' capabilities for critical reasoning, taught them administrative skills, and in general broadened their interests and made them better citizens.[20]

The social life—picnics, excursions, and dances—that trade unions provided filled another important gap in the lives of most female workers. The friendships formed and the knowledge gained through trade union membership gave women workers "a new sense of self-reliance, solidarity, and comradeship," which made it certain "that whatever the difficulties and dangers of the future, they will never again be, like those of the past, without hope."[21] Trade union membership thus benefited women as individuals as well as workers, and in addition, there was the benefit to society in general. According to Macarthur, the ultimate reason why women should join trade unions was that by "living a fuller life they need no longer look to marriage as a way to escape from the monotony and drudgery of existence, but are enabled to undertake its responsibilities more fitted physically and mentally to be the mothers of the coming race."[22]

* * *

American WTUL members offered basically similar reasons for organizing women, but their discussion tended to be couched in a more individualistic framework with only vague references to the concept of class solidarity. Like the British, the Americans defined low pay as the major problem and recognized its negative impact on male wages. However, instead of emphasizing the impact of this downward spiral on the working class as a whole, they focused on its implications for women workers as individuals or as future wives.

Agnes Nestor, an active member of the Chicago league and one of the few women in the country to be an officer of her union at the international level, concentrated on the problem of low pay in an article entitled "Why a Working Girl Should Join a Union," which she wrote for the *Union Labor Advocate*, the publication of the Chicago Federation of Labor. Nestor stressed that only by acting collectively would women be able to resist wage cuts or obtain raises. Since in her industry (glove making) men and women often did the same work, the use of unorganized women to undercut the pay scale won by the organized men was a very real and serious problem. Yet Nestor's essay, which was aimed at women but written for a publication primarily read by men, emphasized the essential injustice of a lower pay scale for women, rather than the problems it created for workers as a whole. Her only reference to the situation of male glove workers came in the context of claiming that women deserved equal pay for equal work, when she noted that "we do not want to crowd the men out of positions; we want to protect their wages as well as our own."[23]

In her presidential address to the 1909 WTUL convention, Margaret Dreier Robins also focused on the rights and needs of women, rather than the working class as a whole. Asserting that even though most women may be transient members of the labor force, it was nonetheless in their best interests to organize, Robins maintained that "if the young woman acts as an underbidder before marriage, then her husband must bring home a lesser wage after marriage . . . and she must suffer a lower standard of living all the remaining years of her life." In addition, because he will have to work longer hours to compensate for the low wage scale, "she will lose for herself the fellowship of a husband" and deprive her children of "the companionship of a father."[24]

The American WTUL considered the possibilities for higher wages, improved working conditions, and shorter hours important reasons for women to join trade unions, but both working-class and ally members of the league also placed considerable emphasis on "the flower realm." Mary Anderson, a Swedish immigrant who was a leading member of the Chicago WTUL as well as a member of the Executive Board of the International Boot and Shoe Workers' Union, wrote, "the best part of the union is that it makes you think," and Agnes Nestor spoke of the organizational skills and knowledge of social issues gained through involvement in a trade union.[25] Nestor commented that "after they have attended meetings and served on committees, the girls begin to feel as though they are waking up and that there is a great deal to be learned through their organizations. . . . And surely we need all the education we can get."[26] Using somewhat loftier and more abstract language, Margaret Dreier Robins wrote of "the incentive it [trade union membership] offers for initiative and social leadership, the call it makes through the common industrial relationship and the common hope upon the moral and reasoning faculties, and the sense of fellowship, independence, and group strength it develops."[27]

Even if decently paid and better informed, women workers would still have social and spiritual needs, and WTUL members promoted unionization as also helping to meet those needs. Agnes Nestor wrote of the social benefits of belonging to a union:

> Life should not be all business and work; we want a little pleasure. There is no way in which we can all meet for a good, social time if not through organization. Many a poor girl is lonely in a new place to work; but when she joins her Trade Union the girls are all ready to help her and stand by to be her friends.[28]

As an active member of the Cloth Hat and Cap Makers' Union, Rose Schneiderman learned that the real meaning of trade unionism was much more than "getting that loaf of bread, buttered or not." It was "the spirit of trade unionism" that was most important, "the service of fellowship, the feeling that the hurt of one is the concern of all and the work of the individual benefits all." Through her union involvement, Schneiderman "came to see that poverty is not ordained by Heaven, that we could help ourselves, that we could bring about a decent standard of living for all and work hours that would leave us time for intellectual and spiritual growth."[29]

A final reason put forward by the American WTUL as to why women workers should be organized was that their total lack of control over their work was contrary to American democratic ideals. This was a perspective specific to the American WTUL, and within the league it was particularly stressed by Margaret Dreier Robins, although it was echoed by other WTUL members. Allowing women workers to organize was seen as "the next step in the human struggle for liberty and social justice," and the WTUL explained its commitment to the organization of women as a consequence of its belief in "a government of the people, by the people, and for the people in industry as in politics." Robins maintained that if the conditions resulting from women being unorganized were allowed to continue, they "will destroy the ideals and promise of our individual and national life."[30]

Thus, while the British and American leagues essentially perceived a common set of reasons as to why women workers should be organized, there was an interesting difference in tone. They both recognized the ways low pay, long hours, and poor working conditions were detrimental to women as workers and as individuals, but the British emphasized the advantages of the organization of women for the working class as a whole, while the Americans focused on the benefits to the individual woman worker and to society in general.

* * *

Both leagues soon learned, however, how difficult it was to get women workers to join or form trade unions, and their similar assessments of this problem are significant. Drawing on the experience of the Women's Protective and Provident League, members of the British WTUL in the 1890s and early 1900s were aware of the complexity of the task they had undertaken. However, the American WTUL, dominated by enthusiastic allies at its inception, began its work with the naive belief that it "only need tell of the improvements organization could bring about in industry to have the working girls respond with equal enthusiasm."[31] The Americans soon realized this assumption was unrealistic, and WTUL records reveal that by 1907 a more sophisticated understanding of the problem was being articulated. The Americans developed these new insights independently of British influence, which makes all the more interesting the fact that the two organizations shared essentially similar perceptions of what were the most significant elements impeding the organization of women workers.

Discussions in both leagues focused on the serious obstacles posed by the position of women within the labor force and the absorption by women workers of cultural norms regarding appropriate female behavior. Speaking to the first part of the problem, Mary Macarthur commented that "the low

27

standard of living may be stated to be at once the cause and consequence of women's lack of organization."[32] The low wages, long hours, and miserable working conditions of women workers made it extremely difficult for them to find the money, time, and energy necessary to develop and sustain union locals. In addition, the fact that women workers tended to be physically dispersed—some doing their work in small workshops, others in their own homes, and yet others in factories—meant that it was difficult for organizers to reach large numbers of women employed in any given trade. Moreover, since women tended to be unskilled and clustered in trades that had seasonal cycles, it was not uncommon for them to work in several different trades in the course of their years in the labor force.[33]

Similar obstacles hindered the organization of unskilled and low-paid men, but prevailing patterns of female socialization compounded the problems caused by the structural situation of women workers. Cultural norms prescribed dependence and submissiveness for women and inculcated in them the assumption that marriage and homemaking were their ultimate goals. As a result, most women entered the labor force with the assumption that working was a temporary phase in their life cycle, and they possessed little knowledge of or interest in the dynamics of the industrial world or the labor movement. As Rose Pfanstil, a cigar worker active in her union, told a 1907 American WTUL conference:

> The great mass of men are committed to a life of work in some gainful occupation as wage earners; hence they are more easily interested in organizations destined to protect them as such. On the other hand the great mass of women . . . only expect to work at gainful occupations for a short time . . . hence they have not that interest in the future of the trade . . . which actuates men. There is no question but what . . . women work cheaper than men. This I hold is not due to a natural intention on the part of women to work cheaper than men, but rather from a multiplicity of other causes, chief among which is an utter lack of understanding of economic conditions and the disastrous effect of cheap labor.[34]

To illustrate, she told of an organizing campaign she had undertaken at the request of the Cigar Makers' Union. Sent to a particularly exploitative shop, where she was paid $7.00 a week for the same work for which she had been paid $18.00 a week in her organized shop, she discovered that most of the women in this shop were making $6.00 a week or less. She talked with them about the advantages of joining the union and found that many of them were not interested. As one woman told her, "I am engaged. I am going to be married soon; it is not necessary for me to work anymore." Pfanstil pointed out to her that her fiancé, who was also working in an unorganized shop, was earning only $12.00 a week, but the young woman remained uninterested. Pfanstil concluded her account to the conference by saying that so long as workers remained unorganized and women were willing to work for less than men, this woman's fiancé "could not make over $12.00 a week to save his life." The engaged woman had "thought she was going to live a life of luxury" once married, but recent news of the couple's situation had left Pfanstil with the impression that "she would join the union now if she could."[35]

A collection of statements by British labor organizers in a 1900 issue of the *Women's Trades Union Review* (a publication of the British WTUL) pointed to similar attitudes among British women workers, creating major obstacles to their unionization. One of the organizers, however, perceived another, more subtle dimension to patterns of female socialization. Confessing that the struggle to organize women was "a most disheartening and painful one," she asserted that "the fault does not lie with the women themselves . . . for trade unionism means rebellion and the orthodox teaching for women is submission." Continuing her assessment of how sexism undercut working-class solidarity, she stated:

> The indifference, and more than indifference, of parents and husbands about their daughters and wives being Trade Unionists is more widespread than many people notice, and . . . is . . . the surviving remnant of the old jealousy and rivalry between the sexes. . . . Real Trade Unionism for women means a moral and industrial revolution, and many people dread a revolution. They prefer stagnation, particularly for women.[36]

Mary Macarthur considered women more liable to exploitation by unscrupulous employers than men because they were "more pliable, more inclined to underestimate their own value (industrially), and on the whole more conscientious."[37]

Recalling the early years of the American WTUL, Mary Dreier, a New York league activist, wrote that the ally members of the WTUL "knew that trade unions were anathematized by employers," but they were unprepared for the degree of fear and timidity which characterized women workers' responses to organizing efforts.[38]

These apprehensive feelings stemmed not only from realistic fears that union involvement meant risking their jobs, but also from the sense that being a committed trade unionist conflicted with accepted notions of feminine behavior. Trade unions were seen as fine for men but inappropriate for women. Even when women were able to overcome these inhibitions and their domestic responsibilities did not keep them from attending meetings, they often encountered opposition from their families or boyfriends, who did not approve of such activities.[39] As noted, Rose Schneiderman's mother was unhappy about her daughter's involvement in the Cloth Hat and Cap Makers' Union, fearing that no man would want to marry a woman who was independent and devoted to a cause.

Even women who did join trade unions consciously or unconsciously felt that union participation was not entirely compatible with accepted models of feminine behavior. Women trade unionists tended to play passive and subordinate roles in union meetings, elected men to lead and represent them, and sometimes even passed up opportunities to improve their position in the labor force. The (British) Bolton and District Power Loom Weavers' Association was fairly typical: although it consisted of 5,800 women and 520 men in 1908, all its officials were males.[40] One of the few women active in the union told an interviewer of her impatience with male and female workers for putting concepts of feminine weakness and modesty ahead of the fight against discriminatory practices:

> There are now in this town posted notices that women touching their machines during meal times are in violation of the factory acts, while the men are allowed to clean theirs and thus gain a half hour or so in work time. Moreover, according to the standard log worked out between the organized operatives and the employers, men and women are supposed to receive the same pay for mule spinning work, yet there is no woman trade unionist in charge of these machines.[41]

The reason the workers (male and female) did not encourage women to assert their rights to run these machines was that "women would be obliged to turn in the neck of their waists [blouses] and go stockingless on account of the humidity necessary in these rooms." It was considered shameful and offensive for women so to deviate from prevailing notions of proper feminine appearance.[42]

Female trade unionists' reliance on male leadership stemmed in part from their ignorance of procedures. Women were unaccustomed to running meetings, were unfamiliar with parliamentary procedure, and were inexperienced in dealing with the financial affairs of organizations. In addition, they rarely had the political and economic knowledge or experience to be confident about conducting negotiations with their employers. Mary Macarthur recounted with amusement an incident that happened early in her career as an organizer, which made her realize that women workers had to be taught how trade unions functioned. Addressing the 1909 American WTUL convention, she told the delegates:

> About the first time I started an open-air meeting I got a number of girls around me on a street corner and I told them about Unionism. I was very enthusiastic, and perhaps I gave it to them in too glowing terms. They believed me, and gave me their names to join the Union. Ten days afterwards the girls looked more inclined to mob me than anything else, and I asked them what was the matter. "Oh, we've been ten days in the Union and our wages haven't gone up yet!" Of course that taught me it was a mistake. I never speak at a meeting of non-Union girls without telling them the Union is not an automatic machine.[43]

The unrealistic expectations of these women may have been encouraged by Macarthur's enthusiasm, but they also reflected common attitudes and realities. Given their low wages, paying union dues meant some degree of financial sacrifice for women. For this reason and because they assumed they would soon be marrying and leaving the work force, it was often difficult to keep them organized if they did not receive immediate benefits from union membership. Women workers were often criticized for being apathetic, selfish, and short-sighted about becoming unionized. There is some justification for such charges, but deciding that women could therefore not be organized, as many British and American male trade unionists did, was simply not to face the problem. Thus, for the organization of women to progress, the Women's Trade Union Leagues (and the British and American labor movements) had to understand their special problems and then develop organizing strategies relevant to women's social as well as economic situation.

To members of both leagues it often seemed that attempting to organize women involved as many setbacks as rewards. Rose Schneiderman became an organizer for the New York WTUL in 1908, when a wealthy ally volunteered to pay her salary. Happy to leave her factory job, Schneiderman worked hard for several years to form unions among box makers and garment workers on the Lower East Side of New York and then worked briefly as a traveling organizer for the ILGWU. She discovered that "organizing is a hard job, too, and often very frustrating. You work and work and work and seem to be getting nowhere." To be an organizer meant "hours and hours of standing on corners in all sorts of weather to distribute handbills to the women as they come from work." It also meant "calling an endless number of meetings and never knowing if anyone will show up." Moreover, "on top of all this, you never have a life of your own, for there is no limit to the time you can put into the job." Nonetheless, the hard work and personal sacrifices paid off, for "just when you feel that it is no use going on, something happens. There is a reduction in pay or a faithful worker is discharged. Then the workers remember that there is help waiting for them."[44]

Members of the British league encountered similar discouragements, but they too persevered, sharing Schneiderman's faith in the power of trade unionism and her belief "in every cell of [her] body that what you were doing in urging them to organize was absolutely right for them."[45] One British WTUL member recalled an organizing campaign in an industrial area of North London when "meeting after meeting was held in slush or snow or driving rain with audiences of one or two."[46] One evening, having announced that she would be at a certain street corner at a specific time, Mary Macarthur "stood for an hour, in a snowstorm so blinding that her companion could hardly see her, while shadowy girls darted past to shelter and none thought of staying to make a meeting." Yet as they trudged home, dripping wet and chilled to the bone, Macarthur turned to her colleague and said, "It seems hard to go on like this, but you must take no notice of it. It is all in the work."[47]

Both leagues found that women were often most receptive to unionizing when they had become discontented enough to initiate a spontaneous strike. Because these strikes were not planned and because the workers did not have a union strike fund to support them through a period of unemployment, such strikes were usually of short duration and rarely resulted in significant gains for the workers. They were useful moments, however, for WTUL organizers to convince the workers of the need for organization so that they could benefit more fully from the power of collective action.

The British league's involvement in an unsuccessful strike of Dundee jute workers is noteworthy both as an example of this dynamic and because it was the precipitating incident in the creation of the National Federation of Women Workers. Labor unrest among the women workers had led to a lockout in March 1906, and the local Trades Council requested the assistance of the WTUL in settling the dispute. Mary Macarthur immediately went to Dundee, where she found the living and working conditions of the workers appallingly substandard. As she stated in an interview a few days after her arrival, "I don't know of any community where textile workers are largely employed which can in the least compare with the backward state of matters existing in Dundee."[48]

Although the women had every justification for striking, Macarthur quickly realized that they had little chance of sustaining the strike. They had no funds to carry them through a prolonged struggle, the employers were well aware of this crucial weakness, and male labor leaders in the area were reluctant to help the women financially, claiming that they could not be made into serious unionists. Deciding that the best that could be done was to use this occasion to build a union among the women so they would be able to fight more effectively in the future, Macarthur conveyed this message to countless meetings. She told the women how the Lancashire operatives had created a strong union by paying weekly dues of 3*d*., 4*d*., 6*d*., and even 9*d*. a week, and the reaction of the jute workers at one of these meetings was described by a local reporter:

> There was a wail of despair as the figure mounted so far, but the speaker [Macarthur] quickly turned the feeling of hopelessness into one of amusement and optimism by exclaiming: —"I know you cannot pay that now. I know that 2d. is the most we could expect you to pay, but when your Union has been formed and has fought its battles then you will be able to invest as much as the Lancashire weavers."[49]

Even though Macarthur hated to have to advise the workers to return to work on the old terms of 10*s*. a week, she did just that, but in the process she gained the confidence of the women and convinced them of the value of unionization. When she left Dundee at the end of a week, the Dundee Union of Jute and Flax Workers had been created, and it already had a membership of 3,000 women.[50]

Despite this spectacular success, Macarthur returned to London discouraged about the survival prospects of this group and the other scattered and impoverished unions of women workers the WTUL had organized. Musing over this problem, she decided the only solution was to unite all these disparate groups into a single national organization. This organization, in contrast to the WTUL, would be composed solely of women workers; as such, it would be eligible to affiliate with the Trades Union Congress and with the General Federation of Trades Unions, a strike insurance fund created by the TUC in 1899. As branches of a larger organization, these women's unions would presumably benefit financially, be in a more powerful position in negotiations with employers, and feel a greater sense of identification with the national labor movement.

Thus, taking advantage of developments in the British labor movement that made possible the creation of a general labor union, the WTUL established the National Federation of Women Workers later in 1906. Membership in the NFWW was open to all women working in unorganized trades or in trades where they were not admitted to the existing men's union. By establishing the NFWW, the WTUL gave women workers hitherto outside of, excluded from, or on the periphery of the male-dominated labor movement the opportunity to become an integral part of the Trades Union Congress.

Mary Macarthur served as the executive secretary of the NFWW as well as the WTUL, and although structurally autonomous, the two groups essentially share a joint history.[51] The NFWW functioned as the trade union arm of the WTUL, and the members of both organizations worked together closely in carrying out organizing campaigns and providing support during strikes of organized and unorganized women workers. Local branches of the NFWW were formed throughout Britain, and even though 73 percent of the women in the labor force still remained unorganized in 1921, the activities of the WTUL and the NFWW had significantly enhanced the visibility of women workers and made them seem an important segment of the labor movement and of society in general. As a contemporary noted:

> With the Federation and the Women's Trade Union League, Mary Macarthur and Miss Tuckwell wrought miracles. With all their camp followers in attendance they were no more than a stage army, but they said that they were the women workers of Great Britain, and they made so much noise that they came to be believed.[52]

* * *

The British WTUL promoted the unionization of women workers out of a commitment to feminist ideals as well as out of a commitment to class solidarity. Aware of the special disabilities that resulted from women workers' dual roles as women and as workers, the league consistently gave priority to its organizing work, believing that the solution to the problems of women workers lay in their becoming respected and committed members of the labor movement.

Although the American WTUL consistently articulated the same belief, it was less successful in effecting increases even as limited as those of the British in the number of women union members. A complex set of obstacles impeded the unionization of women in both countries, but the American WTUL's organizing efforts were further hindered by the vast physical size of the United States, the high proportion of immigrants in the labor force, and the lack of receptivity of the American labor movement to the organization of unskilled workers in general and to women workers in particular.

As a result, the American WTUL increasingly took a more diffuse and indirect approach to unionizing. The league emphasized education and propaganda, believing that such work was a prerequisite for furthering the organization of women workers.

The British WTUL did not eschew education and propaganda, but it undertook such activities as a way of extending its organizing efforts and imbuing greater numbers of working-class women and men with an understanding of why the unionization of women was crucial to the achievement of working-class solidarity. The history of the American WTUL, however, reveals a tendency to have its educational programs replace organizing campaigns. By taking this approach, the American WTUL emphasized a more exclusively feminist vision of women of all classes uniting to work for improvements in the position of American women workers.

THREE

The Potential of Education

In addition to their involvement in specific strikes and organizing campaigns, the British and American Women's Trade Union Leagues sought and created opportunities for reaching women workers, trade union men, and "the general public" with propaganda and programs that they hoped would facilitate women's active participation in the labor movement. Both leagues considered these activities a necessary and important aspect of their work, but they occupy a much more prominent role in the history of the American WTUL than in the British.

Somewhat disillusioned by the problems it encountered in its initial organizing efforts, the American WTUL increasingly devoted its energies to educational programs, hoping thereby to generate greater moral and financial support for its work among middle-class women and trade union men and greater interest in the labor movement among women workers. The British WTUL focused its energies on actually organizing women, assuming that there would be a snowball effect to its efforts in this area—as more women were unionized, there would be greater interest in and support for the organization of women, and with experience in local unions, women would gradually become more knowledgeable and more active participants in the broader labor movement.

* * *

Both leagues published national journals. The British *Women's Trades Union Review* and *Woman Worker* and the American *Life and Labor* give an overall picture of WTUL activities and thus serve as a valuable source for assessing the leagues' concerns and priorities. They are most interesting, however, as documents of the leagues' attempts to reach simultaneously their three constituencies—women workers, trade union men, and middle-class sympathizers.

The *Women's Trades Union Review* was a quarterly report published by the British WTUL from 1891 to 1920. It served primarily as a record of WTUL activities, although it also included some general news of issues and events affecting women workers. Edited by Gertrude Tuckwell, the middle-class secretary and later president of the WTUL, it was a sober and rather dry journal, which was about women workers but not really for them. Deciding on the basis of experience that women workers "are not great readers," the WTUL relied primarily on personal contacts to reach this group.[1] Essentially the *Review* was seen as a vehicle for gaining support for the league's work among male labor leaders and the middle-class public.

The tone and format of the *Review* remained virtually unchanged throughout the years. Its contents regularly consisted of reports on WTUL policy decisions, organizing and social activities, legislative and legal issues pertinent to the league's work, meetings and events relevant to the labor movement in general and women workers in particular, and the state of women's unions affiliated to the WTUL. Letting the information speak for itself, articles were straightforward and not embellished with "human interest" or emotional passages underlining the plight of women workers. While this approach did not make the *Review* compelling reading, it did convey respect and avoid patronizing overtones. The *Review* thus kept before the public the problems and needs of women workers, and it projected an image of the WTUL as a serious and dedicated organization that needed broad-based support to achieve its goals.

As a complement to the *Women's Trades Union Review*, Mary Macarthur, the dynamic executive secretary of the WTUL and the National Federation of Women Workers, created *Woman Worker* in September 1907. Designed to supplement the organizing efforts of the WTUL and the NFWW, the *Woman Worker* was published as the official organ of the NFWW. Initially edited by Macarthur, it was consistently directed primarily at women workers. The journal met with an enthusiastic response, and after a few months as a monthly publication, it became a weekly paper with a circulation of over 25,000.

Although Mary Macarthur's close friends "laughed at her literary pretensions and told her that she handled a pen like a walking stick," she was ardently involved in this new project and undaunted by this good-natured criticism.[2] However, editing a weekly paper and serving as an organizer and agitator proved too demanding even for someone with Macarthur's supply of energy and verve. She reluctantly came to the conclusion that she could not serve effectively in both capacities. When a choice had to be made, she unhesitatingly gave up the paper. She announced her resignation as editor in the December 30, 1908, issue, telling her readers that she had learned that "one cannot be agitator and editor at the same time; and . . . I am agitator first."[3] Propaganda, however effective, remained secondary for the British movement.

The paper continued as a weekly under a series of different editors until the middle of 1910, but it no longer functioned as the official journal of the NFWW.[4] Its orientation increasingly shifted from women workers to women in general, and its name was changed to *Women Folk*. It ceased publication entirely for several years, but in January 1916 Mary Macarthur revived the journal as *Woman Worker*. Reverting to its original monthly format and to its function as the official organ of the NFWW, the journal once again became a publication directed at women workers. Edited by Macarthur for the first few months of 1916, *Woman Worker* remained in existence until the NFWW was dissolved in 1921.

During the years the journal was published under the auspices of the NFWW, its goals remained those articulated by Macarthur in the first issue: "to teach the need for unity; to help improve working conditions; to present a picture of the many activities of women Trade Unionists; and to discuss all questions affecting the interests and welfare of women." Macarthur intended to have the paper "touch the life of women workers at every point," hoping that it would thereby bring women workers "together in friendship and unity" and impressing upon organized women the necessity of unionizing.[5]

In contrast to the *Women's Trades Union Review*, *Woman Worker* was a lively, easily readable publication. Its contents did indeed "touch the life of women workers at every point," for the paper covered topics relevant to the private and working life of women, married and single. Along with various forms of exhortations to unorganized women to join or form trade unions, the journal featured news of the NFWW, the WTUL, and the women's labor movement in general. However, its pages were also interspersed with book reviews, poetry, serialized fiction, accounts of the suffrage movement, and recipe, fashion, and health columns. Contributions from readers were encouraged, and *Woman Worker* published their descriptions of job conditions, statements on the situation of women workers—organized and unorganized—and even bits of creative writing. The quality and quantity of these contributions led Macarthur after a few months to recognize that it was the paper's unanticipated function "to call out these latent gifts" among women workers throughout the country.[6]

Underlying and unifying these various features was a strong strain of class-conscious feminism. The journal was a feminist publication that advocated the broader participation of women in the public sphere; it also encouraged women to see themselves as individuals and to become more independent in their relationships with men. *Woman Worker* did not, however, hold out a vision of cross-class female solidarity, for it strongly argued that improvements in the conditions of women workers were ultimately dependent on getting working-class women and men to join together in collective action. Essentially *Woman Worker* was dedicated to convincing women workers that they needed to become more assertive and more committed to sustained participation in trade unions; at the same time it realized that for this to happen, trade union men needed to become more willing to accept women as genuine colleagues, both in the work force and in the labor movement itself.

In an early editorial Mary Macarthur wrote of her desire to make *Woman Worker* "an effective force in stimulating the spirit of organized resistance to capitalistic wrong, and in teaching the need for class loyalty and collective action." She looked "with confidence" to trade union men "for assistance and support," for only with joint effort would women cease to be "the weak link in the Trade Union chain." *Woman Worker* was simultaneously committed to "stirring working women to take a deeper interest in all questions affecting their welfare and freedom" and to making men realize the necessity of having "the women with them in the struggle for improved conditions."[7]

While the pages of *Woman Worker* were filled with discussions of why women should organize, the journal also reflected an awareness that men did not always make it easy for women to participate. "Put to the Proof," one of the first stories published in *Woman Worker*, concerned a young woman who was trying to organize a union among the women workers in her factory. Her fiancé, who held traditional views about women's roles, belittled and then resented her involvement in the labor movement. When she told him that she had to return early from a Sunday outing with him to attend an important meeting, he condescendingly replied, "All right, dear. Of course you must have your little amusements—and you shall call them 'business' and 'duty' if you like."[8] As plans for a strike developed, the woman became increasingly caught up in union affairs, and the young man was angry that she seemed to care as much about her union as she did about him. He told her that she would have to choose between the union and him. Not without considerable pain, she decided that she could not desert her sister workers and their fledgling union just as a strike was about to begin. The story ended with the man announcing his engagement to another, more docile woman, and the woman bringing the strike to a successful resolution. Feeling enormous pride and satisfaction in her role in the strike, she found strength and companionship in her relationships with her sister workers and came to realize that if she were to be happily married, it would have to be to a man who accepted her as both a labor activist and a woman. Determined to help women develop strength and independence as individuals, *Woman Worker* pledged its "sympathetic support to all sections of the women's movement which make for freedom and a larger life."[9]

The journal consistently reported on the activities of the various woman suffrage groups, while criticizing the class bias of the woman suffrage movement. A two-part article entitled "To Ladies in Revolt" castigated middle-class feminists for not showing more interest in working-class women. Since a major purpose of *Woman Worker* was "to quicken hope and discontent in the breasts of hopeless women," it was a distressing commentary on the feminist movement that this publication had been greeted by middle-class women with "a certain coldness," rather than with the "frank and sisterly welcome" it merited.[10] That comment was prompted by an incident at a suffrage rally, where, after setting up a literature table, NFWW members had been told that they would not be allowed to display or sell copies of *Woman Worker*. The article pointed out to suffragists that this suppression of a publication that gave voice to their sentiments among women workers only did harm to the suffrage cause. It played into the hands of politicians who claimed that only a small minority of women wanted the vote, and it made women workers wonder whether suffragists were their enemies or their allies.

A letter to the editor in a subsequent issue echoed this last concern. Written by a woman who described herself as a suffragist and a worker, after thinking carefully about the suffrage movement, she had come to the following conclusions:

1) There are at the head of the Suffragist movement ladies of wealth and position.
2) Wealth, position, &c., have been hitherto responsible for capitalism and its disastrous effects upon male workers.
3) London Suffragist at-homes are held at which evening-dress is worn. Is this intended to debar servants, laundresses, &c.?

4)   Unless all women workers force themselves into the Suffragist movement before the vote is won, and throw the weight of their influence on the side of workers, we may find ourselves eventually dominated and exploited.[11]

Woman Worker was very successful in reaching the women workers to whom it was directed. Its pages exuded warmth and camaraderie, and many readers found the journal enjoyable to read and useful in their attempts to rouse other women to social action. A typical response was a letter written by a factory worker in a Midland town. Published under the title "No time to think," the letter said in part:

> I have been trying for two years to get the other girls to join the Union. A good many have joined, but there are still many others outside. Our weakness is taken advantage of by the employer. We have often to pay fines which are not fair, and sometimes we do not get the full wage we work for.
> We must all work together, and, if necessary, stop work together; then the employers might listen. I wish all the girls could do this, but some of them just grumble and grumble, and do nothing else. We have not much time to think. But I have got a number of girls to take the *Woman Worker*. They enjoyed it. We do so need a paper that will always speak up for us, and will help us to get better conditions.[12]

Other readers wrote in asking for advice or simply used the journal as a forum for expressing their views. The tone, content, and extent of these letters make it clear that a large number of British women workers regarded *Women Worker* as "their" paper and were pleased to have a journal that addressed itself to topics relevant to their lives as women and as workers.

A cross-class feminist perspective was more prominent from the start in *Life and Labor*, the American WTUL's combined version of the *Women's Trades Union Review* and the *Woman Worker*. Begun in January 1911, it appeared monthly until October 1921, when it was discontinued for financial reasons.[13] Prior to the establishment of *Life and Labor*, the WTUL had been given space for a "Woman's Department" in the *Union Labor Advocate*, a monthly labor journal published in Chicago. While this arrangement limited the WTUL in some ways, it was not as expensive or time-consuming for the league as publishing an entire journal on its own, and it was an effective way of reaching trade union men. As Alice Henry, a Chicago ally who served as editor of the "Woman's Department," told the delegates to the 1909 WTUL convention:

The place we occupy, filling a department in a general paper, indeed in what may be called, strictly speaking, a man's paper, and one which circulates chiefly in the labor world, is a position which offers peculiar advantages for propaganda work. We are holding up the woman's end all the time, and yet what we print is read chiefly by men. There is no other way in which we could reach such a large number of men, unless we could enjoy the advantages of having our department a part of some national journal.[14]

However, in the spring of 1910, the WTUL national executive board concluded that the circulation of the *Union Labor Advocate* was too restricted to the Chicago area and, in the hope of reaching a larger and more socially diverse audience, decided to undertake the publication of its own journal.

Although trade union members of the WTUL contributed articles of various sorts over the years, they were never represented on *Life and Labor*'s editorial staff, which was composed solely of ally members of the WTUL. Since these women (in contrast to their counterparts in the British league) had stronger personal, cultural, and political ties to the feminist movement than to the labor movement, *Life and Labor* stressed the ideal of cross-class sisterhood more than the notion of working-class solidarity. The editorial in the first issue called for radical change through cooperation within the entire community:

Every intelligent person who has given attention to social and industrial conditions in America knows that these are all wrong, so wrong that a radical change in the industrial basis of our civilization is as imperative as it is inevitable.

Such a radical change can come only in one of two ways. If the whole burden of remedying unfair industrial inequities is left to the oppressed social group we have the cruel and primitive method of revolution.

To this the only alternative is for the whole community, through cooperative action, to undertake the removal of industrial wrongs and the placing of industry upon a basis just and fair to the worker.

Since *Life and Labor* stands primarily for the bringing about of just such social conditions, we hope to do our share in making possible that mutual understanding which must precede and accompany effective cooperative action.[15]

Thus, for the Americans, propaganda was as important as unionization in bringing about necessary social reforms.

As a reflection of this point of view, the concerns of *Life and Labor* were somewhat broader in scope than those of the *Women's Trades Union Review* and *Woman Worker* combined. *Life and Labor* regularly included reports on foreign labor legislation, working conditions, strikes involving women, and feminist activities. Like the British publications, *Life and Labor* contained book reviews, poetry, and serialized stories; it also of course featured news of the WTUL and of the labor movement in general. However, it devoted considerably more attention to the suffrage movement, to reports of meetings of social feminist organizations (such as the General Federation of Women's Clubs), and to various topics in women's history—articles on nineteenth-century labor uprisings among women workers, on pioneer women educators, and on the development of the suffrage movement. Indicating the range of its concerns, *Life and Labor* published several articles on the problems of blacks in the United States. This attention to racial prejudice was rare in labor or feminist journals of the period, but, given the composition of the industrial labor force at the time, it is somewhat surprising that *Life and Labor* contained more articles on the situation of blacks than of immigrants.[16] In response to requests, the journal staff experimented briefly with Italian, German, and Yiddish translations of editorials, but other than this, relatively little reflected the WTUL's awareness of the ethnic diversity of the female labor force.[17]

Many of the editorials and articles stressed the benefits of belonging to a trade union and encouraged women workers to organize and take a more active role in the labor movement. But this theme was generally not reflected in the fiction published in *Life and Labor*. None of the stories in the first year dealt with topics or featured characters particularly relevant to women in the industrial labor force. Concerned about this lack, one working-class member of the New York WTUL, a Jewish immigrant, wrote an earnest letter, which appeared in the December 1911 issue. She said that *Life and Labor* was not particularly popular with the women in her factory. She urged the staff to make a greater effort to publish stories that would give women workers "new heart and new courage" to struggle for improved conditions:

> I do not know if I can tell you in English, but I will try, to tell you why I think the stories of *Life and Labor* do not mean much to the Jewish girls. You see, they are all *pleasant stories*, and we Jewish people have suffered too much to like just "pleasant stories." We want stories that tell of struggle and that tell of people who want justice—passionately. You see, with the people in your pleasant stories we have no fellowship. They do not seem real.[18]

Despite such pointed criticism, the fiction in *Life and Labor* remained escapist. Many of the stories had rural settings and stressed the joys of living in the country. Of the stories that did have industrial themes, several dealt primarily with male workers, and women appeared in them only as supportive wives. There were, however, a few stories over the years that concerned women workers and reflected a feminist perspective as well as an awareness of class differences.

The most forceful one of this genre was "The White Satin Gown," published in the December 1914 issue. The heroine is a seamstress who worked in a dressmaking shop that catered to wealthy, fashionable women. Envying these women for their beautiful clothes and their easy lives, Eva, the young seamstress, was particularly captivated by what she considered the Cinderella story of Mrs. Copley, the woman for whom the white satin gown was being made. As far as Eva was concerned, Mrs. Copley was perfect, and she was everything Eva dreamed of being.

Eva knew, from having read of the Copley wedding in the paper, that Mrs. Copley was from a Southern family that had suffered financial reverses. Mr. Copley, a wealthy Northern businessman, held the mortgage on her family's plantation. Intending to foreclose the mortgage because the family could not keep up payments, Mr. Copley had gone to visit the family. However, he was charmed by the daughter, and he ended up giving the title of the property back to the family and marrying the young woman, bringing her back to his mansion in a northern city.

Anxious to see the Copley home and to catch a glimpse of Mr. Copley, whom Eva imagined to be as handsome and charming as his wife, Eva volunteered to deliver the dress when it was finished. The mansion was even more elegant than she had envisioned, but she was amazed and appalled to discover that Mr. Copley was a "stout, red-faced, cross, little man," who was extremely unpleasant to his wife. Realizing that Mrs. Copley had married him only because his money would save her family and that despite her beauty, her extensive wardrobe, and her magnificent home, her life was miserable, Eva left the Copleys with a new sense of appreciation for her own independence.[19]

Prior to the visit, she had been resenting the fact that she could not afford to buy a new outfit to wear to a Christmas ball she would be attending the next night with a handsome, but poor, young man. However, upon leaving the Copley mansion, she "squared her shoulders under her old coat like some gallant little soldier," seeing "quite suddenly and plainly that she was a soldier in the army of industry fighting for woman's freedom." Deciding that she could at least afford a new sash for her old dress, she stopped at a shop to make this purchase, where in response to a friendly comment from the storekeeper, she declared, "I ought to have a good time. I came by the money honestly that buys this sash, there's a raise coming to me the first of the month and I'm going to a ball tomorrow night with the finest fellow you ever set your eyes on." The story concludes with "Eva tripping out of the shop, her head held high, her eyes shining like some princess in a fairy tale who has been awakened from a long sleep."[20]

The political themes underlying this story make it an interesting, although unrepresentative, illustration of the fiction published in *Life and Labor*. By portraying Mrs. Copley as a beautiful and wealthy but fundamentally unhappy and dependent woman, it indicated to working-class women that women of the upper classes also had problems. However, the fact that it essentially concerned a woman worker who becomes more content with her situation, rather than struggles against the oppressive aspects of her job (it is mentioned in passing at the beginning that she was earning only $3.50 a week; the raise she was promised would bring her salary to $4.50, which was still low for that period) reveals that even in stories with political content, *Life and Labor* never provided women workers with the kind of fiction requested by the author of the 1911 letter.

There is some indication that WTUL leaders were aware that by trying to publish a magazine that appealed to both middle- and working-class women, they ended up with a publication that did not speak very effectively to either group. Alice Henry, the professional journalist and writer who served as editor from 1911 to 1915, deeply believed in the ideals for which *Life and Labor* stood, but she confessed that it was extremely difficult to produce a journal that was supposed to fill so many functions and appeal to such a diverse audience.[21] In the face of *Life and Labor*'s disappointingly low circulation, Margaret Dreier Robins reluctantly raised the possibility in 1913 that the WTUL should cease publishing it.[22] She had hoped that the journal would appeal "to the great middle class of America as well as to the working people," but she recognized that "we have not reached many of the middle class" and that the average working girl cannot be reached by *Life and Labor*. She believed that with time and increased publicity, *Life and Labor* would be an effective vehicle for rousing the middle class to greater action on behalf of women workers, but she was skeptical that in its current format it would ever be read by many working women not already involved in the WTUL. She elaborated: "Such tired out and undeveloped minds as these girls present, through no fault of their own as you and I both know, need the educational method used with little children. They have to have their minds stirred continuously by short statements or stories which they can take in almost at a glance."[23]

Robins did not express these same thoughts at the 1913 WTUL convention, where the future of *Life and Labor* was considered. After a lengthy discussion of the journal, the delegates voted that it should be continued. Over the next two years, the WTUL intensified its efforts to increase the journal's sale among feminist and labor groups, and special appeals for contributions were sent to wealthy allies. Financial problems led to a reduction in the journal's size and staff in 1915, but it remained a regular publication until the summer of 1921.

Believing that "the educational and constructive work is the most important that we can undertake," Margaret Dreier Robins essentially underwrote the publication of *Life and Labor* in its first two years, and she continued to provide the bulk of the money that allowed the magazine to continue after 1913.[24] She was full of ideas for articles and features (which she generally expected others to write) and was anxious to have *Life and Labor* become a "more human and more intimate" publication.[25] It was never clear just what she meant by this; it seems to reflect an inchoate vision of *Life and Labor* as a journal that appealed to a cross-class readership.

Alice Henry shared Robins's commitment to the journal, but she increasingly resented Robins's behavior toward the journal staff. In one of the very few instances of a WTUL member expressing criticism of Robins directly to her, Henry bluntly wrote that because of her work for *Life and Labor*:

> I have no time to read a book . . . and as for recreation, I dare not spare the time to take even a walk. I know you would say "Read the book," "Take the walk," but how can I? You yourself never enter the office without suggestions for yet more to be done, yet fresh fields to conquer.

She felt that Robins did not realize that often some suggestion that takes a minute to make may take days in the carrying out, and that as a result of Robins's tendency to get the WTUL started on "too many new things without adequate preparation," the staff was suffering under an unduly heavy work load.

> It is surely not your idea, it is surely not the ideal of the League that we, who carry so much of its administration should be leading lives utterly at variance with what we are standing for. We work night after night, because, partly owing to work, and partly to the innumerable distractions of an enquiry office, such as

47

this has to be, it is impossible to get either the time or the quietness to attend to the correspondence and writing during the daylight hours. So many things come up in our movement that have to be attended to courteously, completely and immediately.[26]

There is no question that Robins also worked long, intense hours for the WTUL, but she had the luxury of retreating to a home in Florida for periodic vacations, and it was during one of these periods that Henry wrote the letter. Although Henry does not express overt resentment of this difference in their situations, it is likely that some degree of resentment underlay the feelings she articulated so forcefully. This impression is strengthened by a comment in a letter written several months later by Stella Franklin, who was then WTUL secretary-treasurer and coeditor of *Life and Labor*. Returning to Chicago from a trip to visit the Philadelphia and New York local leagues, she found that "Mrs. Robins has already gone to Florida again" and that Alice Henry was "at the breaking point with everything left on her hands and $800 owing this very minute on *Life and Labor*."[27]

Henry resigned in March 1915, although she remained active in the WTUL, serving as the league's official lecturer. Stella Franklin became the sole editor of *Life and Labor*, but she too resigned by the end of the year. Like Henry, Franklin was a middle-class woman by background, but she had become a member of the Stenographers and Typists' Union when she joined the WTUL staff in 1911. Single and needing to support herself, she tended to feel a greater sense of identification with the working class than with the ally members of the WTUL, and she was especially close to Agnes Nestor, the glove worker who was president of the Chicago league. In a letter to Nestor written several months after her resignation (from her position as secretary-treasurer as well as editor of *Life and Labor*), Franklin mentioned conflicts with Robins:

> There is nothing I should have liked so much as to edit *Life and Labor*, and try and make it a real working woman's publication . . . but Mrs. Robins having expressed her desire to exterminate me . . . and having acted accordingly there was nothing else to be done.[28]

Franklin also noted that although *Life and Labor* had been in serious financial straits during 1915, as soon as she bowed to pressure and resigned, Margaret Dreier Robins proceeded to produce the necessary funds "now that she had got her own way."[29] This cryptic comment is one of the few explicit references indicating that Robins probably frequently used her financial resources directly and indirectly to exert control over the direction and content of WTUL policies, programs, and publications.

During the ten years that *Life and Labor* was published, the WTUL expended a considerable amount of energy and money on it. It is questionable, however, whether it was ultimately worth this investment of human and financial capital. Despite the WTUL's efforts to publicize the journal, it never achieved a very wide circulation; furthermore, there is no direct evidence indicating that it led to increased support for the WTUL among middle-class women or trade union men or to an increased interest in the labor movement among unorganized women workers. Given the WTUL's limited finances and personnel, publishing *Life and Labor* deflected resources from direct organizing work. However, by the time *Life and Labor* was established, many WTUL members (most notably Margaret Dreier Robins) were already beginning to feel that significant improvements in the situation of women workers would not take place until there was more widespread understanding of why they needed to be organized. *Life and Labor* might have contributed to this understanding, but as a stimulus to broadly based social action in the interests of women workers, it seems to have been ineffectual.

Nevertheless, *Life and Labor* served an important function within the league by keeping WTUL members throughout the country abreast of activities at the national and local levels. Moreover, it was the only journal published in this period that simultaneously attempted to interpret the feminist movement to women workers and to educate middle-class feminists regarding the position of women in the industrial labor force.

* * *

In addition to their publications, both leagues of course attempted to reach women workers directly through "soap box" speeches in industrial areas and through addresses at formal meetings. Considering *Woman Worker* definitely secondary to this direct approach, the British WTUL did not hesitate to suspend its publication when it was infringing on time needed for organizing work. The British league concentrated on direct contact with women workers, viewing this approach as the most effective way to rouse women to the necessity and possibility of improving their working conditions through trade unionism.

The Americans, on the other hand, as their decision to put so much time and money into the continued publication of *Life and Labor* partially indicates, placed a much higher priority on the need for education and propaganda to pave the way for actual organization. Consequently, the Americans responded to the problem of unionizing women workers with a much more diffuse range of educational activities.

Reflecting its disillusionment with the results of its early organizing efforts, the New York WTUL, which, of the three initial local leagues, had been the most involved in unionizing, reported in 1908 that it now recognized "that the direct work of organization will be done by the women themselves and that its own work is largely educational." The New York league's statement that "the strength of the league lies in its capacity to train wage-earning women for the work of organization" characterizes the basic position of the WTUL as a whole;[30] increasingly the WTUL devoted its energies to imbuing women workers with the motivation to organize and providing them with skills necessary to function comfortably and effectively in the labor movement.

To this end, early issues of *Life and Labor* contained explanations of parliamentary procedure and concrete guidelines for writing business letters.[31] In addition, several leagues established reference libraries, and most local leagues sponsored lecture series on trade union practices. Initially on their own and eventually (by World War I) in frequent conjunction with city labor federations, many local leagues offered or arranged for classes on labor history, parliamentary procedure, and public speaking, which were held on weeknights or Sunday afternoons.

As an indication of the league's interest in the totality of women workers' lives, the local league libraries contained works of fiction, poetry, and history, as well as books on industrial issues. The Chicago league reported at the end of 1911 that its library now contained almost 600 volumes. Because the Chicago public libraries were closed on Sundays, the one day most women workers were free, ally members of the Chicago WTUL library committee took advantage of their more flexible schedules to borrow and then return public library books for working-class league members.[32] In addition to providing women workers with a broad range of reading material, local leagues regularly invited experts to speak on topics such as health and hygiene and the evolution of women's roles in world history.

Realizing that Italian cultural values about appropriate roles for women seriously impeded the organization of Italian women workers, the New York WTUL hired an Italian (man) to meet with Italian women workers and their families as one of its early educational projects. The hope was that by convincing "the entire family as to the desirability and value of trade union organization," it would become more acceptable among the Italian community for its young women to participate in the labor movement.[33] The early organizing efforts of the New York league had also made its members aware that many American-born women resisted joining trade unions because they did not want to associate with immigrants. To combat this prejudice, the New York WTUL in 1909 presented a series of talks on "What American girls have done for trade organization in several typical trades" to branches of the Working Girls' Club, a friendly society type of organization composed primarily of nonimmigrant women workers.[34]

One of the WTUL's earliest and most interesting educational ventures was the establishment of free English classes for immigrant women where they could simultaneously learn English and the value of trade unionism. By the summer of 1908 the New York league reported that its educational committee was conducting weekly classes in settlement houses for three groups of Russian (i.e., Jewish) and one group of Italian women.[35] The Chicago WTUL instituted similar classes in early 1911 after the 1910 garment strike in that city made clear how employers exploited non-English-speaking workers and how language differences interfered with the worker solidarity necessary to create a strong labor movement. The Chicago WTUL concentrated its efforts on Italian workers, and it organized six different classes that met weekly in homes of Italian women. The women who attended these classes in both cities were encouraged to improve their English-language skills through discussing their problems at work.

Discovering that it was difficult to find appropriate material for use in such classes, Violet Pike, a recent Vassar graduate who was a member of the New York WTUL, developed a series of lessons for students who already knew some basic English vocabulary and grammar. These lessons, which were published as a primer entitled *New World Lessons for Old World Peoples*, appeared in *Life and Labor* in February 1912 and were subsequently published in trade union, socialist, and settlement house publications in the hope that such groups would adopt them for use by their own organizations.

The lessons consisted of a series of didactic texts and stories dealing with situations facing immigrant women workers. They were designed to stimulate discussion, and some of the topics introduced were the tendency of employers to pay immigrants lower wages than American workers, the value of learning a trade, how the practice of homework undermined the wages of factory

51

workers, the existence of factory laws and the need to have them enforced more rigorously, and above all, the value of belonging to a trade union.

The primer begins with a lesson entitled "Looking for Work":

> I go to the factory.
> I see a sign on the door.
> I read the sign: Girls Wanted.
> I go upstairs.
> I see the boss.
> I say: I want some work.
> The boss says: I will pay you five dollars a week.
> I say: That is not enough.
> You pay American girls nine dollars a week.
> I can do good work.
> I can do as good work as the American girls.
> I live now in America.
> I live like American girls.
> I am an American.[36]

Lessons IV and V contrast the conditions between unorganized and organized workplaces and emphasize the importance of maintaining a union local once it is established:

> *A Trade Without a Union*
> I go to work at eight o'clock.
> I work until six o'clock.
> I have only half an hour for lunch.
> I work overtime in the busy season.
> I do not get extra pay for overtime work.
> I earn eight dollars a week in the busy season.
> I earn three or four dollars a week in the slow season.
> I have no work at all for three months.
> I pay for my needles and thread.
> I pay for the electric power.
> My trade is a bad trade.
> Once my trade was a good trade.
> The season was longer.
> The workers got more pay.
> They did not work overtime.
> They went home at five o'clock.
> I wish that those girls had kept the prices up.
> It would be easier for us girls now.
> It is always easier to keep up prices than to get them again.

A Trade With a Union
I met a friend yesterday.
She works at a good trade.
She goes home at five o'clock.
She goes home at twelve o'clock on Saturday.
She has one hour for lunch every day.
She earns twelve dollars a week.
Sometimes she works overtime in the busy season.
She gets extra pay for overtime.
She belongs to the Union in her trade,
She says: "Our trade was once a bad trade.
Then we girls formed a Union.
We wanted to make our trade a good trade for the workers.
It took a long time.
It took a great deal of hard work.
But now our Union is strong.
We girls are proud of it because we made it.
It was worth the hard work."[37]

The social aspects of belonging to a union enter into another lesson, which describes the process of joining a union. The new member is told of the dances the union often holds and the sick benefits available to its members. The narrator of the account (the new union member) goes on to talk about how warmly she is welcomed at union meetings, where the "Union girls . . . call me sister."[38]

One of the stories illustrates the protective value of working in a union shop. The heroine, Becky, reports to a factory inspector that the workers in her shop are being forced to work more than the legal ten hours a day. As a result of her action, her employer is fined and conditions in the shop improve, but Becky is fired for getting her employer in trouble. It takes her a long time to find another job "because the boss told the other bosses about her," but she eventually finds work in a union shop. The story concludes with this account of an incident at her new job:

One day Becky found that the factory doors were locked. She knew that it was against the law. She knew this was dangerous. She told her shop chairman. The shop chairman spoke to the boss. The doors were unlocked that day. Becky did not lose her job. The boss knew that in a union shop the girls all stand together.[39]

53

Ethnic conflicts impeded the organization of immigrant workers. In recognition of this problem, one of the vignettes tells the story of Sonia, a Russian Jew, and Francesca, an Italian, who worked side by side in the same shop and were close friends despite their religious, cultural, and temperamental differences.

> Francesca and Sonia were friends. . . . Francesca came from Italy, Sonia came from Russia. Francesca went to the Catholic Church. Sonia went to the Jewish Church. Still they were friends. Sonia was a quiet girl. She spoke English very well. She liked to read and study. Francesca could not read, even in Italian. She liked to have a good time and was always smiling and happy. The other workers . . . used to laugh at the two friends. But Sonia and Francesca did not care. They kept right on being friends.[40]

The story goes on to tell of the formation of a union in the shop where the two young women work, of a subsequent strike over the issue of whether the workers would have to pay for the thread they used in their work, of the initial willingness of Italian women (including Francesca) to serve as scabs, and of the ultimate conversion of the Italian workers to the union cause. The last scene has Francesca and Sonia hugging each other; their friendship, which had been disrupted by their different reactions to the strike, now cemented by their common political perspective.

The primary intent of the story was to show that women of different ethnic backgrounds can achieve political solidarity and become friends. But this tale also reveals a tendency within the WTUL to deal with immigrants in terms of prevailing ethnic stereotypes. The characterization of Sonia, the Jew, as literate, studious, politically aware and active (she was made the leader of the strike) contrasts with the portrayal of Francesca as the typical Italian—illiterate, happy-go-lucky, and unconcerned (at least initially) with the principles of trade unionism. The reference to Sonia attending "the Jewish Church," which appeared in both the pamphlet and the *Life and Labor* versions of the primer, may be regarded as one of those trivial errors that reveal a more serious problem—a lack of understanding of the world of Jewish women, who were one of the primary constituencies the WTUL was attempting to reach.

Although the New York league had been the first to offer English classes, its members decided after a few years that they would rather let other groups, such as trade unions and settlement houses, act as the primary sponsors of such programs, and by 1913 English classes had been dropped from the educational program of the New York WTUL. The Chicago league maintained a more sustained commitment, and as late as 1921 English was one of the most popular classes offered by the Trade Union College, a joint creation of the Chicago WTUL and the Chicago Federation of Labor.[41]

It cannot be said, however, that these English classes occupy a central role in the WTUL's history. Except in Chicago, they were not a consistent aspect of the local leagues' educational programs, and ultimately only a handful of immigrant women participated in them. The classes generally consisted of six to twelve students, so even when a local league was conducting several different classes, the total number of women involved was not large. There is no evidence in WTUL records of whether these classes actually brought the women who attended them into the labor movement, which may indicate that they did not.

Nonetheless, the English classes represented an innovative attempt to respond to one of the barriers to female immigrants' participation in the labor movement. Furthermore, they stand as one of the ways the WTUL pioneered in the development of educational programs for adult workers in the United States. As one of the first documents for use in such programs, Violet Pike's primer deserves recognition. It is also worthy of attention for the insight it provides into the tone and content of WTUL educational programs aimed at women workers and as an example of how a middle-class WTUL member used her skills in the service of her working-class sisters.

* * *

The most ambitious educational project undertaken by the American WTUL was a Training School for Women Organizers, established in 1913. The school was a pioneering venture, the first residential workers' education program established in the United States. Even after similar programs were established in the early 1920s, the WTUL school remained unique because its curriculum included fieldwork as well as academic classes.[42] The school did not have a long history; financial problems and the disruption caused by World War I led to its temporary suspension in 1915 and again in 1918, and it was closed in June 1926. Nonetheless, it occupies an important place in the history of the WTUL and in the history of workers' education in the United States.

The idea of establishing such a school was proposed at the 1913 convention by Margaret Dreier Robins, who felt the creation of a larger pool of female organizers was an essential prerequisite for increasing the number of organized women workers throughout the country. The WTUL national office had received requests for women organizers from groups in nineteen states, and these requests, coupled with the growing number of women workers, convinced the WTUL leadership that there was now not only a need for women organizers but a greatly increased demand for them. Ten years of organizing work had also shown that the scarcity of female organizers contributed to the tendency of gains won by women workers through strikes to disappear because solid unions were not sustained in the aftermath of the crises.

In her presidential address to the 1913 convention, Robins declared that "the great need of the hour in the industrial development of America" was the need for more women trained to serve as organizers and union officials. She went on to say that "the best women organizers without question are the trade union girls," but that "many a girl capable of leadership and service is held within the ranks because neither she as an individual nor her organization has money enough to set her free for service." In recognition of this situation, Robins proposed that "if we are to serve our time as we ought to serve it, representing as we do the hope and aspirations of the great women's working group of America, organized and unorganized," the WTUL should provide funds and training to enable more women with leadership potential to become organizers and labor leaders.[43]

The convention delegates endorsed Robins's proposal, so she immediately appointed a committee to formulate plans for instituting a training program. To head the committee, Robins selected Mary Anderson, a member of the Boot and Shoe Workers' Union who had left her factory job in 1910 for a full-time position with the Chicago WTUL as an organizer. In addition, the committee consisted of three other trade unionists and three allies: Melinda Scott, national vice president and a member of the New York WTUL and the United Hat Trimmers Union; Leonora O'Reilly, a working-class member of the New York WTUL; Stella Franklin, a Chicago league activist, who was national secretary-treasurer and a member of the Stenographers and Typists Union; Laura Eliot, a New York ally; Amy Walker, a Chicago ally; and Mrs. Henry D. Faxon, an ally who was president of the Kansas City WTUL. Once the committee had worked out a preliminary plan, the WTUL wrote to trade unions and labor federations throughout the United States, soliciting their reactions to the school. The responses were uniformly enthusiastic.

The training program consisted of a year's residence in Chicago, where the students were instructed in labor history, industrial relations, labor legislation, the theory and practice of trade agreements, English, public speaking, and parliamentary procedure. The fieldwork component of the program was divided between organizing and administrative activities. Under the supervision of WTUL and union officers, the students gained experience in planning, conducting, and publicizing union meetings, recruiting unorganized workers, handling of employee grievances and negotiations with employers, and writing reports, articles for the press, and business letters. The students spent time in the offices of the WTUL and the Chicago Federation of Labor, where they were exposed to basic bookkeeping procedures and general office practices; this aspect of their fieldwork gave them insight into the bureaucratic functioning of labor organizations.

It was understood from the beginning that the program would consist of full-time study and fieldwork for the duration of the student's stay in Chicago. All the students would have to be on full scholarship; the wage levels of women workers made it inconceivable that applicants would have savings to cover a year of unemployment. Thus, the decision to institute the school signified the willingness of the WTUL to make the school a major financial priority in the leagues' budget. The students would be selected by the WTUL national executive board, based on recommendations from unions and local leagues.

The school actually got underway in the winter of 1914 with the arrival of the first three students: Louisa Mittelstadt, a brewery worker from Kansas City; Myrtle Whitehead, president of a 400-member (all female) local of the Crown, Cork, and Seal Operatives' Union in Baltimore; and Fannia Cohn, a garment worker from New York, who was president of her ILGWU local (Local 41 of the Kimona, Wrappers, and Housedress Workers' Union).

Louisa Mittelstadt, who was secretary of the Kansas City league and a member of the WTUL national executive board, was a capable but diffident young woman. Upon hearing of her selection as one of the first students in the program, she wrote a short letter conveying her "appreciation and thanks for giving me this honor" and earnestly promised to make "every effort to realize your hopes."[44] The first four months of Mittlestadt's year at the school were subsidized by the Kansas City Industrial Council, a local federation of trade unions, and the WTUL was pleased at this indication of support from an AFL body.

Myrtle Whitehead, who had been working in a bottling plant since she was eleven years old, was partially sponsored by the Baltimore WTUL. She was eighteen or nineteen when she arrived at the school and was characterized by Stella Franklin, WTUL secretary-treasurer, as "a splendid girl with plenty of go and good humor and common sense."[45] Margaret Dreier Robins shared Franklin's positive reaction to Whitehead, but she revealed her essentially paternalistic attitudes toward young women workers when she described Whitehead as "one of the dearest children, spontaneous, and full of spirit and an ardent little Methodist."[46]

It is surprising to find virtually no mention of Fannia Cohn in WTUL documents concerning the school, for of all the students who attended it throughout the years, she was the one who achieved the greatest prominence in the labor movement. Cohn became a member of the ILGWU staff in 1919 and worked for the union until her death in 1962. She served as Education Director for most of that time, but was also the executive secretary and a vice president in the course of her career. She developed a national reputation for developing workers' education programs, founding the Workers' Education Bureau of America, and helping to establish Brookwood Labor College. Cohn was "a sensitive, slightly irritable woman," and her personality and her politics (she was a Socialist) may have made her seem aloof and less accepting of the WTUL values and attitudes encountered at the school.[47] The only comment about her in WTUL records during the period she was at the school appears in a set of minutes from a staff meeting that took place shortly after Cohn arrived in March 1914. Presumably in response to a request from Cohn, the staff delegated Alice Henry, a Chicago league activist who was also a Socialist, to put Cohn in touch with leading Socialists in Chicago. This request apparently prompted a series of comments from Margaret Dreier Robins, for the next sentence in the minutes reads, "Mrs. Robins dwelt upon the necessity of getting our revolutionary spirits to do constructive work."[48] Robins, who had a proprietary attitude toward the WTUL in general and the school in particular, was willing to have Socialists in "her" organization, but she was skeptical of their revolutionary theories and accepted them as colleagues only when they proved their willingness to do what she considered constructive work. By 1918 Cohn had apparently met Robins's standards, for in a fund-raising letter she referred to Cohn as "among the finest of our women leaders . . . a woman who is able to move to the best possibilities in them the rank and file of our poorest workers."[49]

In the first year of the school, instruction was primarily provided by WTUL allies, with supplementary sessions conducted by Chicago area (male) labor leaders on trade agreements and judicial decisions affecting labor. A University of Chicago professor was hired to teach a class on public speaking one evening a week; this class and the sessions on trade agreements and labor legislation were open to other women workers as part of the educational program of the Chicago WTUL. The public speaking class attracted more students than could be accommodated. A sense of the tone and content of this class comes from an account in a letter to members of the national executive board:

> Mr. Nelson is a modern, up-to-date man with no professorial taint. . . . He makes the girls really get on their feet and say something clearly and to the point. He is death on digressions and long windedness and altogether the class is a splendid thing. . . . Not only are the new speakers developed but the practiced ones are corrected. Miss Henry has been rebuked for lack of clearness, Mrs. Robins for being too tense and Agnes Nestor for being too talky. You can imagine how this is enjoyed by the lesser mortals and how it encourages them.[50]

Some of the early fieldwork consisted of having the three students attend shop stewards' meetings, distribute leaflets for a union organizational drive, and attend a meeting at Hull House called by "the women of Chicago" to protest police treatment of picketing waitresses on strike at Henrici's restaurant. WTUL leaders felt this Hull House meeting "gave the girls a particularly fine opportunity of seeing the League getting that publicity and co-operation with citizens which is one of the distinctive features of our work in labor troubles."[51]

Even though the WTUL had been able to accept only three students its first year, there was a general sense that the school had gotten off to an encouraging start. All three young women went on to become full-time organizers, although by 1918 two had given up their careers for marriage. Myrtle Whitehead spent 1915 as an apprentice organizer in New York under the supervision of Melinda Scott, president of the New York WTUL, who had done considerable organizing work among garment workers in New York and New Jersey. Whitehead then spent most of the following year as an organizer for the Philadelphia and New York leagues, but she also became engaged that year and resigned her post in November 1916.

Louisa Mittelstadt returned to Kansas City, where she worked as an organizer for the Kansas City Industrial Council and the Brewery Workers' Union. Her career as a labor activist was also ended by her marriage in 1917 or 1918. Fannia Cohn initially remained in Chicago, serving as a general organizer for the ILGWU, and she was instrumental in organizing striking workers at the Herzog Garment Factory into Local 59. She subsequently returned to New York, where she was a member of the ILGWU national staff until her death in 1962.

This first group of students had done academic and fieldwork simultaneously throughout the year. In 1916 the program was reorganized and the year divided into four months of academic work and eight months of fieldwork. This plan was followed until 1922, when financial problems caused the WTUL to reduce the training program to a six-month course—three months of classes and three months of fieldwork. The school staff consistently attempted to work out programs of study and fieldwork assignments that took into account each student's academic background and experience in the labor movement. A few students who did not need the fieldwork component of the program came only for a period of academic study; several others participated only in the fieldwork.

In response to a suggestion in 1920 from Julia O'Connor and Rose Sullivan, telephone operators who attended the school in 1919, the staff decided to add a "short course" to the program. Five students came for an intense three-week session in January 1921, and shortly after returning to her job, one of them wrote the director of the school that what she had learned in her three weeks had enabled her to settle "an organizational dispute" that she would not have been able to handle previously. Explaining the impact of being at the school for even this short time, she wrote, "It put some pep and some very vital facts into my head at a time when I sure needed it."[52]

After the school's first year, WTUL members involved in the school decided its academic goals would be best served by having the students take classes at local educational institutions whenever possible. The WTUL broached this idea to administrators at schools ranging from the University of Chicago to Crane Junior College and generally met with favorable responses. Most of the schools were willing to allow WTUL students to attend as auditors, but the University of Chicago stipulated that they would have to enroll as special students, which meant taking courses for credit. Since the university offered a course entitled "Trade Unionism and Labor Problems," which the school staff felt would be useful, they decided to try placing selected students in the course.

Dora Lipschitz, a garment worker from Philadelphia, and Julia O'Connor enrolled in the course for the fall quarter of 1916, and there was great rejoicing at the league when they passed their first exam with grades of C+ and B+, respectively. A WTUL staff member wrote to Margaret Dreier Robins, jubilantly pointing out that the regular college students had averaged a C on the same exam.[53]

The presence of WTUL students at the University of Chicago provided an additional dimension for the regular students' study of labor problems. Reporting that the two WTUL students who were taking this course in 1920 had done "distinctly creditable work so far," the professor went on to say:

> I am very glad that they have been in the class. They have brought a reality into the discussions which has enlivened the subject for the other students and has enabled the college students better to understand the point of view of the working woman. It is an excellent thing for our students to have two such intelligent women with first hand knowledge of the facts, associated with them.[54]

After 1920, virtually all the WTUL students took some courses at the University of Chicago. However, since most of them had limited educational backgrounds, their attendance was supplemented by intensive tutorials with WTUL staff members. Of the four students who attended the school in 1923, one had gone through the tenth grade, another had reached the seventh grade, and the other two had not finished elementary school.[55] Prior to each class the students met with the director of the school, and together they went over the reading assignment paragraph by paragraph, discussing the meaning of individual words and summarizing the main points of the assignment. As a result, the students were able to participate in classroom discussions "on about the same level as students who have had a great deal more schooling."[56] The same intensive tutoring was given to help the students prepare term papers and English compositions. These college courses expanded the students' intellectual horizons, and discovering that they could do college-level work gave them new confidence in their abilities.

The high point of academic achievement by a WTUL student was an independent study of Canadian minimum wage laws done by Kathleen Derry, a Canadian boot and shoe worker who attended the school in 1920-21. The project was suggested to her by Professor Paul Douglas after she had taken his labor problems course in the fall; he supervised her research, and they produced a coauthored article that was published in the April 1922 issue of the *Journal of Political Economy*. The WTUL extended Derry's scholarship to allow her time to complete this work, and the league's pride in her accomplishment was echoed by Douglas, who remarked, "If anyone needed an argument for workers' education, it was at hand in this piece of work, done by a girl who left school early and had but scant advantages afterwards."[57]

Despite the WTUL's pride in the students' academic achievements, it always kept firmly in mind that the goal of the school was to train young women for leadership positions within the labor movement, not to make them into college students. The league encouraged the students to keep up their ties with their trades by attending meetings of Chicago locals of their unions and stressed the educational value of attending meetings of the Chicago WTUL, the Chicago Federation of Labor, and various public lectures and forums on topics relevant to the labor movement and the women's movement.

Despite valiant fund-raising efforts, the school was beset by financial problems from its inception. In the ten and one-half years it was in operation, the league spent approximately $50,000 on the training program, virtually all of this from contributions from outside the labor movement.[58] Most of the contributors were women, and WTUL fund-raising appeals stressed cross-class sisterhood. In a fund-raising letter describing the school, Margaret Dreier Robins wrote:

> I am very happy to be able to add that all the money which we have received for this work has come to us from women. It seems to me so significant of our time that women of all groups should get together, should learn to understand each other and should be of service one to another.[59]

Some of the fund-raising letters mentioned the need to provide health care for the students. As Robins wrote to one of the WTUL's benefactors, "No one who does not know intimately the terrible drain upon the physical strength and vitality of our young girls can have any conception of the universality of ill health among them." The WTUL did what it could to arrange for medical and dental care, but serious health problems caused the premature departure of three students. Robins felt it would have been beneficial for all students to have a month's rest before coming to the school and deeply regretted that such an arrangement was "of course quite out of the question."[60] A 1922 memo from the director states that an arrangement had been made with a "first class" woman physician to attend WTUL students for the special rate of $3.00 for a full examination and $1.00 to $2.00 for ordinary office consultations. The school staff hoped "that somehow we can meet these small bills."[61]

The league also provided for the physical well-being of the students by including recreational activities in the school's program. The YWCA allowed WTUL students to take swimming and exercise classes free of charge, and in the summers the school arranged picnics in Chicago parks and boat rides on Lake Michigan.

The WTUL national executive board took the process of awarding the scholarships very seriously. Guided by recommendations from members of local leagues and union officials, the board based its selections on an applicant's intellectual abilities, union experience, leadership potential, and seriousness of purpose. The league's desire not to antagonize the AFL was a major factor in its decision not to award a scholarship to a 1923 applicant who was a member of the United Shoe Workers of America, a group that had seceded from the Affiliated International Boot and Shoe Workers' Union.[62] However, that same year the board did select Marjorie Kemp, a black post office worker from Chicago, despite the fact that prejudice in the labor movement might lead to problems in finding fieldwork placements for her. Kemp was a "splendid" young woman who had taken "exceptional interest" in the activities of her union, and league officials felt that with the benefit of training, she would be in a position to do "pioneering work among a group as yet scarcely touched by organization."[63]

The students did not always fulfill expectations. Two students were asked to leave the program in 1917—one partly because of health problems but largely because she did not "give evidence of possessing the qualities of leadership" considered essential; the other because experience in union activities proved too limited to give her the "background to profit by the course of training as outlined for the School."[64]

A compromise of sorts was offered to another student, who became engaged. The executive board decided that it could not justify continuing her scholarship after her marriage. Their rationale was their belief that:

> while being a married women is not in itself any disqualification for either an organizer or a student organizer, the fact remains that very few young brides care to face the great amount of evening work that organizing involves, or the possibility of being sent away from home at short notice and for indefinite periods.[65]

The student's scholarship would be continued for another month and she could use the last two weeks of her grant for her honeymoon. She was invited to continue her program at the school after her marriage at her own expense. There is no evidence in WTUL records indicating whether she returned to complete her year of training, but it is unlikely that she would have been in a position to do so.

Based on experience, WTUL officials were being realistic. But at the same time, this case illustrates their tendency to accept prevailing views about the incompatibility of careers and marriage. Throughout the league's history, most of its most active and committed members (on both the national and local level) were single women who often had ambivalent feelings about women who gave up their roles in the labor movement for marriage. Reporting to the national executive board that Alexia Smith, a student at the school in the academic year 1923-24 and subsequently an organizer for the WTUL, was resigning her position with the league to marry, Elisabeth Christman, the national secretary-treasurer, commented, "While I adore brides and weddings, I find myself wishing that Alexia could have remained with us a while longer!"[66]

A more serious problem was the orientation of the fieldwork program. Although the stated goal of the school was to train women to be union organizers, the fieldwork assignments emphasized bureaucratic and administrative skills and did not provide much supervised experience in day-to-day organizing work.

Dissatisfaction with the fieldwork program was expressed by the six students at the school in the fall of 1916. In a memo to the national executive board, the students affirmed their belief in the "purpose and the possibilities of the School," admitted that they considered "the academic work valuable and entirely worthwhile," but bluntly stated that they found "the opportunities for experience and practice in field work, the most important phase of the School's work . . . to be practically negligible." As far as they were concerned:

> Not a piece of work has been done by the students who are partly or entirely on field work that can be construed as experience in organizing work. We submit that office routine work is distinct from organizing work and that training in the former makes no contribution to the value of the latter.[67]

This astute criticism did not lead to lasting changes. After discussing the students' memo, the executive board decided to ask Mary Anderson, a WTUL organizer, to direct student fieldwork.[68] She took over this aspect of the training program in 1917, adding the students to the group of women she was coordinating in an attempt to unionize the approximately 15,000 women employed in the Chicago stockyards.[69] Anderson left Chicago the following year, and the changes she had effected in the fieldwork program apparently did not survive her departure.

In 1925 Helen Hill, an ally who served as director of the school in 1924-25, voiced reservations similar to those expressed by the students of 1916, noting that it was a "farce" to think the fieldwork was providing the students with experience in organizing. As far as Hill was concerned, her year as director had convinced her that "office and academic work we can do and have to some extent done; insofar as whatever we have taught is transferable we may have increased the potentiality of whoever from our students may become an organizer, but we are not training organizers."[70]

Hill felt the only way to train organizers was actually to require the students to attempt to unionize a group of unorganized workers. "Real training" from her point of view would consist of picking a target group of workers and then having the students explore legislation and union practices pertinent to the industry in question, make a preliminary survey to obtain names of workers in a given shop or shops, visit them to discuss the advantages of unionizing, produce and distribute leaflets, and conduct a series of meetings. Such a program would offer genuine organizing experience and would produce a new, viable group of trade unionists.

Clearly there was a gap between the WTUL's goals for the program and the kind of training it was actually providing. The WTUL was not consciously betraying its commitment to organizing; the bureaucratic emphasis simply reflected the current orientation of the WTUL. From 1913 on, the WTUL, on both the national and local level, put much more time and money into general educational activities, lobbying for protective legislation, and providing generalized support for the cause of women workers than it put into organizing women into trade unions. Accordingly, the students were being taught those skills which would be useful in these activities; reflecting the background and the experiences of the school's leaders, the fieldwork program was producing women better trained to be labor bureaucrats than militant organizers.

Another criticism of the school concerned the interaction between the staff and the students. Despite, or possibly because of, their good intentions, the WTUL personnel most closely involved with the school suffered from a sense of self-righteousness about their exclusive qualifications to run the school. The fact that Florence Adesska, a student who was terminated, went on to do very effective organizing work for the ILGWU in Boston is one indication that the staff was not always correct in its judgments.

The student memo mentioned above also sharply criticized the staff's attitude toward the students as patronizing. Contending that "the School as it is being administered at present must fail of its avowed purpose—the training of trade union girls for leadership among their fellow workers," the students cited the following reasons in support of this view:

1) Because initiative and the qualities that make for leadership are neither permitted nor encouraged to develop.

2) Because past experience and knowledge of the movement are discounted and ignored; we resent being made over.

3) Because the treatment accorded us as students in the School has not been that of equals and co-workers in a great sense, but rather that of distrust and condescension.

4) Because on no matter, great or small, are we considered capable of making a decision for ourselves, although every one of us has for many years been not only permitted but forced by circumstances to meet her own problems and make her own decisions.[71]

Nevertheless, all six of the students who signed the memo remained active in the WTUL. Despite their complaints, they had not been fundamentally alienated from the WTUL. Nor was their grievance a clear instance of class conflict between middle-class allies and working-class trade unionists. The WTUL personnel most closely involved in the administration of the school at the time were primarily trade unionists who now held staff positions with the league.[72]

From its inception in 1913, the school was a serious financial burden for the WTUL. In the face of a steadily decreasing budget and the development of other worker education programs in the 1920s, the 1926 convention voted to discontinue the school, hoping that some of its functions would be carried out less formally by the local leagues.

During the years the training program was in operation, a total of forty-four students attended the school, and at least thirty-three of them went on "to serve the labor movement in some capacity."[73] Information about the specific career patterns of individual students is very sketchy, but of the twenty-three about whom some pieces of information exist, sixteen worked as organizers for trade unions or for the WTUL for at least some period of time. The seven others may also have done some organizing work, but they are known to have been active in WTUL local leagues, as union staff members, or as government officials in labor-related agencies.

The decision to establish the school was a sign of the WTUL's increasingly indirect approach to the organization of women workers. While league leaders deeply regretted that financial constraints limited the number of scholarships that they were able to offer, they were extremely proud of the school and considered it a significant aspect of the WTUL during the years it was in operation and in retrospect.

Overall, the school was a qualified success. It served only a small number of students, and the fieldwork program did not provide them with the best possible training in organizing. Nonetheless, as the first full-time, residential workers' education program, it was important to the history of workers' education in the United States, and it influenced the design of several subsequent programs.[74] A more important measure of success is the fact that 79 percent of the students who attended the school moved on to positions of greater responsibility and prestige than they had held previously. Thus, in a limited way, the WTUL school did increase the number of organized women workers and raise the status of women in the labor movement.

* * *

There are almost no parallels in the British WTUL to this broad spectrum of educational programs for women workers. There were no lectures on health and hygiene or the evolution of women's roles, no classes on labor history, parliamentary procedure, or public speaking, and there was nothing in the British WTUL's history resembling the American School for Women Organizers.

The British WTUL did maintain a lending library established by the Women's Protective and Provident League. Always mentioned in league documents in the 1890s, references to it cease after the turn of the century; either it was discontinued or it was no longer considered important enough to be noted in league reports.

The activity most comparable to the educational work of the American league was the British WTUL's consistent effort to inform women workers about the existence of relevant factory legislation. Gertrude Tuckwell, the middle-class president of the WTUL from 1904 to 1920, was especially interested in this, and over the years she probably gave as many speeches to groups of women workers on their legal rights under the factory acts as she did on why women should be organized. When Tuckwell or other league officials spoke on this topic, they generally left with their audiences leaflets that reminded women workers of their legal rights and urged and instructed them to take advantage of legal protection. Excerpts from one such leaflet illustrate the WTUL's straightforward, uncondescending style:

> If you suffer from heat, cold, bad air, dust or even bad smells. If there are too many people in the room. If you do not get sufficient mealtimes without interruption. If you are kept at work too long. If you are obliged to pay unreasonable fines without notice. There is a remedy for all of these evils.
>
> Although you may not be able to protect yourself *the law* can protect you. The lady inspector has the right to enter any workroom without giving a reason for her visit; so if you prefer not to give your name, you can simply write her a postcard without signature or apply in the way explained below.

The leaflet then summarized existing factory laws and listed the addresses of the Principal Lady Inspector of Factories and Workshops and the WTUL, assuring workers that any complaints would be treated confidentially. The leaflet concluded with a final exhortation to report illegal abuses:

> You do no good to anyone by not complaining.
> You injure your own health.
> You make it harder for others who may not be so strong as you to earn their livings.
> You make it more difficult for good firms to do their duty when they know they are being undercut by those whose employers are willing to break the law.[75]

WTUL annual reports usually concluded with a plea for funds so the league could hire additional organizers, but there is very little mention of these women needing or receiving training. In most cases WTUL and NFWW organizers had been active in their own unions, and this experience was deemed sufficient. The nearest that the WTUL came to providing formal training was having a few women work as assistants to Mary Macarthur. In 1908 a Mrs. Teichman volunteered to underwrite the salary of an organizer, and Macarthur suggested that a promising but relatively inexperienced young woman be hired to work for three months under her direction. This could constitute a training period for her, and if she proved "suitable" she would become a regular organizer. Mrs. Teichman subsidized similar training periods for two other young women in 1910 and 1911, and when the WTUL wanted to keep them on as regular staff members, she contributed additional funds toward their salaries.[76]

Mary Macarthur encouraged trade union women to attend adult education classes such as those sponsored by the Workers' Educational Association, but leaders of the British league placed much less emphasis than did their American counterparts on special training to enable women to function effectively within the labor movement. Macarthur in particular believed that women workers could gain confidence in their own abilities by being more or less forced to rise to the occasion.

Inadequate union budgets, family responsibilities, and discomfort about traveling alone prevented many union women from attending the annual Trades Union Congress. The WTUL nonetheless urged women's unions to send delegates to this important convention. The congress took place every September, and almost all the October issues of the *Women's Trades Union Review* and *Woman Worker* contain reports and admonishing and encouraging comments similar to the following:

> We hope that next year there will be a strong effort made on the part of the Women's Unions to increase the representation. Much as we owe to the advocacy of the men Trade Unionists, we wish that the women would attend and voice their own needs, for however feeble the voice it always meets with careful and hushed attention. . . . Resolutions passed at Congress are a stimulus to Labour Legislation, and resolutions which specially affect women should be moved by a woman.[77]

Understanding the hesitation of women to speak publicly at labor conferences, the WTUL always noted approvingly when women contributed to the congress deliberations. Prominently set off by boldfaced subheadings, *Woman Worker*'s account of the 1917 Trades Union Congress featured two such incidents. "Cheers for Mrs. Fawcett" declared that Mrs. Fawcett, a trade unionist active in the NFWW, "made a sensation when she supported the demand for an eight-hour day for the railway men." The wife of an engineman, "she gave a most graphic account of the peculiar difficulties and trials of their lives," and the delegates "cheered again and again when she said she had been in the last Railway Strike and she hoped she would be in the next." The other incident involving an NFWW woman concerned a Mrs. Mills, who had gone to the congress prepared to second a resolution Mary Macarthur was to propose. However,

> Mrs. Mills deserves a special word of congratulation. The resolution came on unexpectedly while Miss Macarthur was engaged outside the Congress Hall on other business. Mrs. Mills, who had only prepared herself to second, rose to the occasion nobly, and although it was her maiden speech in Congress, it was very much on the spot and was greatly appreciated by the delegates.[78]

69

Further justification for Macarthur's confidence in the abilities of women workers to "rise to the occasion" came from Nora Jones, who recalled her first contact with Macarthur. On a visit to the town outside of Birmingham where Jones lived, Macarthur took her, as one of the most active members of the local NFWW branch, to a meeting of the Local Trades Council. Jones, who was sixteen at the time, worked in a pen factory, where the men were resistant to having the women join "their" union. When the meeting began, Jones was unprepared to have Macarthur introduce her and then "push her to her feet to tell the men why women should be organized." Although she was terrified, Jones made an impromptu (and effective) speech to this group of labor men. In retrospect Jones was extremely grateful to Macarthur for creating this situation, for it gave Jones an expanded sense of her own abilities and was an important influence in her decision to devote her life to the labor movement.[79]

The British WTUL's general lack of involvement in educational programs resulted from three major factors. First, other agencies, such as the Workers' Educational Association, provided a wide range of adult education courses and programs, although the WTUL leadership was aware that not many women participated in them. Second, the British WTUL was dominated by women who did not place the same value on education as did the more middle-class-oriented leadership of the American WTUL.

Finally, due to the structure of the British labor force and labor movement and to the fact that key members of the British WTUL, such as Mary Macarthur and Margaret Bondfield, were highly respected by and had close ties to the national leadership of the TUC, the British WTUL faced fewer obstacles than the American in achieving its organizing goals. Consequently, members of the British league never contemplated diverting their energies into preparatory activities—programs that were designed to lay the groundwork for getting more women to join trade unions but stopped short of actually organizing them.

* * *

Although the two leagues differed in their perceptions of the educational needs of women workers and in the priority they placed on educational programs, they agreed on the need for and value of providing social, recreational, and cultural activities for organized and unorganized women workers. The leagues saw these activities as a means of simultaneously attracting new members to the leagues and to the labor movement in general and improving the quality of life for women workers.

To this end, monthly meetings of the British WTUL and of local American leagues included refreshments and entertainment, such as music, dancing, travel slides, and literary recitations. Several local branches of the American WTUL and the NFWW sponsored annual balls, and in the summer months, virtually all the local groups in both organizations planned picnics and excursions for their members. The British WTUL established a holiday home for women workers in Brighton, and the Chicago WTUL ran a small summer camp for its trade union members.

Even Rose Schneiderman, who was initially skeptical about the American WTUL, finding it hard to believe that "women who were not wage-earners themselves understood the problems that workers faced," became convinced of the value of such activities. Recalling the first New York WTUL meeting she attended in 1904, she wrote, "Not only was the meeting unlike any union meeting I had ever attended, but also I have never seen the Virginia Reel danced before. I was enchanted."[80] Years later when Schneiderman was president of the New York league, it was recommended that the New York WTUL drop the social and recreational aspect of its education program since such activities were available through the YWCA. Schneiderman, however, now felt these activities were an important part of the educational program and insisted that they be maintained.[81]

Recognizing the dual function served by using social activities as a forum for WTUL propaganda, Mary Dreier, president of the New York league from 1905 to 1914, wrote to her sister Margaret Dreier Robins in 1912:

> I am wondering if we could have a dance hall and have a decent place for the girls to meet their friends and have a happy social life. Then we could distribute literature and have a sort of lassoing of girls into the trade-union movement. . . .
> I do feel . . . that the only way to bring trade unionism to the girls is to make the union of social value to them as well.[82]

British WTUL leaders also thought it desirable to link trade unionism with an improved social life for women workers. Mary Macarthur, who was characterized by an extraordinary zest for living life to its fullest, worried terribly that dreary lives would cause many women workers to lose their capacity for pleasure. She always encouraged NFWW chapters to include social and recreational events in their programs, and in recognition of the value she placed on this, a frequent feature of *Woman Worker* from 1916 on was

"How We Play," a compendium of NFWW social activities. Like Mary Dreier, she thought the camaraderie developed through such activities played a crucial role in getting women workers to identify with the labor movement. As she wrote in a *Woman Worker* column:

> There is no better way of bringing the workers in touch with one another than by means of these social gatherings, which combine music and dancing with a certain amount of very useful propaganda. They have the direct effect of encouraging among members that spirit of comradeship and *espirit-de-corps* which is so essential a part of the whole Trade Union movement.[83]

The non-working-class members of both leagues tended to be especially interested in activities that would bring beauty and cultural richness to the lives of working-class women. In the 1890s various wealthy members of the British WTUL conducted a monthly Literary Society, where women workers read and often enacted plays and stories and were treated to a substantial tea. A gesture that could have been lifted from the pages of a Dickens novel satirizing "lady do-gooders" was made by Lady Dilke, who, too ill to attend a meeting, sent her secretary with baskets of violets to distribute to each woman.[84] Even though Mary Macarthur was also concerned about women workers being "shut out of all the higher things of life . . . music, art, science, and literature," after Lady Dilke's death in 1904, activities such as the Literary Society disappeared.[85] Although such activities had never played a major role in the British WTUL, their elimination reflects Macarthur's desire to move the league away from attempts to impose middle-class cultural values and interests on working-class women. Under Macarthur's leadership the league instead became much more actively concerned with class solidarity among women workers.

These cultural activities were, however, a prominent aspect of the American WTUL throughout its history. As part of their educational programs, various local leagues offered music, drama, art, and creative writing classes. The Chicago league's chorus performed at several Hull House functions and at WTUL conventions, and in 1909 it was one of that league's most successful and important activities.[86]

Mary Dreier's 1912 dream of a WTUL clubhouse was realized in 1922 when New York allies raised $20,000 to purchase a five-story brownstone. The second floor was turned into a club room, and it was used several evenings a week for social and cultural activities. Eleanor Roosevelt joined the New York WTUL in the early 1920s, and for several years she spent one evening a week at the clubhouse reading aloud to a group of trade union women. She always brought refreshments to serve while she talked informally with the assembled women about their jobs. According to Rose Schneiderman, the women enjoyed the books she read to them and felt she was genuinely interested in their lives.[87]

Agnes Nestor wrote proudly of the WTUL providing "opportunities for working girls to explore more of the cultural avenues which had been denied them," and she and Rose Schneiderman both mention pottery classes as being especially popular. After harassed days at work, the chance to spend an evening quietly, making things of their own design was welcome and relaxing. A waitress told Nestor "that after working all day at her job she became so nervous that she could not sit half an hour reading, but that in this pottery class she could sit for two hours enjoying it so much that she completely forgot the passage of time."[88]

Although these opportunities for relaxation and cultural enrichment were greatly appreciated by the women and were regarded by both trade union and ally league members as serving a valuable function in bringing women into the labor movement, they were sometimes discussed condescendingly by middle-class members of the WTUL. At a meeting held in conjunction with the 1909 WTUL convention, Margaret Dreier Robins declared:

> Perhaps we can best understand what our task represents in this division of our work if we will remember that it has happily fallen to the lot of the Women's Trade Union League to have charge and supervision of the kindergarten department in the great school of organized labor. It is for this reason that music and merrymaking are so essential a feature of our league work, that books and story-telling and all that makes for color and music and laughter lead to that essential human fellowship—a sure foundation for the industrial union of our younger sisters.[89]

Despite such attitudes, this aspect of the WTUL's work did provide at least some women workers with the uplift and increased personal strength it was intended to impart. Elisabeth Christman believed that through these classes she learned that "the beauty that lies everywhere around us in the world gives inner resources that enable one to overcome difficulties." Christman, a Chicago glove worker who served as national secretary of the WTUL from 1922 to its dissolution in 1950, described herself as one of the many "industrial workers brought to a realization of the world of beauty . . . outside the shop because Mrs. Robins cared about workers as human beings." No wonder she saw Robins as a "great woman" with "prophetic vision, keen human sympathy, and radiant courage," a view shared by many women and one that provides an important counterweight to the temptation to interpret Robins as simply a well-meaning but domineering upper-class woman condescending to women workers.[90]

These social, recreational, and cultural activities were vital and important aspects of the league's programs. They met real needs, they humanized the labor movement for many women, and they reflect the leagues' commitment to a world of "bread and roses" for workers.

* * *

If the Women's Trade Union Leagues were to make lasting gains for women, however, they had to gain the support of trade union men. The records of both leagues indicate the scope of that effort, but they tell little of its content. Essentially, WTUL members wrote articles for labor papers and addressed local, regional, and national labor meetings on the work of the WTUL, the situation of women workers, and the need for union men to support and promote the inclusion of women in the labor movement.

Continuing a practice begun by the Women's Protective and Provident League, the British WTUL held a meeting each year in conjunction with the annual Trades Union Congress for TUC delegates from trades in which significant numbers of women were employed. Various prominent male labor leaders cooperated with the WTUL in planning these meetings and often served as featured speakers. Generally well attended, these meetings often produced requests to the WTUL for organizing help, and the league considered them important.[91]

It is somewhat surprising that the American WTUL never instituted analogous meetings in conjunction with the AFL's annual convention. The most likely explanation is financial. AFL conventions were not always held in cities or states where there were local branches of the WTUL, and the size of the United States made it expensive to send a group to these meetings. The American WTUL always sent one (fraternal) delegate to the AFL convention, but it was obviously unrealistic to expect one woman to organize and conduct a meeting similar to those sponsored by the British league. That the American WTUL chose to spend its funds on projects such as *Life and Labor* and the School for Women Organizers, rather than on sending enough WTUL representatives to AFL conventions to convene conferences on the British model, reflects an important difference in the priority each league accorded to outreach programs directed at trade union men.

The larger American WTUL delegations attended city and state labor federation conventions, and in some cases the local league was able to arrange for an entire morning or afternoon session to be devoted to the topic of women workers.[92] The president of the local WTUL generally presided, and various members spoke on the situation of women workers in that state and explained the goals and work of the WTUL. Even though these sessions usually resulted in favorable resolutions being passed, they rarely led to significant support for the league or to serious efforts by male workers to organize the women in their trades.

Where a block of time was not set aside for the WTUL, members would prepare a set of resolutions for consideration at the convention; thus WTUL representatives would have a chance to speak to the delegates on issues of concern to women workers. A typical set of resolutions would include a request for female factory inspectors, support for legislation to bring about shorter hours and higher wages, and a general statement of support for the principle of organizing women.

Although local branches of the American WTUL were often given full membership in city and state labor federations, the national league was not an official member of the AFL, since it was not actually a trade union. Endorsed by, but not formally affiliated with, the AFL, WTUL representatives could attend AFL conventions only as fraternal delegates; they were generally able to make a short speech, but they did not have voting privileges.

In Britain the National Federation of Women Workers was a bona fide trade union; as such, its representatives had full membership rights at the annual Trades Union Congress. They could not only propose resolutions in the interest of women workers, but also could oppose resolutions they felt harmful to their cause. Mary Macarthur's vehement arguments were a major factor in defeating a proposal of the Amalgamated Society of Brassworkers at the 1908 Trades Union Congress. Claiming that the processes of polishing, turning, and screwing were "unhealthy and unsuitable" for women, the brassworkers asked the TUC to go on record supporting the legal prohibition of the employment of women in these jobs. Macarthur contended that the real reason the brassworkers wanted to prohibit the employment of women was that the women were unorganized and were undercutting the established wage rates. She pointed out that if women were prohibited from working in this industry, they would simply flood other trades, thereby increasing the competition in

75

them. She urged the brassworkers and all other unions to organize the women working in their industries, for only then would employers cease using women to undercut men. Macarthur agreed with the brassworkers that these processes were unhealthy, but she felt that in fairness to all workers, "it is the bad conditions, not the women, that ought to be abolished."[93] This incident illustrates the British WTUL's tendency to argue for women's rights within a solid framework of class solidarity; by taking this tack, WTUL members conveyed to union men that the organization of women was something they should undertake out of self-interest, rather than simply out of altruism.

The American WTUL felt that its own biennial conventions served an important educational function.[94] The league always invited male labor leaders to these conventions, to prove to them that women could be organized, participate intelligently in conference deliberations, and chair meetings—in sum, that women could be committed and capable labor activists. A handful of male labor leaders did attend WTUL conventions over the years, and they generally made warm speeches to the assembled women, praising the work and goals of the WTUL. But this did not lead AFL unions to regard the organization of women or the raising of women's status within the labor movement as a central concern.

Unlike the British WTUL, the American league defined itself as the industrial branch of the woman suffrage movement, and much of its educational work among union men involved appealing for their support on this issue.[95] WTUL members always mentioned suffrage when they spoke at labor conferences or wrote articles for labor journals. When suffrage referenda were pending in states where there was a branch of the WTUL, the local league made special visits to union locals and state labor conventions to urge the men to vote for women's suffrage. The most vigorous campaign was carried on by the New York WTUL, which formed the Industrial Section of the New York State Suffrage Party. In this capacity the WTUL wrote letters to labor papers and traveled throughout the state visiting union meetings. Their telegraphed appeal to the 1914 New York State Federation of Labor Convention was typical:

> The Industrial Section of the New York State Woman Suffrage Party sends fraternal greetings to the State Federation of Labor in convention assembled. Best wishes that achievement will crown your efforts in your deliberations for the effective advance and protection of labor. We work beside you, picket and strike with you and stand by you in your struggle for industrial freedom. Stand by us in our struggle for political freedom next November. Our trade union

brothers have the power to withhold or to bestow this freedom we need and desire. If we win, the workers will double their power. We pin our faith on you.[96]

One of the Industrial Section's major propaganda devices in the 1917 campaign was a series of sixteen letters addressed to labor men.[97] Distributed widely throughout the state, the letters explained why working women and working-class housewives wanted and needed the vote. The next to last letter, entitled "Objections to Votes for Women Answered," illustrates the kinds of arguments the WTUL used in its appeals to trade union men. It begins by citing statistics on the number of women involved in the suffrage movement in New York to prove that women do indeed want the vote. It then declares that in states where women are already enfranchised, they vote in the same proportion as men, thus countering the claim that "women will not use the vote when they get it." The letter goes on to list the following objections and the WTUL's refutation of them:

"Women are represented by their husbands." In New York State there are 1,768,698 married women over 21 years of age; 1,089,529 women are unmarried or widowed. Who represents these women on election day? Who represents the wives of trainmen and traveling salesmen when their husbands are not at home on Election Day?

"Men vote because they are the head of families." Here is a family with father, mother, and five sons—six votes. Another family, mother and five daughters—no vote. Think of the added power and strength the working class would have when you give your wife and daughters the vote.

"Women can get what she wants through her influence." Why go across the State on foot when you can go by train? Influence is slow and uncertain. Adding the vote to your influence increases your influence. It took women a great many years to get a 9 hour work day because they had influence without the vote.

"Women's place is in the home." Voting does not take one out of the home any more than marketing. On the other hand, more than 988,000 are out of the home earning their own living—what about them? We fancy men would find themselves in a dreadful fix if the 988,000 women would come to them for support.

"Who will take care of the children?" Who takes care of the children when the mother goes out working? Who takes care of the scrub woman's children when she leaves them in the dead of night to scrub office floors for the handsome wage of six per week? Give the mothers the vote so that mothers' pension laws can be passed. The mother will then be able to take care of her children.

"It will make women unwomanly." If modern industry has not made women unwomanly, you can rest assured that casting her vote into the ballot box won't . . .

In short, brother, women as well as men are people and there is no real reason why working women should not vote on equal terms with working men.[98]

The American WTUL, like the British, appealed to trade union men in the name of class solidarity. However, in contrast to the British, who rooted their feminism firmly within the context of class solidarity, the Americans tended to make feminist values the essence of their appeals.

This emphasis on feminism rather than class consciousness and the American WTUL's attempt to straddle the feminist and labor movements ultimately left the league on the fringes of both movements. The British WTUL identified much more completely with the British labor movement, and this orientation was reflected in the scope and content of its educational outreach to trade union men. Valuing its autonomy as a woman's organization, the American WTUL resisted being absorbed into the AFL when this possibility was raised in 1924. The British, on the other hand, felt rewarded for their efforts to gain the support of trade union men when the Trades Union Congress in 1920 granted women trade unionists two seats on its Executive Board and when in 1921 the TUC was receptive to the WTUL becoming the Women's Section of its newly formed General Council.

* * *

Not surprisingly, efforts to reach women outside the working class remained much more central to the American WTUL than to the British. After the death of Lady Dilke and the establishment of the NFWW, such concerns became increasingly peripheral to the British WTUL, despite its continued search for financial and moral support from "the general public" during strikes and legislative campaigns. Yet the British league was certainly capable of effective propaganda.

Under Lady Dilke's leadership in the 1890s and early 1900s, non-working-class members of the British WTUL presented the cause of women workers to the public through drawing room meetings organized by WTUL sympathizers, speeches to political and social reform groups such as the Women's Liberal Federation and the Christian Social Union, and articles and essays in books and journals, including, of course, the *Women's Trades Union*

Review. These speeches and publications described the situation of women workers, explained why the organization of women was necessary but difficult, and outlined the work of the WTUL.[99] Essentially they were designed to combat attitudes such as those expressed by the woman who responded to one of Lady Dilke's speeches in the 1890s on the sweated conditions and starvation wages of women workers with the comment, "It is not true, and if it is, it ought to be hushed up."[100]

Like Margaret Dreier Robins, Lady Dilke became involved in the WTUL for a combination of reasons: feminism, political liberalism, moral outrage, and a sense of religious mission. In her speeches and writings on the work of the league, she urged "the claims of this work on all women who feel the sacredness of the tie of our common womanhood."[101] She impressed upon audiences from the leisure class her conviction that "It is not for us to sit idly by taking our pleasure in the purple and fine linen of life while, in their anguish, our working sisters lift up their voices to heaven. Day by day that voice is in our ears; they are crying to us for redemption." Furthermore, the industrial prosperity of England was based on the shameful exploitation of the working class. She warned those in positions of privilege, "If we shut ourselves off from the knowledge of this that lies at our very doors; if we will not understand the teaching of these things, then may we well fear lest their meaning be made plain to us in a lesson of wrath and ruin." If the wages and conditions of the working class were not improved, "these neglected ones, who fill the ranks of the army of labour, may one day shape their giant forces under the wings of an avenging angel, whose mission will be not to bring peace and prosperity to our land, but a sword." Dilke also appealed to the moral sense of her audiences when she spoke of the spiritual rewards that came to women who reached out to help their less fortunate sisters:

> Can any joy that we may win for ourselves ever equal the joy of knowing that by our unselfish effort we have taught the weak and feeble, the ignorant and lonely ones to feel that they are not alone; that we have given them the blessing of self-respect, have brought them to breathe a purer air, or have helped them to win a few shillings more by their weekly toil? I say most emphatically "No." Nothing we can win for ourselves can ever be compared with the happiness that will be ours should we succeed as we fight the battle of life, in lifting ever so little the burden borne by these sorrowful ones.[102]

Even discounting Lady Dilke's Victorian rhetorical style, it is clear that her concept of feminism was dominated by a sense of noblesse oblige rather than by a vision of women of all classes working together as equals in the struggle for social change.

After Lady Dilke's death in 1904, her niece, Gertrude Tuckwell, became the WTUL's leading speaker to non-working-class groups. Described in a 1908 biographical profile in *Woman Worker* as "a great disturber of consciences" who had "a special mission to the leisured," Tuckwell's forthright and moving speeches on the situation of women workers were cited as an important factor in changing the attitudes of wealthy women. The author (Mary Macarthur?) of this profile wrote that "a genuine impulse among wealthy women, a new desire for knowledge of industrial conditions and remorse for past callousness is now too conspicuous to be ignored."[103]

In Mary Macarthur's first few years with the WTUL, she actively participated in this sort of outreach. She wrote a series of articles in the *Penny Pictorial* entitled "The Cry of the Woman Worker," which conveyed "tragically truthful pictures of the life of the sweated women working in factories or at home." She spoke at drawing-room meetings to fashionable West End audiences, telling them of the conditions and wages that lay behind the goods they took for granted. In graphic detail, she described the lives of four-year-old children in the slums of Birmingham working far into the night linking hooks and eyes and of East End women who earned 2*d*. an hour for producing elaborately embroidered baby clothing or who were paid 6*d*. to 8*d*. for making beautiful blouses that were then sold for 25*s*. to 30*s*. in West End shops.[104]

Although Macarthur was generally extremely effective in gaining support for the WTUL's work through these speeches, she was often uneasy and ambivalent about spending time in society she tended to scorn and condemn.[105] She sometimes found herself impatient with her audiences' inability to comprehend the lives of women workers. In one speech she spoke sorrowfully of the conditions under which a group of women lived and worked, but her face brightened when she told of the 2*d*. a day increase they won after two weeks of agitation. Even this small amount was an important gain—it made the difference between no and some milk for a baby, between walking and riding to work, between having to wear shoes with holes and having them repaired—but it had no impact on her West End audience, who appeared "unmoved and bored" by her account. Although she emphasized the need for empathy, 2*d*. was such an insignificant sum to her listeners that they failed to appreciate the difference it could make in the lives of others.[106]

One of the major educational programs undertaken by the British WTUL in the early 1900s was a campaign to create a public demand for leadless glaze pottery. The WTUL distributed hundreds of leaflets and wrote numerous letters explaining the health problems suffered by pottery workers who spent their days exposed to lead. The league also organized several exhibitions of dishes made with leadless glazes to make the public aware that attractive and reasonably priced alternatives existed. Although the WTUL regarded organization and legislation as the ultimate solutions to this problem, it considered its educational work in this area "an unqualified success." As a result of these exhibitions and the publicity surrounding them, there was a significant increase in orders for leadless glazeware from public bodies, clubs, and shipping companies, as well as individual consumers.[107]

The British WTUL directed its appeals for support to a broader public than simply middle-class women. Less dedicated than the American WTUL to a vision of cross-class female solidarity, the British league sought the moral and financial support of men as well as women, although it did often speak of the special obligations of leisure class women to help their "less fortunate sisters." Essentially, however, the primary goal of the WTUL's educational efforts directed at "the general public" was to make visible the needs and problems of women workers, the most invisible and ignored group in the labor force. The problems of women workers were by no means solved by the time the WTUL disbanded in 1921, but to the extent that there was greater public support for the organization of women in 1921 than in 1890, the league's educational work played a critical role.

* * *

The American WTUL was also instrumental in arousing public concern and support for the struggles of women workers but it directed most efforts to middle-class feminists. The league saw itself as the bridge between the feminist movement and the women's labor movement, and its members felt strongly that it was in the interest of both groups to be more closely connected. In the absence of financial support from the labor movement, the WTUL's existence depended on contributions from middle-class sympathizers, and as Rose Schneiderman wrote in 1915, "The general woman movement cannot advance very much further till the great body of working women are enrolled in it."[108] With this in mind, the WTUL devoted considerable energy to making the goals of the feminist movement relevant to women workers and the needs of women workers relevant to middle-class feminists.

Interest in the enfranchisement of women provided the most obvious link between the two groups, and the WTUL was heavily involved in suffrage activities on its own and in coalition with National American Woman Suffrage Association (NAWSA) groups. Viewing itself as the industrial branch of the woman suffrage movement, the WTUL worked hard to develop working-class support for woman suffrage, stressing the value of the vote for women to improve their living and working conditions. At the same time, the WTUL educated NAWSA members and groups regarding the special problems of women workers and their particular need for the vote. The WTUL urged NAWSA organizations and publications to broaden the scope and content of their activities and rhetoric to incorporate the views and participation of women workers. The history of the suffrage movement reveals some changes in this direction. Nevertheless, because of social and political tensions, generated primarily by the class bias of the middle-class suffragists, middle- and working-class women joining together to achieve a common goal was at best a tenuous alliance.[109]

Along with its efforts to influence the suffrage movement, the American WTUL sought to win support for the struggles of women workers from middle-class women's groups. The WTUL consistently sent delegates to national conventions of NAWSA, the YWCA, and the General Federation of Women's Clubs, and whenever possible it sent speakers to meetings of local women's organizations. However, just as the WTUL was not very successful in making the suffrage movement a genuine expression of cross-class female solidarity, league members discovered that sensitivity and commitment to working-class women were even rarer when a common goal such as suffrage was not present.

One of the first activities of the Chicago WTUL after its formation in 1904 was to take up the cause of a group of striking corset workers in Aurora, Illinois. The Chicago league sent out letters to every woman's club in Illinois, telling them of the conditions under which these women worked, explaining their strike demands, and asking the club women to boycott the products of the Kabo Corset Company until the strike was settled. The company's attorney threatened the league with a suit for the boycott letters, and this was called to the attention of the delegates to an Illinois State Federation of Women's Clubs convention by Anna Nichols, a club woman and ally member of the Chicago league. Her action produced so much publicity that the company dropped its threat to sue.[110] WTUL records do not indicate whether the boycott was effective, but there was enough interest in the league and sympathy for its work that the following convention of the Illinois State Federation of Women's Clubs voted to amend its constitution to allow an organization such as the WTUL to affiliate. However, as Agnes Nestor notes in her autobiography, not all the club women supported this move, and one was overheard saying, "Isn't it dreadful! I suppose next year we'll have those corset workers here as members!"[111]

From their inception local leagues sent out circulars to women's groups listing WTUL members available to speak on topics such as "The Objects of the Women's Trade Union League," "Why We Believe in Trade Unions," "Women in Trade Unions," and "Club Women and Trade Union Women."[112] In addition, the national league created the post of official lecturer, a paid staff position filled first by Frances Squire Potter, a University of Minnesota English professor who resigned from her academic position to become corresponding secretary of NAWSA and then left NAWSA to work for the WTUL. In subsequent years Rose Schneiderman and Alice Henry served as the official lecturer. Advertisements soliciting lecture engagements for Schneiderman described her experiences as a labor activist and suffragist and stated, "She has not only been an inspiration to her fellow workers but has the rare power of making other women understand the great modern industrial situation and of bringing them to a sense of sisterhood which knows no class."[113] Working-class WTUL members, however, sometimes found that their appearances did not produce such a sense of sisterhood among middle-class women comfortable with elitism and class-biased stereotypes.

Pushed by Mary McDowell, a settlement resident, WTUL ally, and head of the Industrial Program Committee for the 1905 convention of the Illinois State Federation of Women's Clubs, the State Federation invited Agnes Nestor to speak to its 1905 convention. "It was a bold step" for the club women to consent to have a working woman speak to them on trade unionism, and Nestor was eager to present her case effectively. She splurged and had a white silk blouse trimmed in rose-colored velvet made for the occasion. It was the fanciest garment she owned, and she went off to the convention feeling that she looked "gay as a butterfly." She was pleased to have her speech described as "stirring and informative," but terribly disappointed by a reference to her "dark and shabby appearance."[114]

The blouse won more attention the following year, when Rheta Childe Dorr, a league ally and an active member of the General Federation of

Women's Clubs, arranged for Nestor to speak to the national convention of the GFWC. Nestor told of her experiences as a glove worker and as a trade unionist and urged federation members to support women workers in their legislative fight for an eight-hour day. After her speech a club woman came up to Nestor, felt the material of her blouse, and said accusingly, "You're not a real working girl. Look at the blouse you are wearing!" At least this time, Nestor noted philosophically, "I had the satisfaction that the blouse was recognized for what it was."[115]

A revealing commentary on WTUL priorities is the 1909-1910 Annual Report of the New York WTUL, which mentions in passing that WTUL representatives spoke "constantly" at union meetings but lists in detail the non-union groups addressed by league members. Seven WTUL members constituted the "speaker's bureau" for the league that year, and among them, they spoke at 105 meetings of groups such as the Colony Club, the Woman's Civic Forum, the YWCA, and the Council of Jewish Women.[116] By 1920 an "organizing" trip for Margaret Dreier Robins consisted almost entirely of speaking to various middle-class groups on the situation of women workers. Within a ten-day period she visited Philadelphia, Boston, New York, and Washington, and the following excerpts from her schedule are a tribute to her physical stamina (at age fifty-two) and her commitment to the WTUL:

Philadelphia
March 22, Noon   Spoke on The Value of Collective Bargaining at
                       home of Mrs. Gifford Pinchot.
           Afternoon   Spoke on the Need of Training for Leadership,
                       also at home of Mrs. Pinchot.
           Evening   Spoke on the Value of Collective Bargaining at
                       the YWCA.

Boston
March 24, Noon   Spoke on The Challenge of Present Day
                       Industrial Conditions to the Junior League.
           Evening   Spoke on the National Women's Trade Union
                       League at the home of Mrs. Roland G.
                       Hopkins at Chestnut Hill.
March 25, Morning   Conference at the office of the Boston WTUL.
           Noon   Luncheon with Miss Mabel Gillespie, Miss
                       Anna Weinstock, President and Secretary of the
                       Boston Women's Trade Union League and
                       Miss Ann Withington.

	Evening	Dinner and Address on the Value to the Community of the Trade Union Movement before the Boston Women Voter's League.
March 27		All day meeting of the New England Conference of Trade Union Women called by the Boston Women's Trade Union League; Spoke on the International Congress of Working Women and on The Need of Organization.
	Evening	Dinner at the Women's City Club. Spoke on The Challenge of Present Day Industrial Conditions.[117]

It is true that the WTUL would not have survived as long as it did without the financial contributions from middle- and upper-class women whose sympathies were aroused. Yet the cause of women workers would ultimately have been better served if the WTUL had focused some of this energy on more direct organizing campaigns or had created a body such as the British National Federation of Women Workers.

The response of what Rose Schneiderman called "The Mink Brigade" during the 1909-1910 New York shirtwaist strike probably stands as the most impressive result of the WTUL's efforts to win support from women outside the working class.[118] Socially prominent women such as Alva Vanderbilt Belmont and Josephine Sykes Morgenthau staged fund-raising benefits and served as observers of police treatment of picketing strikers. Their involvement generated extensive publicity for the strike and was a critical factor in creating public support for the striking women. However, as Theresa Malkiel, one of the strikers and a Socialist not inclined to overlook class differences, pointed out after the Hippodrome rally sponsored by Alva Belmont:

> Most of our girls had to walk both ways in order to save their car fare. Many came without dinner, but the collection baskets had more pennies than anything else in them—it was our girls themselves who helped to make it up, and yet there were so many rich women present. And I'm sure the speakers made it plain to them how badly the money was needed, then how comes it that out of the $300 collected there should be $70 in pennies?[119]

As part of the fund-raising effort during that strike, female strikers and WTUL members traveled throughout New York and New England, speaking on college campuses and to local women's groups. A considerable amount of money was raised in this way, but the strikers did not uniformly receive support. Margaret Dreier Robins recalled one such instance many years later:

> One of our very fine young working women, a leader of one of the strikes in New York City, an English-American girl, was not permitted to stay overnight in the YWCA House in a small town in New York state because her name was so well known and the Matron said they would not accommodate any strikers. It was ten o'clock at night when this girl came in good faith to the YWCA for a night's lodging. This and some similar experiences naturally embittered the Trade Union girls against the YWCA.[120]

Life and Labor acknowledged the significant help of the Woman Suffrage Party of Illinois during the 1911 Chicago garment workers' strike, when it contributed over $700 to the strike fund.[121] On the other hand, even supportive women revealed their lack of understanding. When the garment workers' strike spread to Cleveland in the summer of 1911, Pauline Newman and Margaret Dreier Robins went there to arrange a mass meeting to publicize the strike and explain the issues involved. Among the speakers they recruited were two prominent and relatively wealthy suffragists, who made stirring speeches in support of the striking women workers and the work of the WTUL, but then submitted bills for $40 for their services and showed no further interest in the strike or the WTUL.[122]

Like the British league, the American WTUL's educational work made the problems and needs of women workers much better known, but the tangible response of non-working-class women was hardly commensurate with the amount of energy expended by the league. It was able to elicit only limited generosity, sensitivity, and commitment from middle-class feminists.

The American league was more oriented to the middle-class feminist movement than the British for two major reasons. First, many more of the ally members of the American league had ties to women's organizations, such as NAWSA and the General Federation of Women's Clubs. Second, the American WTUL emphasized education and legislation as means of improving the situation of women workers, given the relative indifference of the men in the American labor movement. This shift from direct organizing to educational and legislative activities thus made the WTUL increasingly dependent on the support of middle-class feminists. Yet while the league did form alliances with middle-class feminists over issues of common concern such as suffrage, it met with only limited success in getting middle-class feminists to join women workers in their struggles for better working conditions. Ironically, it was the middle-class feminists whose conscious and unconscious sense of class limited the achievement of cross-class female solidarity. As a result, the WTUL did considerably more for the American women's movement than the women's movement did for the WTUL and the cause of women workers.

FOUR

The Promise of Legislation: Britain

As a complement to their organizing and educational work, both the British and American Women's Trade Union Leagues lobbied for legislation that would improve the situation of women workers. Although both leagues remained firmly committed to unionization as ultimately the only effective solution to the problems of women workers, they realized that women workers' low wages, oppressive working conditions, and long hours tended to create virtually insurmountable barriers to their organization into stable trade unions. In other words, the leagues viewed legislation regulating wages, conditions, and hours as a necessary precondition for lasting unionization. Another factor influencing the leagues' advocacy of legislative measures was their realization that the passage of such laws would benefit more women more quickly than the leagues, with their limited resources, could hope to reach through their organizing campaigns and educational programs.

Even though both leagues shared a common perspective on the value of and need for labor legislation, the political systems of Britain and the United States are distinct enough to require treating each league's legislative efforts separately. It is important to note at the outset two differences between Britain and the United States that significantly affected the leagues' legislative endeavors. The first is that labor legislation in Britain is passed only at the national level, whereas in the United States it falls within the purview of state legislatures as well as Congress. As a result, the British WTUL could concentrate its lobbying efforts on Parliament, while the American WTUL's energies were of necessity more diffused. The second difference was the existence of a Labour Party in Britain, with which the British WTUL closely identified and on which it relied heavily for support. In the absence of a comparable political party in the United States, the American WTUL adhered to a nonpartisan orientation, and consequently it had no guaranteed allies among American politicians.

* * *

The British WTUL's advocacy of various legislative proposals between 1890 and 1920 represented a reversal of the policy followed in the previous fifteen years by the Women's Protective and Provident League. Throughout the late 1870s and 1880s the league actively opposed special labor legislation for women; it considered classifying together wage-earning women and children a demeaning restriction on women's rights as adults to make contracts with their employers. Emma Paterson, founder of the Women's Protective and Provident League, wrote when a bill limiting the hours of women's work in factories and workshops was before Parliament in 1874, "This Bill is intended to apply also to children, with whom working women are classed, thus conveying and endeavouring to perpetuate, the idea that women are entirely unable to protect themselves."[1] In addition to wanting to establish the principle that women workers be classified with men rather than with children, the WTUL feared that legislation regulating the hours women worked, the wages they received, or the types of jobs open to them would make women's labor less profitable and thereby decrease their opportunities for employment. Motivated more by abstract feminist principles than by genuine insight into the situation of women workers, early members of the Women's Protective and Provident League, strongly influenced by the views of Emma Paterson, regarded the formation of independent women's unions as the only useful solution to the problems of women workers.

Although Paterson was naively optimistic about the possibility of women forming strong and viable independent unions, she distrusted the motivation behind trade union men's support for legislation regulating women's work. Her suspicions were confirmed at the 1877 Trades Union Congress, when, in a discussion on a resolution favoring the extension of legal restrictions on female labor in the cotton industry, several delegates indicated that they not only supported this resolution but were interested in legislation that would exclude women from certain branches of agriculture and chain making. Paterson pointed out that unionization rather than exclusion was the socially responsible answer to the danger of women being employed to undercut male wages, but her arguments were in vain. The Trades Union Congress overwhelmingly passed the resolution, and Henry Broadhurst, secretary of the

TUC Parliamentary Committee, was enthusiastically cheered when he summarized the dominant position. Rhetorically acknowledging that "it was very natural for ladies to be impatient of restraint at any time," he then told the women that they must realize:

> They [the men] had the future of their country and children to consider, and it was their duty as men and husbands to use their utmost efforts to bring about a condition of things, where their wives should be in their proper sphere at home, instead of being dragged into competition for livelihood against the great and strong men of the world.[2]

Unwilling to let men define women's proper sphere, the WTUL often in the 1880s opposed the legislative proposals of men's unions.[3] The most protracted conflict occurred over the role of women in the metal trades. It began in 1882, when, in accordance with the wishes of the Black County metal unions, Broadhurst introduced a bill into Parliament calling for barring girls under fourteen from working as blacksmiths. Apprehensive that this bill, ostensibly motivated by a concern for child labor, was a prelude to legislation prohibiting the employment of females of all ages, the WTUL asked that the bill be extended to cover boys under fourteen.

The ensuing debate between the league and the unions proved that the women's apprehensions were well founded. The men resisted the league's proposal and did not deny that their goal was the exclusion of women from this industry. Refusing to acknowledge that their primary objection was that women were used to undercut male wage rates, the men instead argued for the exclusion of women on the grounds that "the women working side by side with the men were exposed to the grossest possible language and conduct." The WTUL refused to be swayed by this appeal to conventional social values and responded that such a state of affairs "was a libel on the men and no reflection on their [the female] sex."[4]

Unmoved, the delegates endorsed the Broadhurst bill, claiming that "the condition of things described [half-nude women working with men in the same state of undress] is a disgrace to the nation" and that as trade union men, they felt compelled "to stand out against the iniquitous system of female labour."[5] The bill, however, did not pass through Parliament, for ironically and unwittingly, the WTUL's feminist stance provided a useful cover for employers, whose interest in maintaining a pool of cheap labor led them forcefully to oppose this measure. It was of course primarily their influence, rather than the WTUL's, that was responsible for the bill's defeat.

91

The metalworkers continued to lobby for legislation limiting the employment of women in their industry. With dissenting votes cast only by the two women delegates, the 1887 Trades Union Congress passed a resolution submitted by the Midland Trades Federation advocating the introduction of "such amendments to the Factory and Workshops Act as shall prevent the employment of females in the making of chains, nails, rivets, bolts, etc., such work not being adapted to their constitution." However, by the following congress, the league's efforts to convince the metalworkers of the validity of its point of view had succeeded. Mr. Juggins, the Midland Trades Federation representative who had moved the previous year's resolution, announced that he "had come to the conclusion that nothing but better pay for women could cure the evil, and they [the federation] had therefore resolved to organize women as soon as possible."[6] He now supported a resolution calling for equal pay for equal work. It passed unanimously, and the Midlands Trades Federation immediately requested the WTUL's assistance in organizing the women chain makers of Cradley Heath.[7]

Although opposed to labor legislation affecting only women workers, the WTUL strongly supported the principle of labor legislation and was especially concerned that laws regulating working conditions (e.g., ventilation and sanitary standards) be more rigorously enforced. Factories and workshops that primarily employed women were often neglected by inspectors and women workers were often intimidated by male inspectors (particularly when it came to reporting violations of sanitation regulations). So the WTUL began lobbying in 1878 for the appointment of women factory inspectors.

Emma Paterson objected to the ambiguity of a resolution before the 1878 Trades Union Congress calling for the appointment of "practical persons" (i.e., workers) as factory inspectors, and she moved to amend the wording to "practical men and women." Considering this proposal inconsistent with Paterson's views on protective legislation, the chairman ridiculed her suggestion, and the male delegates' initial response was that "the ladies truly had strange ambitions!"[8] Despite this reaction, Paterson's amendment passed by a slim majority, but it took thirteen more years before the men were willing to propose this revised wording on their own. At each Trades Union Congress between 1879 and 1891 a male delegate moved a resolution calling for "persons," a WTUL delegate moved to amend the resolution to "men and women," and the amendment passed. Finally in 1892 the initial resolution incorporated the WTUL's amendment; it passed unanimously, and in the following year the Home Secretary did in fact appoint a WTUL member as the first woman factory inspector.[9]

* * *

The league had begun to reconsider its policy on labor legislation for women in the late 1880s because its attempts to form stable trade unions among women workers had met with limited success. The obstacles to effective organization were far greater than the WTUL had originally realized. When Emma Paterson died in 1886, it was clear that changes in the league's approach were necessary. The first public indication that the WTUL was reevaluating its policies was a resolution passed at its 1886 annual meeting, which declared "the best way to extend the work of the League is to lay stress on its *protective* as distinct from its *provident* element and . . . for the League to use its influence to support all other modes of action which may tend to bring about a better distribution of wealth."[10]

It was largely as the result of its efforts to organize laundry workers in Wandsworth and Fulham that the league came to regard legislation as a useful "mode of action."[11] These women worked fourteen- to sixteen-hour days and earned approximately twelve shillings a week. They lacked the time and money to develop stable unions. Moreover, as unskilled, easily replaceable workers, they were more vulnerable to their employers' attempts to squelch incipient signs of labor unrest than the relatively skilled female bookbinders, tailors, and upholsterers the league had previously organized. A WTUL canvass of the laundry workers revealed overwhelming interest in legislative regulation, so the WTUL mounted a campaign to secure the inclusion of laundresses in the 1891 Factory and Workshops Bill.[12] Although the agitation was not successful, it was an important moment in the history of the WTUL, for it was the first time the league advocated, rather than opposed, special legislation for women.[13] The league formally announced its new policy in 1891, stating that it now "conceded . . . the principle that the State has a right to interfere with the labour of women and children, if the moral and physical well-being of the country demands it."[14]

Despite this concession, the league was initially reluctant "to appeal to State legislation except as a last resource."[15] Feeling that women shop assistants were in a strong enough position not to warrant special legislation, the WTUL instructed its delegates to an 1892 national conference on shop assistants' hours "to vote only in favour of such legislation as would place men and

93

women shop assistants on an equal footing"; they were to oppose "any proposals for separate legislation for women."[16]

However, insights gained by WTUL members who undertook the provincial organizing tours begun in the early 1890s and reports of newly appointed women factory inspectors in the mid-1890s made the league realize that the hours and wages of most women workers were so low that without some legislative changes, efforts at organizing were doomed. As Clementina Black, one of the earliest converts to a pro-legislation policy, wrote, "Like most middle-class people who have no personal acquaintance with working-class life, I set out with a prejudice against 'State Interference'," but meeting women workers and visiting factories and workshops had taught her the value of legislative regulation.[17] Throughout the 1890s the WTUL devoted increasing time to legislative lobbying, so much so that by 1897 the league was proudly claiming that "no legislation, Order of the Secretary of State, or regulation of any description concerning working women has been brought forward without the League's attention being directed to the matter, and appropriate action being taken."[18]

This fundamental shift in the WTUL's policy and behavior reflected its open-mindedness and its willingness to question the standard feminist doctrine that men and women should always be treated equally. Middle-class feminists, anxious to abolish the legal barriers that denied females access to the professions, tended to equate protective legislation for women workers with existing laws that restricted their own access to education and employment.[19] The WTUL, however, had come to reject the notion that women of all classes should be treated as free agents, able to sell their labor as they wished; women who entered the labor force with the double disabilities of sex and class were not genuine free agents but instead were bound by considerably more severe social and economic constraints than either working-class men or middle-class women.

With this change in its thinking, the WTUL strengthened its ties to the labor movement and severed its links with the middle-class feminist movement, which remained steadfastly opposed to special legislation regulating female employment. After the WTUL's 1891 statement, the Society for Promoting the Employment of Women, which had joined forces with the league to oppose factory legislation for women, denounced its former ally and attempted to discredit the WTUL's lobbying efforts in connection with the 1895 Factory Act.[20] Going even farther, former WTUL members Lady Balfour, Lady

Knightsly, and Jessie Boucherett founded the Freedom of Labour Defense League, whose stated purpose was:

> to protect workers, especially adult women workers, from the restrictive legislation which would lessen their wage-earning capacity, limit their personal liberty, and inconvenience them in their private lives, and also to maintain the right of women to the same amount of liberty enjoyed by men, in regard to the nature, hours, and conditions of employment.[21]

Boucherett, who was also editor of the *Englishwoman's Review*, a middle-class feminist journal, published a book in 1898 contending that factory legislation was responsible for a decline in women's wages. Aside from the fact that her argument was based on suspect statistics, the book revealed how far she was from understanding the reality of women workers' lives. In addition to opposing the legal regulation of hours, wages, and nature of employment open to women, she argued against regulations dictating special health and safety standards for factories and workshops employing women, on the grounds that:

> Every year gives us a long list of accidents with bicycles, carriages, and horses. Yet it is on the whole better that women should be allowed to enjoy these amusements. . . . No doubt a few young ladies die every year from colds caught at balls. . . . It is better that a few delicate persons should suffer in health than that hundreds should be exposed to the misery of being turned out of work.[22]

Unlike the American WTUL, which actively sought to convert middle-class feminists to its position, the British league generally ignored this opposition. Middle-class women who refused to support factory legislation were, however, severely criticized by Beatrice Webb, who edited *The Case for Factory Legislation* as "a counterblast to the persistent opposition to factory legislation on the part of the 'women's rights' movement reinforced by employers' wives." Webb held these women responsible for blocking extensions of the Factory Acts, and she defined the opposition as consisting of "a few blatant agitators, who would not count for much if they were not backed up by many 'society' women who belong to the governing clique."[23] Lady Dilke also publicly dissociated the league from "the clamour" raised by those women vehemently calling for total legal equality between the sexes. Furthermore, she chastised those women for "retard[ing] the advance of public opinion in the direction of practical or needed reform."[24]

In this she was in harmony with her husband, Sir Charles Dilke, M.P. for Chelsea. Dilke, a well-known and highly respected Radical Liberal, representing first Chelsea and then the Forest of Dean, a mining area in Gloucestershire. He was consistently a dedicated advocate of labor and from 1892 on he served as the WTUL's parliamentary spokesman. Sidney Webb praised Dilke's role as a labor supporter:

> No one will ever know how much the Progressive Movement, in all its manifestations owed to his counsel, his great knowledge, and his unsparing helpfulness. Trade Unionism among women as well as men, the movement for amending and extending factory legislation, the organization of Labour forces in the House of Commons are only some of the causes in which I have myself witnessed the extraordinary effectiveness which his participation aided.[25]

When Dilke died in 1911, the WTUL noted, "The fact that a public man of his eminence concerned himself with the details of women's work gave the subject an importance which it never had before."[26]

Thus, under the influence of the Dilkes, the WTUL in the late 1880s and 1890s moved away from the individualistic Liberal policies that had characterized the league under Emma Paterson's leadership. Lady Dilke died in 1904, and although her post as president was subsequently filled by her niece Gertrude Tuckwell, it was Mary Macarthur, who had been appointed executive secretary in 1903, who quickly became the WTUL's leading figure. Prior to her involvement in the WTUL, Macarthur had been active in the Shop Assistants' Union, serving on its national executive board and as president of the union's Scottish National District Council. Thus she came to the WTUL with stronger political and personal ties to the labor movement and the Labour Party than either Emma Paterson or Lady Dilke had had, and under her leadership the league greatly expanded its legislative functions and became solidly linked to the Labour Party.

WTUL literature now listed legislation as one of the league's three main objects (the others were organization and "social work") and characterized the league as "the agent of women Trade Unionists in stirring up Government Authorities or Parliamentary Committees."[27] Macarthur and three other WTUL activists were among the founding members of the Women's Labour League, an organization established by Margaret MacDonald (wife of J. Ramsay MacDonald) in 1906 to give women a greater role in Labour Party politics. The WTUL's already close ties to the Labour Party were strengthened in 1911 when Mary Macarthur married Will Anderson, a Scottish shop assistant by background, who had risen through the ranks of union and labor politics to become a leading figure in the Independent Labour Party. Elected to Parliament in 1914 as M.P. for the Attercliffe division of Sheffield, Anderson, like Dilke before him, served as the WTUL's primary parliamentary spokesman during World War I, an especially active period of government involvement in the position of women workers.

Of all the legislative measures supported by the league from 1891 to 1920, its role in the creation of a system of Trade Boards empowered to set minimum wage rates in sweated industries was its most significant legislative achievement.[28] The 1909 Trade Boards Bill stands as a landmark in the history of British labor legislation, and the WTUL's response to its passage illustrates its commitment to using legislation as a foundation for further unionization. Women in sweated industries constituted the most oppressed sector of the labor force. Appallingly poor, overworked, and isolated in homes or scattered in small workshops and factories, these workers could hardly improve their situation through collective action. The WTUL considered low wages to be the major obstacle to effective organization, and it turned to legislative intervention as a necessary first step in the campaign to raise the standard of living for workers in sweated trades. If minimum wage rates could be legislated and enforced, the WTUL reasoned, organization might then follow.

Trade boards had been established in Victoria, Australia, in 1896 for five sweated industries: clothing, boot- and shoemaking, shirtmaking, furniture, and bread making. These boards consisted of an equal number of representatives of labor and management and an outside chairman. They were instituted in the face of considerable opposition from employers but rather quickly came to be seen as serving the interests of both groups, for they provided an effective curb on ruthless competition through exploitative wage rates. By 1907 trade boards had been established for forty-four additional industries.

Influenced by the Australian example and by his wife's involvement in the WTUL, Sir Charles Dilke introduced a private members' bill in 1898 advocating the creation of British boards on the Australian model.[29] Dilke continued to raise the issue each year, but there was little public or parliamentary support until the WTUL began an active campaign to rouse public opinion in 1905. Stirred to action by the suffering she had observed in her two years as WTUL secretary, Mary Macarthur appealed to A. G. Gardiner, the sympathetic editor of the *Daily News*, for help in publicizing the plight of sweated workers, who were predominantly female, and the need for legislation on their behalf. Gardiner had been impressed by the impact of a public exhibition on sweated industries held recently in Berlin, and he proposed that a similar exhibition be staged in London. Macarthur responded enthusiastically to this suggestion, feeling that it had considerably more dramatic potential than a series of meetings or articles describing the problems of these workers.

Although the exhibition, which was held in the spring of 1906, was officially sponsored by the *Daily News*, the WTUL did much of the actual work in planning it. The league assembled artificial-flower makers, hook-and-eye and button carders, sack sewers, shirtmakers, fur stitchers, tennis-ball makers, box makers, and various other workers representing a total of forty-five sweated trades to demonstrate to the public the conditions under which these articles were produced. Posters indicating wage rates and family budgets accompanied each exhibit, a handbook on sweated industries was prepared, and several league members gave daily lectures, explaining the cause and cure for sweating. Hundreds of thousands of people visited the exhibition, and many came away shocked by what they had seen.[30]

As a result of the exhibition, the Anti-Sweating League was formed in June 1906 to promote legislation to combat the worst aspects of the sweated trades. Several WTUL members were on the executive board of the league, and they successfully argued for trade boards, rather than a licensing system, as the legislative remedy to be advocated. Once the Anti-Sweating League had come to this position, its next step was to seek support of the labor movement for its proposal.

Three hundred trade union delegates attended a three-day conference called by the Anti-Sweating League in October, where WTUL leaders, social reformers, and several male labor leaders spoke about the problems of sweating and the value of trade boards. For the first two days the conference seemed to be proceeding smoothly toward an endorsement of minimum wage legislation through a system of trade boards. On the third day, however, vigorous opposition was voiced by a series of speakers, all of whom were members of the Social Democratic Federation. They denounced the concept of trade boards as "a middle class dodge, a mere palliative designed to put off the day of real thoroughgoing change." The trade unionist chairing the meeting attempted to respond to these objections, but he was shouted down. As the tumult increased and it seemed that the opponents were gaining the upper hand, Mary Macarthur stepped forward to speak. Rather than directly refuting the arguments that had been raised against legislative intervention, she appealed to the audience to remember the circumstances they had come together to discuss. She spoke emotionally of the misery of sweated workers, of the countless women and children in London slums "toiling day and night, with aching fingers, burning eyes, and breaking hearts." As she spoke, "the Guildhall with its ornate ornamentation disappeared; silence fell upon the floor; the struggle of contending tacticians was forgotten." When she finished, the delegates rose as one, passing the resolution by acclamation, "amid resounding cheers." Dissolved in tears of emotional exhaustion, Macarthur saw and heard the end of the conference through a blur, but she recognized that a major victory had been won: the trade union movement had committed itself to the principle of a minimum wage for selected workers through trade boards.[31]

Labour Party victories in the 1906 election created a broader base of support in the House of Commons labor legislation. In June 1907 a Select Committee of Home Work was appointed, charged with considering and reporting on "the conditions of labour in trades in which Home Work is prevalent and on the proposals, including those for the establishment of wages boards and the licensing of work places, which have been made for the remedying of existing abuses."[32] Although the WTUL was disappointed that the committee's charge was limited to home work, since the problem extended to workshops and factories as well, it saw the establishment of the Select Committee as an important opening wedge in the struggle to gain minimum wage legislation for all sweated workers.

Both Gertrude Tuckwell and Mary Macarthur testified before the committee, and they stressed that it was difficult to separate sweated conditions of home workers from factory workers. Macarthur acknowledged that women home workers, whose wages she estimated averaged 4s. 6d. a week, were the most oppressed group of sweated workers, but even among women employed in factories and workshops (except in textiles), wages averaged barely 7s. a week.[33] According to Tuckwell, as Macarthur spoke, "the hard face of the Chairman and the rather bored faces of the Committee were gradually roused to an almost smiling and sympathetic interest as she told him of her personal experiences in London."[34]

Macarthur's presentation was particularly effective because she spoke about the value of trade boards from the employer's point of view as well as the workers'. The "good" employer, committed in principle to decent conditions and wages, was unable to put his principles into practice because another, less scrupulous employer down the street was paying lower rates. Drawing on her own experiences, she cited numerous examples of employers who had told her they would be willing to raise wages if it was being done throughout the industry. Impressed by the comprehensiveness of Macarthur's testimony, one committee member told her, "Your evidence, to my mind has brought Wage Boards within the sphere of practical politics."[35]

The committee chairman said he would like to hear from sweated workers themselves in a private session and asked Macarthur if she could arrange this. In complying with this request, Macarthur inadvertently supplied the campaign for legislative intervention with a dramatic episode. Venturing into one of London's worst slum areas, she visited a young woman who made lace-trimmed baby garments for which she was paid a penny apiece. The woman owned no bed linen and covered herself at night with the garments she was making. Unknown to Macarthur or the young woman, she had incipient diphtheria, and after visiting her and handling the garments, Macarthur came down with the disease. Since these contaminated garments were destined for middle-class homes, this incident forcefully brought to public attention that the proposed reforms were necessary for the well-being of the entire British population; self-interest as well as altruism dictated their passage.[36]

Despite the success of this first round of hearings, it took another year and a half of agitation before the government was ready to introduce a bill advocating the creation of trade boards. However, once introduced in March 1909, the proposal met with little resistance in the House of Commons. It was passed by the House of Lords the following fall, and it received Royal Assent on January 1, 1910. The act called for the establishment of trade boards in four industries, all of which relied primarily on female labor: chain making, cardboard box making, lace finishing, and wholesale tailoring. In each district where these trades were prevalent, boards representing workers and employers were to be formed. Their first task was to study the conditions of the trade in that area, and on the basis of their findings, determine a schedule of minimum rates by piece or hour, taking into account the general cost of living for the area. The act provided for a three-month grace period once the new rates were set, but after that any manufacturer found to be in violation of the board's standards would be fined and required to make up the difference in lost wages to his employees.

Like all legislation, the strength of the Trade Boards Bill depended on enforcement. But the WTUL was optimistic about the act's potential to bring about important changes in the situation of sweated workers. Mary Macarthur told the delegates to the American WTUL's 1909 convention, "I don't think England quite realizes what has been done. It is simply a revolution. It means a revolution in our industrial conditions."[37] The British WTUL was especially pleased that the bill provided for the extension of trade boards to industries beyond the original four. The "inquiry clause" established that any trade union, district trade council, or any six people—employers or workers—representing a given trade could request that a board be constituted for an unregulated industry. Upon receiving such a request, the Home Secretary was required to institute an investigation of the trade, and the WTUL assumed that virtually all such investigations would result in the creation of a new trade board. According to Constance Smith, a WTUL member and a lady factory inspector:

> The immense value of this procedure in the case of women workers can only be fully appreciated by the workers themselves and by those who have striven to act as their friends. In a very large number of cases, the difficulty, for women and girls, of obtaining access to their employer, and of laying their grievances before him are considerable.[38]

Of the four trade boards scheduled under the 1909 act, the one for Cradley Heath was established first. The situation of these women chain makers, who worked at their backyard forges for 5s. or 6s. a week, was considered a national scandal. The WTUL had long recognized the plight of these workers, and the league's work on their behalf in 1910 illustrates the complementary nature of its legislative and organizing activities.

The chain makers asked Mary Macarthur to serve as one of their representatives on the trade board, and the negotiations, which began in January 1910, went on for five full months before the two sides reached an agreement on new wage rates. Macarthur, who was adding the negotiations in Cradley Heath to her already full schedule at the WTUL in London, was unprepared for their length and bitterness. Macarthur was enraged by some of the employers' representatives on the board who were insensitive to the suffering they perpetuated in the interest of their own material well-being. "Neither patience nor tolerance were natural virtues with her [Macarthur], and both were sorely tried as meeting after meeting ended with no agreement on a rate and it looked as though the deadlock was insoluble."[39]

An acceptable compromise on new rates was eventually reached, although the wage scale was considerably lower than the workers' representatives had hoped it would be. But, feeling that "any ordered system of payment" was useful in the face of the chaos that characterized this industry, they accepted the new rates as the best they could do for the moment, viewing them as "the basis upon which improvement in the future could be built."[40] To strengthen the workers' position on future negotiations, the National Federation of Women Workers, the trade union arm of the WTUL, immediately began an organizing campaign, reasoning that even with this small increase in wage rates, the workers would for the first time be able to support the formation of a union. However, before the NFWW had a chance to make much headway in its organizing drive, it was confronted with a situation that called for a bold and forceful response.

The threat came from certain employers who took advantage of a "contracting-out" provision in the Trade Board Act. In addition to the three-month grace period the law granted employers before the new rates had to be put into effect, the act allowed them to request their employees waive their rights to the new rates for a further six months. Intimidated, illiterate, and ignorant of their rights, hundreds of women workers signed documents agreeing to this further delay.

These same employers simultaneously instituted a production speedup, which the WTUL was convinced was meant to create a large stockpile of chains when they finally would have to begin paying the higher wage rates. This oversupply would then be used as a justification for laying off workers and thus was a calculated attempt to arouse opposition to minimum wages by making it appear that the board's rulings created unemployment rather than raised the workers' standard of living. This reinforced the WTUL's belief that legislation alone could never be a solution; without organization, workers would remain vulnerable to their employers' greater economic and social power.

These first trade boards were viewed as an experiment. Fearful that the consequences of this contracting-out process would call into question the entire system of legislated minimum wage rates, the WTUL and NFWW were determined that this attempt to circumvent the spirit, if not the letter, of the Trade Board Act be resisted. Since solid organization among the chain makers had not yet been achieved, the workers were not accustomed to acting collectively. Moreover, to urge them to resist their employers' demands literally meant asking them to risk starvation; these workers had no savings, no possibilities of alternative employment, and there was no local union strike fund to see them through a struggle.

Mary Macarthur, however, was convinced that if the women were willing to go on strike, public opinion could be mobilized to support them. People would see the chain makers as fighting not only for themselves but for the principle of a minimum wage. Thus, cognizant of the risks but confident of success, the NFWW called a mass meeting of the workers. Macarthur eloquently explained the situation, and she then urged the women who had already signed the contracting-out agreements to renounce them and encouraged those who had not yet signed to refrain from doing so. Following the leadership of an older woman who declared she "should drop dead rather than sign a contracting-out paper," the entire assembly pledged its collective resistance and its willingness to go out on strike.[41]

Most of the employers contracting out were relatively small entrepreneurs who did not belong to the industry's Manufacturers' Association but who nonetheless employed about 1,000 women. Rather than immediately dealing with these employers, the WTUL arranged a meeting between the Manufacturers' Association and representatives of the chain makers. The Manufacturers' Association pleaded its willingness to begin paying the new rates immediately *if* its member employers could be assured that they would not be undercut by employers outside the association. In other words, the association was asking the WTUL and NFWW to guarantee that women working for other employers would refuse to work for the old rates. Gambling that public support would provide a large enough fund to sustain those workers forced to strike to pressure their employers to implement the new rates, the NFWW called a strike of the workers whose employers were attempting to put the contracting-out provision into effect.

Leaving the daily management of the strike to C. H. Sitch, a male labor leader, and Julia Varley, an NFWW organizer, Mary Macarthur returned to London to publicize the struggle and raise a strike fund. Through letters, leaflets, speeches, and articles, she brilliantly conveyed the plight of these workers whose employers were refusing to raise their wages by a few pennies an hour. The labor movement and the general public responded generously to Macarthur's appeals, contributing nearly £4,000 to the strike fund.[42] Without this backing, the workers would not have been able to hold out for a victory; as it was, it took thirteen weeks, but finally every employer in the district agreed to the new rates.

The success of the strike—and the fact that it happened at all—is an impressive tribute to the effectiveness of the WTUL. Its ability to inspire these downtrodden chain makers with a sense of the possibilities of collective action and its skillful management of the negotiations and public relations are evidence of the league's courage, commitment, and skill. Although many members of the WTUL played important parts in this struggle, Mary

103

Macarthur's role, first in the campaign to pass the Trade Board Act and then in the strike, was critical. She obviously could not have accomplished these victories on her own, but without her energy and charismatic leadership, it is unlikely that the same results would have been achieved. A few months after the strike was over, the chain makers, who were now organized by the thousands rather than the hundreds, invited Macarthur back to Cradley Heath to present her with a gold watch as a symbol of their affection and gratitude. Ultimately of course, it is the courage of the women workers themselves that deserves recognition, but it was the legislative and organizing activities of the WTUL that gave these women the structural and psychological tools to improve their lives.

* * *

The league had developed an effective technique of arousing public opinion and then using that concern as a prod for further legislation. By the outbreak of World War I, the WTUL had raised public awareness about the dangers of lead poisoning among pottery workers, necrosis among match makers, and the particularly pernicious effects of industrial hazards on pregnant women and children. Beginning in the 1890s the League had steadily lobbied for revisions in the Truck Act, and its efforts were rewarded in the gradual decline, and in some cases abolition, of fines and charges for materials (such as thread and electricity) that had reduced women workers' already low wages.

The league had also maintained constant pressure on the Home Secretary to increase the number of female factory inspectors and on Parliament to strengthen and extend factory acts regulating hours and working conditions in industries employing large numbers of women.[43] In the summer of 1911 the WTUL campaigned intensively for changes in the proposed National Health Insurance Act, and as a result, the act in its final form mandated a scale of payments and benefits that were more equitably correlated to the low pay and seasonal nature of most women's jobs. The WTUL was also able to obtain some recognition for the cyclical rhythm that characterized so many women's participation in the labor force by getting the Insurance Act to include some continuing protection for women who worked prior to marriage, left the labor force during their childbearing years, and reentered later.[44]

* * *

Although the WTUL's lobbying efforts inevitably resulted in legislation that fell short of its ultimate goals, by 1914 the league was nationally recognized and respected as an advocate of the special needs and interests of women workers. The size of the female labor force and the range of jobs open to women dramatically increased during World War I, and the WTUL's response to these changes consolidated its position as an articulate, informed, and effective representative of women in the industrial labor force. The league's work during the war stands out as the culmination of the organizing and legislative policies it adopted in the 1890s, and its wartime activities and arguments were largely responsible for the more solid structural integration of women into the Labour Party and the Trades Union Congress that occurred between 1918 and 1920.

At first the war created serious unemployment for women because the industries most severely disrupted were those such as dressmaking, millinery, confectionery, and cotton textiles, where a high proportion of the female labor force was clustered. By September 1914 male unemployment stood at 8.4 percent compared to 14 percent for females. Male unemployment declined rather quickly as men enlisted in the armed services or found work in the expanding munitions industry, but female unemployment remained abnormally high until the spring of 1915.[45]

Meanwhile, middle-class women were mobilizing to do volunteer work in the national interest, and the WTUL, in conjunction with other women's labor organizations (such as the Women's Labour League and the Women's Cooperative Guild), immediately intervened to try to prevent these volunteers from taking on work that unemployed working-class women might be paid to do. As a result of their prompt action, the Women's Emergency Corps, a coalition of about fifteen women's organizations (including the WTUL) was established in early August 1914 to coordinate women's volunteer efforts and direct these women into activities that would not undercut the potential employment of females who needed jobs.[46] The *Daily Herald*, a labor paper, praised the group's approach:

> The Suffrage Societies are taking a sensible view of the work to be done in the present crisis. Mrs. Fawcett has already drawn attention to the necessity of not interfering with paid Labour, and on behalf of the Women's Freedom League Miss Nina Boyle draws attention to the harm which will be done if women of leisure start making clothes for the troops. . . . Amateur tailoring will not help at all. . . . The ordinary factories can turn out shirts and flannels far better than well-to-do ladies can possibly hope to do.[47]

In addition to the WTUL's participation in the Women's Emergency Corps, the league played a major role in the creation and subsequent functioning of a government committee on female unemployment. Queen Mary took a special interest in this problem of displaced women workers, and she summoned Mary Macarthur to discuss the WTUL's views on the formation of such a committee. As a result of this interview, the Central Committee on Women's Unemployment was established to devise programs for the employment of women who had lost their jobs due to wartime dislocation of the economy. At the request of the queen, Macarthur was made secretary of the Central Committee, and its executive board included several women's labor activists as well as a number of more socially prominent women.[48]

Operating in the chaotic atmosphere of the first months of the war, the Central Committee organized workrooms where women could be put to work at government expense making shirts, socks, and belts for British soldiers. In addition to securing contracts for such government work, the committee also provided training in new trades in an attempt to expand employment possibilities for women after the war. Macarthur, who functioned as the de facto head of the Central Committee, insisted that all the workshops established under the committee's auspices conform to Factory Act regulations and pay wages consistent with Trade Board rulings. By January 1915 these workrooms had provided employment for 14,000 women, 9,000 of whom had already been able to move on to other jobs as the economy adjusted to the demands of the war.[49]

Mary Macarthur was also selected to be one of two labor representatives on the executive board of the Prince of Wales Fund, another government committee created in August 1914 to provide assistance to those whose lives were disrupted by the war. There was much criticism in the labor press of the fund's executive board, which consisted primarily of aristocrats:

> We have no confidence in the composition of the National Executive Committee of the Relief Fund. The persons needed most were those who had intimate knowledge of the lives of the workers, who are going to be the greatest sufferers by this war, and instead we get a very different class of person, with Arthur Henderson [head of the Labour Party] and Mary Macarthur thrown in as make-weight. Titled persons, doubtless with enthusiasm but with little knowledge, will not make up for the deficiency of workers' representatives.[50]

Mary Macarthur and the WTUL had achieved respectability while winning the respect of some of the most important men in the labor movement. A column in the *Daily Sketch* discussing the Prince of Wales Fund characterized Macarthur as "the best of the lot"; it further (in words that reveal subtly sexist attitudes) praised her as "the sanest and most enthusiastic of all women leaders" and noted that her work in the women's labor movement "has been characterized with remarkable knowledge and skill."[51]

By the spring of 1915 the problem of female employment had virtually disappeared due to the number of male workers who joined the armed forces and the expansion of the munitions industry. Between 1915 and 1918, approximately 1.25 million new women entered the labor force, almost 99 percent of them directly or indirectly taking the places of men.[52] This increase in female employment and the hiring of women for jobs formerly done by men dramatically highlighted a problem the WTUL had been confronting for years, and it became the major focus of the league's legislative efforts during the remaining three years of the war: the low wages paid to women workers.

It was largely to discuss this problem that the War Emergency Workers' National Committee, of which the WTUL was a member, called a conference in April 1915 of representatives from women's trade union, labor, socialist, and suffrage organizations. Under the leadership of Mary Macarthur, who was chosen to be the presiding officer, the delegates expressed their concern that the war not be allowed to "unnecessarily depress the standard of living of the workers or the standard of working conditions." To this end, the conference urged the passage of legislation guaranteeing that "where a woman is doing the same work as a man, she receive the same rate of pay and that the principle of equal pay for equal work be rigidly maintained." Furthermore, it was imperative that in "no case" should any woman be employed at less than "an adequate living wage" and that the representatives of organized women workers be included on the government's skill standards Advisory Committee of Workers.[53]

This problem of female wage scales was particularly acute in the munitions industry, which experienced the largest influx of women workers (over one-half million) of any major industry, and it was on this industry that the WTUL focused its most intensive legislative (and organizing) efforts between 1915 and 1918.[54] Prior to the war, munitions were made primarily by skilled workers, and there were virtually no females employed in this industry at any level. The war of course enormously increased the demand for munitions, but this was accompanied by a decreasing supply of skilled (male) workers. In response to these shifts in supply and demand, the skilled processes that had characterized this industry were "diluted" or broken down into components

107

that could be done by semiskilled and unskilled workers, and increasingly it was females who filled the latter category.

The engineering unions, which were conservative, craft-oriented groups whose constitutions generally prohibited the membership of women, were alarmed by these changes in the industry, for they feared that the wage and skill standards that they had struggled to obtain might be lost if munitions work came to be dominated by a labor force of unskilled females. Sharing the unions' concerns, the WTUL supported them in their attempts to resist dilution. Munitions was a highly profitable industry, especially during the war, so, as far as the WTUL was concerned, there was no excuse for paying the women low wages, even when they were doing jobs classified as unskilled. Taking a trade unionist rather than a feminist perspective, the WTUL argued that for the sake of both male and female workers during and after the war, gains achieved by the engineering unions prior to the war must not be undermined as the industry changed. The league consistently insisted that ultimately the interests of men and women workers were the same; women deserved access to this area of work, but they should not be used as "black-legs" to lower standards previously won by the men. Thus, the league supported the entry of women into this industry, but only if women employed in jobs formerly done by men were paid the male rates. The WTUL also maintained that when women were hired to perform processes that resulted from dilution, which generally meant that pay scales had not been established through union negotiations, they nonetheless deserved to be paid a "decent living wage."

In alliance with the Amalgamated Society of Engineers, the WTUL lobbied for the inclusion of minimum wage rates for women workers in the 1915 Munitions Act. Although Lloyd George, who was then the minister of munitions, expressed a desire "to abolish sweating on war work," the act did not deal with the issue of wages. Thus, it left women workers with no legal support for improving their rates of pay, which were at best 15s. a week. Not only did the act not establish minimum wage rates, but it prohibited strikes for the duration of the war. It also made it virtually impossible for munition workers—male or female—to leave a poorly paid job for a better one, for one clause specified that a worker could be prosecuted for leaving a job without a certificate of discharge from the employer. One woman who attempted to transfer from a 10s. a week job with one firm to a 17s. job at another factory was denied a "leaving certificate" by her employer.[55]

The WTUL found this aspect of the Munitions Act particularly odious and throughout the summer of 1915 relentlessly pressured Lloyd George to revise or abolish this clause. Since the act had made the government responsible for conditions in munitions firms, the WTUL could focus its lobbying efforts on the government, rather than having to reach individual employers. The main thrust of the WTUL's argument was that if workers were to be denied the opportunity to seek better jobs, the government had a moral responsibility to insure decent wages and working conditions. The WTUL took its case to the public, and in articles, speeches, and interviews told of fourteen-hour workdays and of how the Home Office was routinely granting employers permission to suspend Factory Act regulations and employ women (and in some cases children) for overtime work on Sundays and at night. For 9s. to 15s. a week, women were working seventy- to eighty-hour weeks in factories that more often than not lacked adequate sanitary facilities.

As a result of the league's pressure, a government Committee of Inquiry was formally established in September 1915, and Mary Macarthur was selected to be one of its members. The committee's recommendations, which were subsequently adopted by the Ministry of Munitions, called for minimum wage schedules to govern the range of jobs done by women munition workers and for the immediate provision of lavatory and cloakroom facilities. Most employers, however, refused to comply with the mandated wage rates, and although the ministry had the legal right to take over firms that disregarded its regulations, it looked the other way.

Critical of the government's laissez-faire attitude, the WTUL capitalized on unrest among a group of female munition makers in Glasgow who were receiving particularly low wages. These workers had been organized into a branch of the National Federation of Women Workers, but their employer had refused to negotiate with or even recognize the union. The only situation in which munition workers could legally go on strike was when an application for arbitration had not been dealt with after a certain period of time had elapsed, so Mary Macarthur encouraged the workers to apply to the Board of Trade for an investigation of their situation. When the time limit had passed and the board had still not responded to the munition makers' request, the WTUL began to mobilize the workers for a strike. The threat of organized resistance proved effective. The workers gave a week's notice of their intention to strike, and within that week the firm began paying the £1 a week stipulated by the ministry after the Committee of Inquiry's report. As Mary Macarthur wrote several months later:

The methods of the Ministry in dealing with the whole question of wages seems to be simply part of its deliberate policy of placating whatever may be the most powerful interest at the moment. In cases where, driven desperate by over-fatigue and under-payment, women munition workers engaged on vital work have revolted and refused to continue, it has been found possible to do more for them in a few hours than has been done for the mass of silent, uncomplaining women in a year.[56]

Once again the league's strategy of legislation complemented by organization improved the lot of women workers.

Encouraged by its success with the Glasgow workers, the WTUL continued to press the government to take a more active role in ameliorating conditions for female munition workers. Its efforts were partially rewarded in January 1916, when the Munitions Act was amended to empower the ministry to set hourly rates of pay for women. The revised act also provided for the establishment of Special Arbitration Tribunals to consider grievances regarding wages and working conditions. Deeply disappointed that the House of Commons defeated a Labour Party proposal to abolish the hated "leaving certificate" clause, the WTUL immediately brought a number of cases before the new tribunals. This produced additional publicity on the hardships of the masses of women working in this industry, and the tribunals' rulings remedied some of the worst problems of low wages and oppressive working conditions. Focusing on the positive results of the WTUL's campaign to revise the Munitions Act, Mary Macarthur told the readers of *Woman Worker*:

> The full history of that struggle will never be known—a struggle carried on largely in the twilight of Government buildings and Trade Union offices—sometimes even in the sanctity of Ministers' rooms, when one is almost choked by a suffocating mist, which is known as the official atmosphere, worse than anything ever experienced on Scottish moors. But with the help of the stalwart Trade Union men who shall not find us ungrateful, we have triumphed for the moment.[57]

Unfortunately, the sense of triumph was short-lived. In July 1916, when the ministry finally issued the long-awaited minimum wage rates, they were shockingly low. Again the WTUL took its case to the public, and in an article entitled "The Great Betrayal," Macarthur wrote:

The rate fixed by Order 447 for piece workers is 4d. an hour, which on a pre-war standard is equivalent to less than 2 3/4d. or lower than the lowest minimum fixed in any sweated trade under the Trade Boards Act. . . .

In radiant words on an historic Saturday afternoon on the Embankment, Mr. Lloyd George envisaged a great move forward for women workers. Under the new Order, on the contrary, they have receded to the days of Queen Elizabeth. The woman worker has waited patiently for the protection of a legal minimum wage; she finds herself thrown back three centuries.[58]

The league soon discovered, however, that even these low rates were not being widely applied. Moreover, the tribunals, after their initial spurt of efficiency in processing cases brought before them, were taking six to nine months to resolve grievances. Macarthur pointed out these problems in a long letter to the *Times*:

I unhesitatingly assert that there are thousands of women to whom no protection has as yet been accorded by statutory orders fixing wages. There are to-day women actually working on munitions of war for 2 3/5d. and 3d. an hour. . . . It is true that Special Arbitration Tribunals exist before which their grievances theoretically may come, but in many cases we have had months of negotiation before reaching the tribunal, and after our case has been heard we have had to wait months for the award. . . . The rates fixed for women on women's work, if valued according to the Board of Trade statistics of the rise in the cost of living, are worth less in real wages to-day than the rates fixed legally for some sweated trades under the Trade Board Acts before the war.[59]

After several more months of intense WTUL lobbying, consisting of public speeches, articles and letters to the daily press, and meetings with M.P.'s, the Ministry of Munitions responded to the pressure. It issued new wage rates and declared that workers should not be expected to work more than forty-eight hours a week. The league considered this reduction of hours as important a victory as the raise in wages, and this shorter workday was one of the lasting industrial benefits of the war period. By the end of the war, the real wages of women munition workers had increased by 50 percent over what they had been in 1914, and as a result of organizing efforts and legislative lobbying, these increases were extended to women in other areas, such as brass finishing, optical instruments, explosives, and rubber manufacture.[60]

During the war women were extravagantly praised by politicians, the press, and employers for their willingness to enter the labor force in unprecedented numbers and for their adaptability to jobs previously regarded as men's work. This gratitude and admiration did not, however, "spontaneously express itself in a desire to pay her (the woman war worker) decent wages."[61] The war brought about major changes in the size of the female labor force and in the range of jobs open to women, but these changes were not accompanied by major revisions in traditional attitudes regarding the economic value of female labor.

As the case of the women munition workers illustrates, some improvement in female wage rates did occur during the war, but each gain came only after a struggle initiated by the WTUL, whose actions were consistently supported by the Labour Party and the Amalgamated Society of Engineers. The WTUL steadfastly fought for higher pay and better conditions for women workers out of a commitment to both feminism and class solidarity. Its appeals for labor movement support were based on the double premise that women as women deserved better treatment and that class interests were best protected when workers—male and female—were paid according to the nature of the job rather than the gender of the worker. Despite the WTUL's efforts, equal pay for equal work was rarely achieved during the war, but the improvements in women's wages and working conditions that did take place between 1915 and 1918 were largely the result of the WTUL's organizing and legislative lobbying.

* * *

Beginning in the 1890s, the WTUL's approach centered on two dominant tactics, and these were accentuated by the league's activities during the war: seeking support from the labor movement for the organization of women and acting as a pressure group on the government. The latter strategy was reinforced and extended in 1916 by the creation of the Standing Joint Committee of Women's Industrial Organizations, a coalition initiated by the WTUL to serve as the voice of working-class women.[62]

The Standing Joint Committee was formed at a meeting convened by Mary Macarthur in February 1916, which was attended by representatives of the major working-class women's organizations: the National Federation of Women Workers, the Women's Co-operative Guild, the Women's Labour League, the Women's Railway Guild (an association of wives of railway workers), and of course the WTUL. Ideas for the role such a coalition might play were discussed, and the group met again the following month to elect officers and adopt a constitution. Mary Macarthur was elected president, a post she was to hold until her death in 1921, and the constitution provided for additional members "from industrial organizations of which a substantial number of the members are women, which are national in character and are accepted by the Committee." Although mixed-sex organizations could become members of the committee, the constitution stipulated that the representatives from each member organization had to be women. The class-based feminist orientation of the Standing Joint Committee was further revealed in the three objects of the organization articulated in the constitution:

1. To prepare and keep up to date a register of women in all parts of the country suitable for membership of any Local or Central Committee which may be set up by the Government or other authorities, for administrative or other work in which women have a special interest.
2. To set forth a joint policy for industrial women on such committees to follow, and to assist them to gain any information they may require.
3. To conduct joint campaigns by means of publications in the press, meetings, deputations, and other methods, on any subject of national importance on which combined action by industrial women may be beneficial.[63]

By the end of the committee's first year of existence, it had developed a register of over 600 working-class or working-class-oriented women "able and suitable" to serve on local and national government committees. It had placed women on many of the Local Pension Committees formed after the passage of the Naval and Military Pensions Act in 1916, although in some cases it took considerable pressure before local authorities were willing to appoint female representatives. Standing Joint Committee representatives also served on various advisory committees on women's war employment and on Local Government Board Maternity Committees. The Joint Committee on Labour Problems After the War asked the Standing Joint Committee to prepare a special report on the position of women, and, with some modifications, its recommendations concerning unemployment insurance for women were accepted and published as part of the Labour Problems report. At the end of this first year, the Standing Joint Committee noted with pride that it had "won recognition from the Government and the Labour Movement as the one body which can represent working-class women from the industrial, social, and political point of view." In addition, the creation of this group had brought its member organizations into closer touch with one another and had promoted greater "cooperation and unity of policy" among them.[64]

Over the next few years the Standing Joint Committee held several conferences to discuss issues of concern to working-class women, and it actively lobbied for legislation covering a wide range of areas: employment, equal pay, housing, food, maternity benefits, and child care.[65] Despite Mary Macarthur's premature death in 1921, the organization was stable enough to carry on. By 1925 its membership had expanded to include "practically the whole of the organized working women in the Labour, Trade Union, and Cooperative movements," and the committee was regularly consulted by the Executive Committee of the Labour Party for advice on legislation affecting women.[66]

* * *

In contrast to this essentially feminist orientation that characterized the WTUL's (and the Standing Joint Committee's) approach to class-specific labor legislation, the WTUL demonstrated its commitment to class solidarity in its response to the purely feminist issue of woman suffrage. Not opposed in principle to the idea of woman suffrage, the WTUL nonetheless remained aloof from that movement, aligning itself instead with the much weaker, labor-based adult suffrage movement.

As in the United States, the campaign for woman suffrage in Britain was carried on primarily by middle-class women. However, the suffrage situation in Britain was quite different from that in America, for although women were excluded from full enfranchisement in both countries, Britain retained a limited franchise for men until 1918.[67] For both strategic and ideological reasons, the British woman suffrage movement did not oppose tying the right to vote to property qualifications; until 1918 its demand, even among the most militant wing of the movement, was suffrage for women "on the same grounds as it is or may be granted to men" (which would have enabled only about 1.5 million women to vote). This demand simultaneously reflected the suffragists' pragmatic assessment that it would be impolitic to ask for broader rights for women than those already granted to men and the movement's willingness to accommodate those women who were interested only in extending the franchise to themselves and others in their social position. It is important to note that not all advocates of a limited women's bill regarded it as a prelude to further franchise reform that would ultimately result in universal adult suffrage.

Although a few working-class women's groups, such as the Women's Cooperative Guild and the Manchester Women's Trades and Labour Council, were active supporters of the woman suffrage movement, the WTUL was critical of the class-based nature and demands of the movement, and unlike the American WTUL, the British league was uninterested in bringing together the woman suffrage and women's labor movements.[68] It gave a certain amount of publicity in *Woman Worker* to the activities of various woman suffrage groups, but the WTUL never participated in a demonstration or identified suffragists as a group from whom it might expect financial and/or moral support.

When the Labour Party began its campaign for universal adult suffrage, the WTUL enthusiastically supported this move in principle, but in practice it did not participate actively in developing wider public acceptance for the concept.[69] Sympathetic to "the necessity of an Adult Suffrage organization," the WTUL executive committee nonetheless decided that "it was outside the scope of the League's work" to do more than go on record indicating its support for this broader struggle for franchise extension.[70] The WTUL felt that obtaining the right to vote certainly would not hurt the position of women workers, but it was skeptical about its real, as opposed to its symbolic, value in helping women workers solve their problems. Addressing herself to the relationship between women being granted the right to vote and a rise in women's wages, Mary Macarthur told an American audience in 1909, "There are men in England who have the franchise and whose wages are only a few dollars a week. The only way to increase wages is by trades unions. . . . As for our trades women, suffrage is not a burning question with them . . . they have other things to think about and not much time."[71]

Although the WTUL consistently eschewed participation in suffrage activities in favor of its organizing and legislative work, it did play an important role in the Labour Party's 1912 decision to commit itself unequivocally to the enfranchisement of women. From its inception, the Labour Party had advocated universal adult suffrage, by which it clearly meant the enfranchisement of all men and women over the age of twenty-one.[72] However, there were conflicting views within the party about the position Labour M.P.'s should take on legislation that would extend the franchise only to women or would create manhood suffrage (universal suffrage for men but not for women). By 1912 various Labour Party leaders who had hitherto been unwilling to support bills that would simply enfranchise women with the same property qualifications as men had come to feel that the government had not dealt fairly with women suffragists, and they decided it was time for the

Labour Party to live up to its democratic principles and make explicit its concern for woman suffrage.

After consulting with officials of the WTUL and the Women's Labour League, Arthur Henderson (chairman of the Labour Party) and Will Anderson drafted a suffrage resolution, which they presented to the 1912 Labour Party Conference "in speeches which showed the highest degree of tact as well as the utmost sincerity and conviction." The resolution, which called for the inclusion of adult suffrage in the Reform Bill to be introduced in the coming session of Parliament, included the phrase, "no Bill can be acceptable to the Labour and Socialist Movement which does not include women."[73] This phrase provoked considerable opposition, especially from the Miners' Federation, which supported adult suffrage but was opposed to the Labour Party refusing to support a bill for manhood suffrage "if it was found impossible to get women included."[74] Reminding the conference delegates of her past opposition to any bill extending the franchise only to women who met existing property qualifications, Mary Macarthur appealed to the miners to withdraw their opposition to this resolution, forcefully arguing that the time had come for men to pledge their firm support to women.[75] Although she was unable to sway the miners, a majority of the delegates did vote for the resolution, and it was adopted as official Labour Party policy.

As a result of this decision and of suffrage-related events in Parliament the following year, the WTUL shifted from a negative to a neutral stance on the issue of a limited woman suffrage bill. For the same reasons, over the next few years an increasing number of Labour Party M.P.'s became willing to vote for a limited woman suffrage bill, regarding it as a step to universal adult suffrage.

Although the franchise bill passed in 1918 was touted as a reward for service rendered by men and women during the war, it excluded the largest group of women war workers—it extended the franchise to all men over twenty-one but only to women over thirty. The WTUL noted the irony of this move; due to male deaths in World War I, enfranchising women over twenty-one would produce an electoral majority of females. The WTUL felt this compromise move represented a great injustice to women war workers, for it denied many of them their share of the reward for service to their country. In addition, it would leave the majority of women workers in the postwar period disfranchised. The bill did, however, represent a major, if not a total, victory for the proponents of both adult and woman suffrage: it abolished the connection between property and the vote; and it established the principle that women deserved full political citizenship, which was finally granted in 1928 when the franchise was extended to women between twenty-one and thirty.

* * *

As a result of these events, between 1918 and 1920 the Labour Party and the TUC evinced a new willingness to treat women as serious and integral members of the labor movement. The industrial and political activities of the women's labor movement, heightened by the influx of women into the labor force during the war, had legitimated the role of the woman worker and had created a new awareness of how the entire working class was affected by her social and economic disabilities. The 1918 suffrage act, which, although a disappointment in some respects, was generally regarded as an implicit promise that universal adult suffrage would be granted before long.

In 1918 the Labour Party revised its constitution to extend membership to women on the same basis as it was granted to men, and WTUL members played a major role in the decision. In response to this important structural change, the Women's Labour League, an organization in which many WTUL members had been active since its inception in 1906, disbanded, feeling that there was no longer a need for a separate women's organization, now that women would be "full and direct" members of the party.[76]

Symbolizing the new position of women, Mary Macarthur was nominated to stand as the first female Labour Party candidate, in Stourbridge in the summer of 1918. She was convinced by her work prior to and during the war that legislation provided an essential foundation for improving the situation of women workers. The war had left a legacy of major social and economic issues that could best be solved through political action, and she was eager to join men "in the gigantic task of rebuilding a world that lies in ruins."[77] Regarding herself as a labor politician first and a woman second, she based her campaign on the full Labour Party platform, emphasizing her commitment to peace more than advocacy of women's interests. However, in the Khaki election of 1918, she, along with many other labor leaders, was defeated at the polls. She lost the election primarily because of her identification with the pacifist wing of the Labour Party, but another important factor was election officials' insistence that she appear on the ballot as Mary Anderson, her married name, rather than as Mary Macarthur, as she was publicly known.[78]

She returned to her work for the WTUL, feeling that the time had come for the NFWW and the WTUL to abandon their autonomous status. The executive boards of both organizations shared Macarthur's views on this issue, and negotiations with male labor leaders resulted in the absorption of the NFWW into the National Union of General Workers and the transformation of the WTUL into the Women's Section of the TUC. Thus, building on the foundation laid by its organizing, educational, and legislative work prior to the war, the WTUL effectively used changes brought about by the war—increased employment of women and more direct government intervention in industry—to solidify its own position and to achieve the full structural integration of women into the labor movement.

FIVE

The Promise of Legislation: United States

In contrast to the British WTUL, whose legislative activities strengthened its role as a labor organization and its ties to the British labor movement, the American WTUL's legislative program accentuated its identity as a feminist organization and linked the league more firmly to the American women's movement than to the labor movement. Like the British league, the American WTUL advocated protective legislation as a necessary underpinning to the unionization of women workers, since it too recognized that their long hours, low wages, and miserable working conditions impeded their entry into the labor movement. However, the Americans' commitment to unionization increasingly became one of rhetoric rather than practice, as the American WTUL increasingly concentrated its resources on legislative lobbying.

Legislative activities formed a component of the WTUL's program from its inception in 1903, when it declared as one of its objectives "to secure new legislation to protect women workers and to obtain a better enforcement of existing laws."[1] The 1913 WTUL convention decided to establish a national legislative committee to supplement the legislative programs of the local leagues. This decision was significant, "further emphasizing the need for industrial legislation as a supplementary arm of trade union organization."[2] By the end of its second decade of work, legislative lobbying had become the primary focus of WTUL activities, and in 1929 the league moved its national headquarters from Chicago to Washington D.C.

The WTUL's emphasis on legislation was a logical if not inevitable response to the problems it encountered in its organizing attempts. The labor movement essentially was unreceptive to the inclusion of women, a situation even as ardent a trade unionist as Rose Schneiderman acknowledged when she declared in 1915, "We have come to the American Federation of Labor and said to them, 'Come and help us organize the American working girl,'. . . but nothing was done."[3] Thus, out of frustration and disappointment, the league looked to the government for help in ameliorating the position of women workers. The WTUL's growing emphasis on the state as an agent of social change was characteristic of many reform organizations in this period; there was a general trend of organizations that had initially emphasized local, grass-roots approaches shifting to a more national orientation and focusing on legislative solutions to social problems.[4]

Women workers had special problems simply because they were women. This stress on their identity as women rather than as workers rooted the league firmly within the American feminist movement. In other words, the league's advocacy of protective legislation was based on women workers' social and biological roles as women.

A critical obstacle to the organization of women workers was their tendency to be temporary members of the labor force, and this was reinforced by the fact that women tended to see themselves and be seen by others primarily as future wives and mothers. For workers to be seriously interested in unionizing, they must place greater emphasis on their identity as workers. At the same time, however, it was precisely because of women workers' roles as the bearers of children that the league considered it so important that their working conditions be improved; women's reproductive roles made them more physically vulnerable than men to the deleterious effects of their jobs. Although the contention that protective legislation was in the best interests of women became a controversial issue within feminist ranks in the 1920s, the idea that women were in a special position because of their roles as actual or potential mothers was widely accepted by most feminists well into the twentieth century.

A major impetus to the WTUL's legislative program was the 1908 Supreme Court decision upholding an Oregon ten-hour law for women.[5] The WTUL and other feminist groups, most notably the National Consumers' League, whose secretary, Josephine Goldmark, served as Louis D. Brandeis's research assistant in the preparation of the brief defending the Oregon law, regarded this Supreme Court decision as a major breakthrough for the cause of women workers. The line of reasoning argued by Brandeis and accepted by the court was that protective legislation for women did not violate the right of individuals to make contracts guaranteed by the Fourteenth Amendment; because women were physically weaker than men and because of women workers' roles as "the future mothers of the race," the state had the right and obligation to invoke its police powers to protect them. "Healthy mothers," declared the court, "are essential to vigorous offspring," and it was deemed to be in the public interest for women's working conditions to be legally regulated since the physical well-being of women was necessary "to preserve the strength and vigor of the race."[6]

The basic premise underlying this ruling and the WTUL's legislative program was that because women entered the labor force with inherent social and biological disadvantages, they were more vulnerable than men to exploitation and less able to protect themselves through collective action. Special legislation for women was thus compensatory; to feminists in this period it was a way of equalizing and standardizing the position of men and women in the industrial labor force. As one WTUL member contended in a statement comparing the hours and wages of men and women workers, "The laws for women will help to equalize that situation, because they will strengthen the bargaining power of women. It is only by obtaining equal bargaining power with men that women can have equal opportunity in industry or equal pay for equal work."[7]

* * *

Over the years the WTUL lobbied for a wide range of legislative measures, but its most consistent concern was with limiting the hours of women's work. The league began to develop a legislative program in 1904, when it called for legislation mandating an eight-hour day and a fifty-hour week for women workers and for laws prohibiting the employment of women after nine o'clock at night.[8] Encouraged by the 1908 Supreme Court decision, the WTUL broadened its legislative program at its 1909 convention, adopting the following set of goals:

1. The eight-hour day.
2. Elimination of night work.
3. Protected machinery.
4. Sanitary workshops.
5. Separate toilet rooms.
6. Seats for women and permission for their use when work allows.
7. Prohibition of the employment of pregnant women two months before and after child-birth.
8. Pensions for working mothers during the lying-in period.
9. An increased number of women factory inspectors, based on the percentage of women workers in the State.

10. The appointment of women physicians as health inspectors, whose duty it shall be to visit all workshops where women and children are employed to examine into the physical condition of the workers.
11. A legal minimum wage in the sweated trades.[9]

It was up to each local league to decide how much time and energy to devote to legislative lobbying and which, if any, of these measures it would promote. Although the WTUL did not begin working actively for legislation as a national organization until 1913, after this 1909 program was adopted, the league publicized it as an expression of the views of organized women workers and encouraged other organizations interested in labor legislation, such as the National Consumers' League and the American Association of Labor Legislation, to incorporate these proposals in their programs.

The Chicago WTUL had the most active legislative program prior to 1913. In 1905 it had begun investigating the conditions of women workers in Illinois, and the project culminated in a 1908 conference on the need for industrial legislation for women, jointly sponsored by the Chicago WTUL and the Chicago Federation of Labor. In conjunction with the conference, the league mounted an exhibit depicting the living and working conditions of women in sweatshops, which impelled the governor of Illinois to appoint a commission to study this problem and to recommend legislation designed to protect the health and safety of women workers in that state.

As a corollary to these initial efforts to create support for new labor laws, the Chicago WTUL called two more conferences in the spring of 1908. The first was for members of "women's clubs and other societies sympathetic with the work of bettering women's working conditions," and the second was for "women delegates from trade unions having women members." The decision of both groups was that securing an eight-hour day for women workers should be the league's highest priority, although there was considerable feeling that, given the Oregon precedent, it would be more expedient to ask for a ten-hour bill.[10]

When it looked as if the league would propose a ten-hour bill, Elizabeth Maloney, a member of the Chicago WTUL and of the Chicago Waitresses' Union, expressed her disgust and irritation with this conservative approach: "If this group does not want to introduce an eight-hour-day bill, my waitresses' union will introduce it!" She and her colleague, Anna Willard, precipitously left the WTUL meeting, went to their union office where they secured a copy of the Oregon bill, drafted an eight-hour version of it, and then took a train to Springfield. In Springfield they managed to see the speaker of the House, who directed them to "one of the least influential and most irresponsible members of the house."[11] Although this legislator fulfilled his promise to introduce their bill, he showed no further interest in it and it languished in committee.

More politically sophisticated, Margaret Dreier Robins, who was then president of the Chicago league as well as the national organization, realized that an eight-hour bill had no chance of being passed unless it was carefully drafted and then introduced by an influential politician strongly committed to the proposal. Once the Chicago league decided to push for an eight- rather than a ten-hour bill, she turned to her attorney and friend, Harold L. Ickes, for help. Ickes drafted the bill and then discussed it with Governor Deneen, who in turn asked Senator Walter Clyde Jones to sponsor it.

The bill, which would establish an eight-hour day for women working "in any mechanical establishment, or factory, or laundry, or hotel, or restaurant," was duly raised for consideration in the state Senate. The WTUL's lobbying efforts were spearheaded by four trade union members of the Chicago league: Agnes Nestor, a glove worker who headed the league's legislative committee; Elizabeth Maloney and Anna Willard, waitresses who initially introduced an eight-hour bill into the Illinois House of Representatives; and Lulu Holliday, a laundry worker. While they were in Springfield, they were the guests of Mr. and Mrs. George Lee, a wealthy couple sympathetic to the league. The Lees' home was a gathering place for many prominent liberals and intellectuals, and Agnes Nestor valued this exposure to such interesting people and noted how important the Lees' continuing moral and financial support were to the WTUL's lobbying efforts.[12]

Women workers were for the first time lobbying and testifying on their own behalf, and there was considerable popular support for what became known as "the girls' bill." As Margaret Dreier Robins wrote to a friend, "Every elevator man in the State Capitol, every janitor and page boy, every clerk and stenographer as well as the clerks in the hotels did all they could to push 'the girls' bill.' "[13] The bill without question aroused the greatest interest during the 1909 session of the legislature. Ultimately, however, the WTUL was forced to accept a compromise; the bill that finally passed excluded hotel and restaurant workers and mandated a ten-hour day rather than the hoped for eight-hour day.

Passage of the new law was nonetheless regarded as an important victory for the principle of protective legislation and the cause of women workers. The

Chicago league vowed to continue the fight for an eight-hour day, and it did just that, little dreaming that it would take twenty-eight years to get such a bill through the Illinois legislature.[14] Agnes Nestor, who was president of the Chicago league from 1913 until her death in 1948, appeared before every session of the state legislature from 1909 until the eight-hour bill was finally passed in 1937. "We knew that year we had lined up enough votes to see it passed," she notes, "but until the roll had been called in the house there was uncertainty; so often we had stood hopeful in that gallery only to hear at the last moment that we had lost, sometimes by only a single vote." There was, however, a bittersweet quality to the victory. "My own emotions were mixed. The victory did not seem as thrilling as that of the passage of the Women's Ten-Hour-Day Law more than twenty-five years before. We had been so young then, and in between there had been so many defeats. Also, so many of us who had begun the fight were gone."[15]

* * *

The WTUL's concern with the physical conditions of factories and workshops was heightened by the Triangle Shirtwaist Company fire in March 1911. Since its occurrence, this fire has been regarded as a symbol of the plight of women workers in the early twentieth century, and the WTUL's response illustrates its growing emphasis on legislation.

The Triangle Shirtwaist Company was one of the largest garment factories in New York City, occupying the top three floors of a ten-story building just off Washington Square.[16] The company had resisted efforts to unionize its workers during the 1909 garment workers' strike, and as a nonunion shop, its workers had been unable to reduce their Saturday hours to a half-day. On the afternoon of Saturday, March 25, five hundred employees, most of them young, immigrant women, were at work in the factory, and just at closing time a fire broke out at one of the cutting tables. It spread rapidly through the work areas, feeding on the wooden tables and floors, paper patterns, and bolts of cloth, and it was quickly out of control. The fire department responded immediately, but its equipment was inadequate, its longest hose and ladder reaching only to the sixth floor of the burning building.

There had never been a fire drill to prepare the workers for such an emergency, and many of them were unaware of the single fire escape that did exist within the building. Their exit was further impeded by the fact that the management kept the doors to one of the two stairways locked from the outside to prevent the workers from leaving at the end of the day without passing through an inspection to make sure they were not carrying out stolen shirtwaists. Before the elevators and one accessible stairway were engulfed in flames, many of the workers managed to escape through these exit routes, but as these exits became blocked and then useless, the remaining workers in desperation jumped out the windows to the pavement below. A spectator reported that objects that looked "like bales of dark dress goods" came flying out of the windows; another bystander commented that the management was trying to save "the best cloth."[17] A moment later the two men realized with horror that the bundles being flung from the windows were the women workers trapped inside the building.

One hundred and forty-six workers lost their lives as a result of the fire. This dramatic revelation of working conditions led to an outpouring of public guilt and outrage; relief centers were organized to provide financial assistance to the families of victims, and there were widespread calls for reforms in building codes, fire laws, and factory inspection. Although the New York WTUL ultimately took the lead in forming a citizens committee to devise measures to preclude similar tragedies, the league's first hope was that the fire would strengthen the labor movement's commitment to unionizing women and women's commitment to unionization. In an emotional and moving speech at a memorial meeting called by the New York league a week after the fire, Rose Schneiderman told the mixed-class audience:

> I would be a traitor to those poor burned bodies if I were to come here to talk good fellowship. We have tried you good people of the public—and we have found you wanting. . . . I can't talk fellowship to you who are gathered here. Too much blood has been spilled. I know from experience it is up to the working people to save themselves. And the only way is through a strong working-class movement.[18]

The International Ladies' Garment Workers' Union was one of the main agencies coordinating relief efforts, and its leaders participated in marches and meetings mourning the victims of the fire and decrying the conditions that had led to this tragedy. The union did not, however, intensify its efforts to organize women garment workers.[19] Frustrated and disillusioned by the ILGWU's inaction, the New York WTUL channeled its anger about the fire into legislative activities rather than into an organizing campaign of its own.

The league played a leading role in the creation of a Bureau of Fire Prevention for New York City and in the expansion of the powers and duties of the fire commissioner. It was also the main force behind the formation of a New York City Citizens Committee on Safety, whose recommendations led to the establishment of the New York State Factory Investigating Commission, a group empowered by the governor to investigate industrial conditions throughout the state and to recommend improvements to existing legislation and new regulations.

Mary Dreier, president of the New York WTUL, was one of the twelve charter members of the Factory Investigating Commission, and several members of the New York league served as investigators or testified at commission hearings. The commission concerned itself with more than just fire safety issues; by 1915 it was responsible for thirty-six new laws, and "The four-year term of the Commission marks the beginning of what is generally recognized as 'the golden era in remedial factory legislation' in the state of New York."[20] The WTUL's goals were reflected in the legislation proposed by the commission; new laws passed limiting the hours of work for women and children, prohibiting their employment at night and the employment of women immediately after childbirth, and mandating that seats (with backs) be provided for women workers.[21] Other local leagues began lobbying for better factory inspection and more stringent fire safety regulations, and at the WTUL's 1911 convention, fire safety work was added to the league's legislative program.

* * *

As long as the WTUL lobbied mainly for shorter hours and better working conditions for women, it had the tacit and on occasion the active support of the AFL, but when it began seriously working for minimum wage legislation, it did so in the face of the explicit opposition of the labor movement. In contrast to the British labor movement, which was actively involved in the creation of the Labour Party to serve as its political voice, the American labor movement in the early twentieth century was wary of achieving reforms through government intervention. The AFL did wage a concerted campaign for a legislated eight-hour day for all workers in the late nineteenth and early twentieth centuries, but by 1914 it supported such legislation only for children, minors, and women, having decided that adult men were better off gaining such protection through unionization. As Samuel Gompers, president of the AFL, wrote:

The A.F. of L. is opposed to limiting, by legal statutory authority, the hours of work for men. . . . The A.F. of L. has apprehensions as to the wisdom of placing in the hands of the government additional powers which may be used to the detriment of the working people. It particularly opposes this policy when the things can be done by the workmen themselves.[22]

The AFL supported statutory regulation for women on the grounds that women needed special protection. Even though they were adults, they were weaker and more vulnerable than men.

When it came to minimum wage legislation, however, the AFL stressed the similarities between male and female workers, arguing that "the industrial problems of women are not isolated but are inextricably associated with those of men, and are becoming identical with them."[23] Essentially the AFL feared that legislated minimum wage rates would in practice become maximum rates, and it viewed such legislation as an intolerable interference with workers' freedom. "The establishment of such a policy or practice . . . would infringe upon the liberty of women, and would directly or indirectly affect that of men," declared Gompers, who was apprehensive that "once the state is allowed to fix a minimum rate, the state would also take the right to compel men or women to work at that rate."[24] It was tempting "to resort to legislative devices that palliate the ills," but the AFL placed greater emphasis on the concept of individual freedom, maintaining that minimum wage legislation would not help women develop the qualities necessary for real freedom—"self-discipline, the development of individual responsibility, and initiative."[25]

After the WTUL reiterated its commitment to minimum wage legislation at its 1915 convention, the AFL explicitly warned the league that it was weakening its labor orientation in favor of its identification with the women's movement. The AFL supported the WTUL's involvement in the fight for woman suffrage, noting that "the discussions and addresses at the convention indicate that women realize they cannot establish and maintain industrial freedom and responsibility unless they also have political freedom and responsibility." However, the AFL felt strongly that "industrial freedom must be fought out on the industrial field. . . . Protection and regulation may offer immediate relief—but they are not freedom." The AFL praised the WTUL as having "tremendous opportunity and promise," but warned that for just those reasons, "it is confronted by dangers and pitfalls and must protect itself against attempts to dominate it and use it for other purposes." Unwilling to examine forthrightly its own record in helping women workers to gain industrial freedom through unionization, the AFL contended that "the fight of women for industrial freedom is made doubly difficult . . . by patronizing social workers and by those who would protect woman in order to keep her from exercising her own will power and becoming a member of society upon equality with all."[26] (Despite the opposition of the AFL, legislated minimum wage rates for women were instituted in nine states by 1915.)

The WTUL had endorsed a minimum wage scale as part of the five-point platform adopted at the league's first biennial convention in 1907, and in 1913 Margaret Dreier Robins made this issue a central topic in her presidential address. "Representing as we do the organized women workers in America, it was natural that we should be among the first to understand the need of such legislation." She did not mention the labor movement's reservations, emphasizing instead the growing support among the general public, for, as she told the delegates, "Today . . . thoughtful men and women everywhere are realizing the individual and social menace of the low wage and there is a general recognition of the fact that in a great, rich, empty country, able bodied men and women should find it possible to earn their living by their day's work." In favor of a minimum wage for men as well as women, Robins considered it especially important for women, since their wage scales were so much lower than men's. Furthermore, minimum wage legislation should be promoted because of "the close relationship between the low wage and the social evil." Women workers "who maintained the integrity of their womanhood" generally did so "in the face of great personal suffering and self-sacrifice, as well as in the face of grave temptation." Finally, Robins cited the success of wage boards in Australia and England and claimed that the establishment of similar boards in the United States would bring "the least of the littlest girls . . . the opportunity of organization and self-government."[27]

Prior to the 1915 convention, the minimum wage plank in the WTUL's legislative program was passed with little discussion. However, in 1915 considerable debate preceded its adoption. Opposition to it came primarily from the New York WTUL, where it had become a matter of great internal controversy the previous year. After the 1913 convention, the New York WTUL had consulted with the New York State Federation of Labor and had been told that the labor movement did not favor such legislation. Not wanting to antagonize their "brothers of the labor movement," the New York league decided not to push for the creation of minimum wage boards in that state.[28] However, Mary Dreier's work on the Factory Investigating Commission strengthened her conviction that minimum wage legislation would be helpful to the vast majority of New York's working women. Commission-sponsored investigations concluded that $9.00 a week was the minimum for subsistence in New York City, but many women workers earned less than that.[29]

Dreier began urging league members to make lobbying for minimum wage legislation a priority:

> What I feel very keenly is that the Women's Trade Union League has a real opportunity to be of service to the hard-pressed, unorganized, young or old working women, as for instance, the girls in the paper box trades, in the millinery, flower, retail clerks, and candy trades, and in the kimona and white goods industry. . . . It seemed to me that in arousing public sentiment, first among the workers themselves, and second among the general public, for the minimum wage the League could proclaim to those women who know nothing about organization, who are so hard-pressed that there seems little chance of organizing them, that the Women's Trade Union League is a friend to them in their extremity.[30]

Dreier's views were not fully shared by the other members of the New York WTUL's executive board. When the issue was put to a vote in November 1914, the board voted six to four not to work for minimum wage legislation, the majority either accepting the AFL's arguments against legislation or not wanting the league to stand for legislation the AFL did not support. It is interesting to note, however, that the division did not break down along class lines—there were trade unionists and allies on both sides of the issue.

The New York league's decision precipitated an extensive discussion at the 1915 convention when the national legislative committee proposed that the WTUL reaffirm its support for minimum wage legislation. Specifically, the committee recommended that each local league seek to secure in its state "a minimum wage commission to establish wage boards for each industry, having an equal representation of employers and workers and representation from the public." The issue was discussed from both a theoretical and a strategic point of view, and as in the New York league, trade unionist and ally members were found among both the supporters and the opponents. Louisa Mittelstadt, the brewery worker from Kansas City who had spent 1914 at the WTUL Training School, argued at one point, "This is not a question of whether we believe in the minimum wage or not; it is a question of standing for labor." On the other hand, Mary McEnerny, a Chicago bindery worker active in her union, drew on her own experience to argue that trade union men had not shown much concern about women being paid decent wages, and Pauline Newman, one of the most class-conscious working-class members of the WTUL, emphasized what she termed "the human side of the question." "Regardless of our viewpoint in regard to the labor organizations," she declared, "not one of us, in or out of the labor movement, has a right to say to the underdog: 'You wait until you have become convinced of the necessity of organization and then get all you want through your organization'!" As far as Newman was concerned, the needs of underpaid women workers were so compelling that "if the state, which is supposed to serve its people, can help these people to get 2 or 3 dollars a week more . . . not one of us has the right to say to the girls: 'Don't accept it. Starve rather than accept money from the state.' "[31]

Other speakers refuted the notion that a minimum wage would become the maximum, noting that organized workers could and would use their collective power to raise their wages. As one woman declared, "There are many, many things we have got to do by organization that we cannot do by legislation; but the two go hand in hand together and we must have both in order to get industrial justice."[32] A Boston delegate reinforced this point by citing how minimum wage legislation had facilitated the Boston WTUL's organizing efforts:

> This minimum wage, when it goes into effect, enables the WTUL to get hold of a group of girls they could get hold of in no other way. It is impossible to get a group of girls from some factories to come to a union meeting, but when they are brought together by a commission appointed by the state it is easy to get hold of them. In the brush factories we had girls come to the meetings after they had been to the meetings called by the state and we were able to talk to them about a union. We were never able to get hold of them before. . . . If it makes them understand there is such a thing as a union that will help them of their own accord to get a raise, then, by all means the minimum wage ought to be given a chance.[33]

When the issue finally came to a vote, it was approved by a large majority. Margaret Dreier Robins reminded the delegates that by voting for it, they were supporting the principle of minimum wage legislation and that each local league remained free to decide if and when it wanted to lobby for such legislation in its own state. By 1916 the New York WTUL had reversed its original position, and like the rest of the local leagues and the national organization, its energies during the war and subsequently were much more oriented toward developing and extending protective legislation than actually organizing women into trade unions.

'hus, by World War I, a period of greatly increased focus on the power and
: of the federal government, the WTUL had shifted from organizing to
l. slative lobbying. It had emerged on the public scene as a lobby
re, resenting feminist concerns in the name of women workers, and its work
during the war reinforced its legislative orientation. In contrast to the leaders
of the British WTUL, who came to public prominence solidly based in the
labor movement, American WTUL activists were much more identified with
the women's movement than with the American labor movement.

* * *

The most lasting monument to the WTUL and its commitment to the cause
of women workers is the Women's Bureau in the Department of Labor.
Created in 1920, it represented the culmination of eleven years of agitation by
the WTUL, which interpreted this victory as an indication "that women in
industry were [now considered] an important asset to the nation and that the
federal government was ready to assume responsibility for their well-being."[34]
The WTUL's persistent efforts to have a federal Women's Bureau established
reflected its adherence to the progressive approach to solving social problems.
Like other reform organizations of this period, it placed a high value on the
role official bureaus and commissions could play in mobilizing public support
for social change. It assumed that such agencies would be staffed by
knowledgeable and concerned individuals and that the information they
collected and disseminated would provide useful and compelling guidelines for
social reform.

The WTUL began its campaign for the creation of a Women's Bureau in
1909, arguing that such an agency was the logical and necessary consequence
of the information revealed in the comprehensive federal survey of women and
child wage-earners carried out from 1907 to 1909.[35] The idea for the study
was proposed at a 1905 meeting of the Chicago WTUL, which subsequently
asked the national league to constitute a committee to lobby for a federal
investigation of the condition of women in industry. This committee, which
was headed by Mary McDowell, a WTUL activist well known for her work
in the settlement house movement, appeared before the 1906 convention of
the General Federation of Women's Clubs and won this group's backing. A
conference with President Theodore Roosevelt and Charles P. Neill,
commissioner of the Bureau of Labor in the Department of Commerce and
Labor, led to their support for a study, which they felt should be broadened

to include children as well as women. In January 1907 Congress passed a bill authorizing the secretary of Commerce and Labor:

> to investigate and report on the industrial, social, moral, educational, and physical condition of women and child workers in the United States wherever employed, with special reference to their age, hours of labor, term of employment, health, illiteracy, sanitary and other conditions surrounding their occupation, and the means employed for the protection of their health, person, and morals.[36]

This study, which resulted in a nineteen-volume report, produced valuable and disturbing evidence of the working and living conditions prevalent among women and child wage earners. It also indicated a need for continuing information on this sector of the labor force, and a Women's Division in the Bureau of Labor Statistics was formed to provide these data. The WTUL regarded this move as only a partial victory, for it had hoped for the creation of an agency to function as an advocate of the needs of women workers as well as to collect statistical data about them. As it turned out, however, the Women's Division was not even able to provide very much useful information about women wage earners, for, like the women it was supposed to investigate, the Women's Division was the object of considerable discrimination. Compared to the salary scale of male investigators who worked for the Bureau of Labor Statistics, the salaries paid females with comparable jobs in the Women's Division were insultingly low. Moreover, bureau authorities frequently reallocated funds slated to cover Women's Division projects to other divisions of the bureau. As far as the women in the bureau were concerned, the ultimate indignity came when the commissioner of labor statistics revised a Women's Division study in such a way that the women who had carried out the investigation did not want their names associated with the final report.[37] Within a very short time the Women's Division had virtually ceased to exist. The original staff members resigned and new women were unwilling to take their places.

By 1916, under pressure from various women's organizations led by the WTUL, the secretary of labor had come to advocate the reorganization of the Women's Division as a separate unit within the Department of Labor. A bill to this effect was presented in Congress that year, but there was little interest in it. The women's cause was further hindered by the AFL's refusal to support this proposed legislation. The WTUL had asked the 1916 AFL convention to endorse the bill, but the delegates rejected the resolution, claiming that the proposed bureau would simply create positions for "silk-stockinged" women.[38]

With America's entry into World War I the following year, the situation of women workers took on a new importance and urgency, and early in 1918 a Women's Division of the Ordnance Department was created to develop standards for women employed in the munitions industry. Mary Van Kleeck, head of the Committee on Women's Work and Industrial Studies at the Russell Sage Foundation, was appointed director of this agency, and she asked Mary Anderson of the WTUL and the Boot and Shoe Workers' Union to be assistant director.[39] A few months later the Committee on National Defense recommended that the Women's Division be renamed the Woman-in-Industry Service and that it be transferred to the Department of Labor. Van Kleeck and Anderson were retained as director and assistant director, and although the agency continued to be primarily concerned with women in war-related jobs, its mandate was broadened to include investigating and recommending standards for women working in all areas of the economy.[40]

Created as a temporary wartime agency, the life of the Woman-in-Industry Service was extended for a year in February 1919 so it could aid in the postwar reconstruction process.[41] Mary Van Kleeck resigned in August and Mary Anderson was promoted to director, but the agency's appropriation had been cut from $150,000 to $40,000 and its future was precarious. Led by the WTUL, a coalition of women's organizations intensified their efforts to have the Woman-in-Industry Service maintained as a permanent institution, and after considerable struggle they secured passage of a bill in June 1920 authorizing a permanent Women's Bureau in the Department of Labor. Building on the work begun by the Woman-in-Industry Service, the Women's Bureau was to "formulate standards and policies which shall promote the welfare of wage-earning women, improve their working conditions, and advance their opportunities for profitable employment."[42] Mary Anderson was named director, a post she held until her retirement in 1944, and the establishment of this bureau and the appointment of Anderson, a working-class woman, stand as landmark events in American women's labor history.

Although the WTUL felt a great sense of accomplishment when the Women's Bureau was established and a WTUL member was chosen to head it, the struggle was not over.[43] The bill creating a permanent bureau had an appropriation of only $75,000, half the amount requested by the secretary of labor. Women's Bureau employees were denied the $240 war bonus awarded all other federal employees, and in contrast to the Bureau of Labor Statistics, where (male) statisticians earned $3,000 and other experts $2,280 to $2,760, Congress stipulated that the Women's Bureau could not pay anyone more than $2,000. When supporters of the bureau protested these inequities, one senator responded, "Why, $2,000 is enough for any woman," and another stated that there was no danger of the low salary levels keeping women from accepting jobs in the bureau for "the employment condition is going to be so serious that they will be glad to work there at *any* price."[44] The WTUL strenuously lobbied for increased funding for the Women's Bureau, and by 1925 its appropriation had been raised to $107,380.

Standing for "equal opportunity in industry, freedom of choice in occupation, and equal pay for equal work," the Women's Bureau's investigations and legislative recommendations were designed to promote the economic rights and status of women wage earners.[45] Bureau reports advocating legislation regulating hours and working conditions usually emphasized that the recommendations should not be interpreted as relevant *only* to female workers, but rather as necessary *especially* for them. The bureau based this distinction on the fact that wage-earning women were mothers as well as workers, and it considered the long-term social consequences of women working in unhealthy situations much more severe than those resulting from men working in similar situations. Although the Women's Bureau has never had the power to do more than make policy recommendations, it has functioned as an official advocate of women wage-earners and has consistently provided extremely useful data on the position of women in the American economy.[46]

* * *

Eager to utilize American women's new political power as voters, a group of women's organizations formed the Women's Joint Congressional Committee (WJCC) in December 1920 to coordinate lobbying efforts for national legislation of interest to women.[47] Although superficially analogous in form and function to the British Standing Joint Committee of Industrial Women's Organizations, the WJCC differed from the British coalition in three important respects. First, although the British WTUL played a central role in the establishment and leadership of the Standing Joint Committee, the American league was only peripherally involved in the formation and functioning of the WJCC. This difference resulted in part from the different organizational structures of the two coalitions and from the fact that the

American WTUL's national headquarters were still in Chicago, not in Washington, but it was also a reflection of the American league's declining financial and personnel resources by the early 1920s.

The other, and more fundamental, differences between the two coalitions were the types of organizations belonging to each joint committee and the political perspective of the two groups. Whereas the Standing Joint Committee was composed entirely of working-class or working-class-oriented women's organizations, the WJCC consisted primarily of middle-class professional and social reform groups. Thus the Standing Joint Committee's legislative interests were dictated by a class-conscious feminist perspective; the WJCC eschewed concepts of class and saw itself as representing the interests of all women.

Although the American WTUL joined the WJCC at its inception, several WTUL national officers were initially reluctant to have the league participate in the committee. The WTUL had been represented at the meeting called by the League of Women Voters in November 1920 to discuss the possible formation of such a coalition by Ethel Smith, the WTUL's legislative secretary who was based in Washington.[48] Smith, a white-collar worker by background, wrote an enthusiastic report of the meeting to WTUL national officers, strongly recommending that the league join the proposed coalition.[49] The five WTUL national officers living in Chicago (two allies and three trade unionists) did not, however, share Smith's positive reaction to the idea.[50] It would be useful to have the support of other members of the coalition on legislation favored by the league, but they feared that participating in the WJCC would oblige the WTUL to lobby for bills that did not directly pertain to women workers.

Smith responded by pointing out that the WJCC was designed to function essentially as a series of subcommittees, each member organization participating only on those subcommittees working for legislation the organization had independently decided to support. Given this structure, Smith urged WTUL officers to reconsider; she felt the league would be making a serious tactical error if it did not join the coalition. Citing instances of lobbying support the WTUL had received from some organizations that would be in the WJCC, Smith argued that the league could not expect similar support in the future unless it became a member. If the league refused to participate in the coalition, Smith felt she would be put in the position of having to say to past allies, "My organization is unwilling to have any connection with yours, or to sit in conference with yours—but we want you nonetheless to assist our measures, to follow our lead as to tactics on such bills, and to spend your money on

135

telegrams, etc. to get our bills passed." Furthermore, the WTUL would be passing up a critical opportunity to influence these other organizations to lobby for legislation the league considered important. Worried about the headway the National Manufacturers' Association was making in influencing the YWCA and the General Federation of Women's Clubs to reconsider their industrial programs, Smith contended that "for us to refuse to sit in conference with the organizations of women composed of women from the groups from which our allies come, is for us ourselves to draw a line which will promptly be taken advantage of by the employer's agents who are now trying to work their way into those grounds.[51]

The final thrust of Smith's response revealed the value she placed on feminist rather than class solidarity:

> To me the ideal of women for women—*all* women—is so big and potent that it grieves me to the heart to think that my own group should be the one—the only one—to desert that standard at this critical time. The League has what it has through the efforts of its allies as well as of its trade union members. Such national legislation as it has obtained it could never have obtained without these very organizations who are now inviting us into their councils. Our refusal cannot possibly be made graciously. Not by any possibility can we do it, in my judgment, without looking selfish and unfriendly, and without forsaking our claims of loyalty, woman to woman.[52]

Convinced by the force of Smith's arguments, the WTUL Executive Board decided the league should be represented on the WJCC, and the league thus became one of the ten charter members of the coalition.[53]

These ten organizations had a combined membership of over 10,000,000 women, and the WJCC quickly gained a reputation as one of the most powerful lobbies in Washington. One of its first major efforts was to rally support for the Sheppard-Towner Maternity and Infancy Protection Act, a bill passed by Congress in 1921 that represented the federal government's "first venture . . . into social welfare legislation."[54]

Between 1920 and 1925 WJCC membership grew to twenty-one organizations, and a high proportion of the legislative measures supported by WJCC subcommittees was passed by Congress, which took seriously the idea of a female bloc vote.[55] The issues supported by the WJCC clearly identify the coalition as an instrument of social feminism rather than as a force for women's rights per se. The WJCC did lobby for some legislation specifically dealing with women's rights, such as independent citizenship for women married to foreign nationals, but it strenuously opposed the National Woman's Party's early attempts to institute the equal rights amendment. In addition to the Sheppard-Towner Act, some of the measures the WJCC successfully fought for in the early 1920s were increased appropriations for the Women's Bureau and the Children's Bureau, the child labor amendment, independent citizenship for married women, a federal prison for women, revisions in civil service classifications, and more stringent interstate commerce regulations regarding the fat content in milk.[56] Although the WTUL supported all of these issues in principle, it actively participated only on subcommittees concerned with legislation directly relevant to women workers. This clear sense of WTUL priorities was reflected in Ethel Smith, the WTUL's representative on the WJCC, assuming the chairmanship of WJCC subcommittees on the Women's Bureau, civil service reclassification, and the equal rights amendment.[57]

Despite this promising beginning, the WJCC's influence diminished rapidly after the mid-1920s. This was partly due to politicians realizing that factors other than gender dictated women's political views and the enfranchisement of women did not result in a female bloc vote. It was also the result of a rising conservative tide that caused many women's organizations to pull back from progressive social reform causes. Those organizations, such as the WTUL, whose concerns were not tempered by this shift in the national mood, thus found decreasing support for their legislative interests among many of their former WJCC allies. Moreover, the 1924 election produced a more conservative Congress, so for reasons of both pragmatism and principle, there were fewer politicians sympathetic to WJCC subcommittees lobbying for liberal measures.

A further serious blow to the WJCC's influence and to the cause of social feminism in general was the intense red-baiting to which the WJCC and several of its more liberal member organizations were subjected in the mid-1920s. Although opponents of woman suffrage had attempted to discredit the suffrage movement through similar tactics—circulating articles with titles such as "The Indissoluble Alliance: Socialism, Suffragism, and Feminism"[58]—such attacks were generally ignored by feminists prior to World War I. However, by the mid-1920s this red-baiting had escalated to such an extent that the organizations and individuals under attack felt compelled to respond.[59]

Central to these attacks was the widely circulated Spider Web Chart, an elaborate diagram linking a number of reform organizations and their leaders. The chart was produced by an official in the War Department in 1924, and it carried the caption "The Socialist Pacifist Movement in America is an Absolutely Fundamental and Integral Part of International Socialism."[60] The Spider Web Chart placed the WJCC at the center of this alleged conspiracy to promote communism within the United States, and articles accompanying the chart singled out Margaret Dreier Robins, Mary Anderson, and the WTUL in general as among the most subversive individuals and groups in the country. Although WJCC protests resulted in the secretary of war promising to destroy all the War Department copies of this slanderous material, it continued to be circulated through Henry Ford's *Dearborn Independent* and much of it was reprinted in pamphlet form by various state manufacturers' associations opposed to labor legislation.

These smear tactics, which charged those individuals and groups promoting labor legislation with acting under orders from Moscow, created distrust and confusion within the ranks of social feminists and generally put more liberal groups on the defensive. The child labor amendment, a measure strongly backed by a large number of WJCC member organizations, was a victim of this red-baiting. Passed by Congress in 1924, the amendment was soundly defeated in state after state between 1924 and 1926, and it was generally agreed that a major factor was the popular belief that it was communist inspired.

Although the WTUL and the WJCC remained in existence beyond the mid-1920s, neither organization recovered from these setbacks. Membership in both groups declined throughout the late 1920s, and they were forced to reorient their legislative programs to focus on preventing the erosion of gains achieved in the early 1920s rather than building on their successes and pushing for the extension of progressive legislation. Nonetheless, even though the WJCC was unable to have the long-term progressive impact its founders had anticipated, the feminist movement did not suddenly collapse with the granting of women's suffrage. Moreover, the concerns of social feminists, as represented by the WJCC, paved the way for public acceptance of much of the legislation proposed in the 1930s as part of Roosevelt's New Deal. As Josephine Goldmark, a social feminist whose career spanned the Progressive Era to the New Deal and whose research and writings on the need for labor legislation for women provided the basis for several important legal decisions in the early twentieth century, commented at the end of her life, "The truth is that New Deal legislation did not spring full blown. Its roots lie in the preceding thirty years or more."[61] Thus, directly and indirectly, the WJCC influenced American feminism and social reform in general. The WTUL's decision to join the

WJCC reflects its belief in the possibility of cross-class sisterhood, and the fact that the WTUL consistently participated only on those WJCC subcommittees dealing with women's labor issues reveals its unwavering and focused commitment to the cause of women workers.

* * *

After years of working for special legislation for women workers and seeking support for its lobbying efforts from women outside the labor movement, the WTUL was confronted with a potentially devastating threat to its legislative program, a campaign by a group of feminists to abolish the principle and practice of sex-specific legislation. The campaign, which was initiated by the National Woman's Party (NWP) in 1921, had as its goal the adoption of a federal equal rights amendment. The WTUL bitterly and forcefully opposed such an amendment, fearing that it would nullify or at least jeopardize gains won for women workers through protective legislation. This conflict between the WTUL and the NWP, which preoccupied the league throughout the early 1920s, reveals many of the complexities inherent in the concept of feminism as an ideology with cross-class dimensions.

The ERA was proposed as a way of institutionalizing legal equality between the sexes, and most feminists in the 1920s agreed that despite the granting of woman suffrage, women still faced many forms of legal and political discrimination. For many feminists, however, the ERA was a problematic solution to this situation because of its probable negative impact on protective labor legislation. It was this aspect of the amendment that made it so controversial, and it was for this reason that the WTUL played such a leading role in opposing it.

The controversy over the ERA partially reflected genuine philosophical differences among feminists that had been muted during the years when they at least superficially united to work for woman suffrage. However, the controversy more fundamentally reflected the injection of class interests into feminism, for the ERA was primarily supported by those who felt it would help the advancement of women in professional jobs, while its major opponents were more concerned about the position of women in the industrial labor force. The supporters of the ERA tended to be motivated by an abstract commitment to the ideal of sexual equality; for them, the concept and fact of protective labor legislation represented a regressive position, since it implied that women were not capable of taking care of themselves. By contrast, the

139

opponents of the ERA tended to emphasize the special role of women as mothers and focus on social realities, which indicated to them that the needs and problems of men and women, especially men and women workers, were in many way quite different. For these feminists, protective labor legislation was progressive and realistic.

The conflict within feminist ranks generated by the NWP's introduction of the ERA in early 1921 was foreshadowed in an exchange of views published in *Life and Labor* in the spring of 1920. The WTUL at that time was actively supporting passage of legislation in New York that would make it illegal for women to work more than nine hours a day and after ten o'clock at night. Marguerite Mooers Marshall, a journalist, wrote to *Life and Labor*, protesting the league's efforts to secure passage of this legislation. Basically sympathetic to the WTUL and its general aims, she nonetheless considered its advocacy of "special privileges" for women workers "unfair, old-fashioned, and distinctly short-sighted." She contended that the league was adhering to "the typical anti-suffragist, anti-feminist attitude—that women must be protected, that they must shrink from meeting men on the level ground of equality, that the dear, shrinking creatures must be shielded against themselves, if necessary, for their own welfare and that of the race."[62]

Marshall's views on protective legislation were largely shaped by her own work experience, where her willingness to accept night assignments had been crucial to her professional advancement. Her motivation to work longer hours stemmed not only from a desire to be promoted but also from her commitment to not giving "new life to a prejudice now becoming slightly moribund—that 'a newspaper office is no place for women.'" Concern about the latter made her disdainful of women workers, such as most of the stenographers in her office, who, preferring "social life to professional advancement . . . won't work overtime or cut into evenings to help out in an emergency." In Marshall's experience, such women did not need protective legislation to control their working hours; as far as she could see, it simply served to "penalize . . . the ambitious woman . . . who doesn't work with her eye on the clock, who is willing to do extra work, to stay after hours, to prove that she is a little bigger than her present job and so earn promotion to a better one."[63]

Marshall furthermore argued that the struggle of American women for economic and professional equality was not yet won and that the WTUL, which she expected to support women waging this fight, was instead "launching a flank attack at us." She regarded "the ambitious young man working beside us" and "the conservative male employer" as "the natural antagonists" of self-supporting women and charged the WTUL with playing into their hands by continuing to promote protective legislation. "How can we ask for 'equal pay for equal work' when the hours and conditions of our work are hedged about by taboos and thou-shalt-nots which do not apply to the young man with whom we are in competition?" Marshall had fervently hoped that women would use the franchise "to end the paternal legislation of the past," and it was "with a sense of ironic despair" that she saw the WTUL "altruistically and determinedly beginning the *maternal* legislation of the future."[64]

Three members of the WTUL—Margaret Dreier Robins, Rose Schneiderman, and Pauline Newman, a garment worker active in the Philadelphia league—replied to Marshall's letter. Taken together, their responses contained all the themes the league was to emphasize in the coming years in arguing against the ERA. First of all, like other legislation promoted by the WTUL, this bill was designed to affect only women in factories and mercantile establishments; it would not in any way impinge on professional women's "freedom" to work as many hours as they pleased. More important, Robins, Schneiderman, and Newman pointed out that Marshall's views on protective legislation reflected her position as a professional woman who had a job she liked and one that offered "self-expression instead of monotony."[65] As Schneiderman wrote, "I dare say. . . . if Miss Marshall had to dip chocolates in a temperature of 63 degrees, using her fingers a certain way, she would realize at the end of the day what a blessing an eight-hour law would be and her strong feminist principles would come into harmony with facts."[66]

Robins argued that women who were anxious to leave office jobs at the end of the day should not necessarily be regarded as "slackers"; it was just as likely that they had other interests and responsibilities that could not be fulfilled during their hours at work. Furthermore, in the absence of widespread unionization among women, legislation was an effective and orderly means of standardizing industrial conditions and "the more industry is standardized, the greater the opportunity for women in the various trades and occupations."[67]

Newman and Schneiderman both took issue with Marshall's views on the possibilities for promotion, considering it an irrelevant issue for most women workers. As Newman sarcastically wrote, "Promotion to what . . . packing more boxes of candy or tending another loom? Or does Miss Marshall really think that we can have a world of all foreladies?" Shifting to a more serious consideration of social and economic realities, Newman explained:

> We cannot all be managers and superintendents. Somebody has got to do the work. And it is that "somebody" who needs protection from all sorts of exploitation. She and her co-workers form the great mass of women toilers. She it is who is being taken advantage of, not because there *is* protective legislation, but because there is *not*. She it is who, at the age of 35 is an old and worn out woman. And she it is whom Miss Marshall would like to see "free" from protective legislation! And it is just because of that "somebody" that Miss Marshall and we differ.

Finally, Newman astutely attributed a major source of the differences between Marshall's views and those of the WTUL to the fact that "Miss Marshall is . . . a strong individualist; as such she . . . disregards the problems of the many and has in mind only the problems of the few."[68]

Genuinely sympathetic to the problems facing women seeking access to professional jobs, the WTUL considered protective legislation to be in the best interests of the majority of women workers, who, as far as the league was concerned, suffered more acutely from being exploited in jobs they already held than from being excluded from jobs they might like to hold. Although Robins, Schneiderman, and Newman did not know it at the time, they and other WTUL members would be repeating this set of arguments with increasing frequency throughout the decade.

The WTUL had little reason to suspect that its legislative efforts in the postsuffrage period would be fought so strenuously by the NWP, for several of its leading members had also been members of the WTUL and active supporters of the women's labor movement. The National Woman's Party had its origins in the Congressional Union, a group formed in 1913 by women critical of the strategy and tactics being employed by the National American Woman Suffrage Association. Led from its inception by Alice Paul, who had recently returned from living in England where she had been associated with the militant wing of the British suffrage movement, the NWP injected a note of militancy into the last years of the suffrage struggle in the United States. Paul, a "dynamo" and a "tireless champion of single causes," was a member of the WTUL before she decided to devote herself exclusively to the cause of woman suffrage.[69] She was still considered a friend of the WTUL as late as the fall of 1920. Cornelia Bryce Pinchot, head of the league's finance committee, sought Paul's membership on this committee, feeling that her "spirit and interest . . . would be immensely valuable" to the league.[70] This overture, however, marked the end of cordial feelings on the part of WTUL members toward Alice Paul.

Early in 1921 the NWP invited representatives of all the major women's organizations to a conference in Washington, D.C., to discuss postsuffrage programs. At the conference the NWP, whose members tended to be "impatient with piecemeal, compromise approaches" announced that its new goal was legal equality for women.[71] It intended to lobby for amendments to existing laws, for equal rights legislation in the states, and for an equal rights amendment to the Constitution. Not opposed in principle to the concept of legal equality, the WTUL was nonetheless skeptical of the practical value of such legislation, feeling that it was "so vague and covered such a tremendous field there was no telling what its effect would be."[72] The league was also of course apprehensive that such legislation would undermine the special labor laws for women it considered so important.

The WTUL expressed its reservations to the NWP, whose leaders were initially receptive to revising their proposed federal amendment so that it would not endanger protective labor legislation. Maud Younger, the NWP's legislative chairman, encouraged Ethel Smith, the WTUL's legislative secretary, to submit suggestions for rewording the bill. Younger, who had been made an honorary member of a California waitresses' union in recognition of her involvement in the 1911 campaign to win an eight-hour day for women workers in that state, told Smith:

> We would be glad to find any other form or wording which would better accomplish the object we have in view, namely the removal of all legal discrimination against women without at the same time injuring the eight hour law and other social legislation in which as you know, I am personally deeply interested.[73]

Throughout 1921 both the WTUL and the NWP sought opinions from a wide range of lawyers on the probable impact of an equal rights amendment on protective labor legislation. Although there was some disagreement, the lawyers' responses overwhelmingly indicated that the amendment as currently drafted was likely to invalidate existing protective laws and it would be extremely difficult to frame any equal rights bill that would not call special labor legislation for women into question. George Sutherland, a well-known conservative who later became a Supreme Court justice, stated, "The Supreme Court might take the view that the amendment meant precisely what it said, and that a law which gave unequal advantage to women was as obnoxious to the amendment as one which was unequally to their disadvantage."[74] Felix Frankfurter took the same view, declaring more forcefully, "The proposed amendment . . . undoubtedly will largely retard, if not render impossible, every effort at legislative protection of women workers, for all such effort will encounter the opposition of alleged unconstitutionality."[75]

Frankfurter, who was basically sympathetic to the NWP's interest in removing legal discrimination against women, was nonetheless opposed to blanket equal rights legislation, for "the remedy proposed . . . opens the door to evils far more serious and affecting a vastly greater number of women than the disabilities they would shut out." Furthermore, he thought the NWP was "concentrating upon reforms and upon sentiments of special concern to a comparative handful of professional and leisure class women, who seem either indifferent to or ignorant of the consequences they will bring upon millions of wage-earning women." Given the probable consequences, he shared the WTUL's shock and outrage that the NWP would commit itself to such a goal, for "the proposed amendment threatens the well-being, even the very life, of these millions."[76]

The NWP, however, refused to be swayed from its commitment to equal rights legislation, even though by the end of 1921 it conceded that such legislation would probably nullify protective labor laws. The NWP had begun its campaign asserting that an equal rights amendment would either not affect protective labor legislation or would extend the same regulations to men. In the face of the numerous legal opinions refuting these arguments, the NWP shifted its position and argued that protective legislation hindered women's opportunities for employment. The NWP thus regarded sex-specific labor laws as discriminatory in both theory and practice, maintaining that laws regulating working conditions should either apply to both men and women or not exist.

Once it became clear that the NWP was determined to press for equal rights legislation at the state and federal levels, the WTUL took the lead in organizing opposition. The league held conferences, sent representatives to meetings of labor organizations and women's groups, and mounted a vigorous campaign to prevent the passage of equal rights bills introduced in state legislatures. The WTUL's concern was heightened when the National Manufacturers' Association allied itself with the NWP, and the two groups supported each other's efforts to block the passage of further protective legislation and to secure the passage of equal rights laws. "Stopping blanket equal rights laws and being stopped in turn on protective legislation became a regular occurrence in the 1920s. The two sides inflicted losses by balancing each other in legislative hearings all over the country."[77] Mary Anderson reflected the views of many WTUL members when she expressed her resentment that this struggle with the NWP forced the WTUL "to lay aside the work it was doing to improve conditions for women" in order to defend gains already won; she considered it "a most unfortunate and time-consuming controversy" that seriously impeded other efforts to raise the status of women.[78]

Although there was a theoretical dimension to the ERA controversy, much of the debate focused on whether protective legislation helped or hindered women in the labor force. Both sides cited a variety of case histories to support their position, but the lack of comprehensive and reliable data weakened the force of each side's arguments. To remedy this problem, supporters and opponents of protective legislation at a 1926 Women's Bureau conference on women in industry requested that the bureau undertake an investigation of this issue, each side assuming that the study would validate its point of view.[79]

This investigation became the major project of the Women's Bureau between 1926 and 1928 when it was published. Virtually the entire staff of the bureau was involved in it, and the bulk of the bureau's appropriations for those years was spent on the investigation. The study was planned and carried out with the active assistance of three highly qualified outside experts: Mary Van Kleeck, head of the Russell Sage Foundation's department of industrial studies; Charles P. Neill, a former commissioner of labor who had directed the 1909 study of women and child wage earners; and Lillian Gilbreth, well-known industrial engineer. Information was gathered from 1,661 establishments employing over 660,000 men and women. The study concentrated heavily on factory work, but it also covered restaurant workers, pharmacists, elevator operators, taxi drivers, and street car conductors and ticket agents.[80] When the results were analyzed, they conclusively established that with very few exceptions, "labor legislation was not a handicap to women, that it did not reduce their opportunities, and that it raised standards not only for women but for thousands of men."[81] The opponents of protective legislation were left only with the ideological argument that such legislation sustained the traditional emphasis on the differences between men and women and thereby retarded the development of social, political, and economic equality.

From the standpoint of pure feminist theory, there was considerable justification for the NWP's position; the concepts underlying protective legislation did indeed conflict with the notion of sexual equality. However, from the standpoint of social reality, the WTUL's commitment to protective legislation reflected a more astute assessment of the ways economic equality could be eventually achieved for larger numbers of women. Moreover, the WTUL's support for protective legislation reflected its deep commitment to a vision of feminism as an ideology uniting women across class lines. As one WTUL member wrote:

> We believe that recognition of this principle [that women workers wanted and needed protective legislation] . . . is absolutely necessary to the coherence of the . . . woman movement. Without it . . . working women . . . are bound to come to feel that the women of the middle, professional and leisure classes . . . are unmindful of the labor woman's necessities . . . and class divisions will be created . . . or accentuated.[82]

As support for the ERA increased among women's groups in the late 1920s, the WTUL was left in a relatively isolated position. Its relationship with the labor movement had always been tenuous, and in compensation it had increasingly relied on its identification with the women's movement, hoping that an alliance with feminists would be more fruitful in solving the problems of women workers than its attempts to arouse concern and support among male labor leaders. The conflict over the ERA revealed, however, that the WTUL's relationship with the feminist movement was also problematic. Despite the league's efforts to integrate women workers into both the feminist and labor movements, the needs of women workers remained a peripheral concern of both movements. As women, their problems were neglected by the male-dominated labor movement; as workers, their concerns were slighted by the middle-class-oriented feminist movement.

* * *

Although the legislative programs of the British and American Women's Trade Union Leagues were undertaken out of similar convictions about the value of legislation in facilitating unionization, their work in this area ultimately had very different effects on the history of the two organizations. Since the British WTUL consistently reinforced its legislative victories with organizing campaigns, its legislative activities strengthened its ties to both the British labor movement and Labour Party. The British league was thus able to represent the needs of women workers as a special interest group from an increasingly solid labor base.

By contrast, the American WTUL's legislative activities increasingly substituted for organizing and weakened its ties to the American labor movement. It is interesting to speculate how the existence of an American Labor Party would have affected the history of the WTUL; what is clear is that in the absence of such a party and in response to the league's growing conviction that women workers were a group with special problems and needs because they were women, the American WTUL stressed its role as a feminist organization. Its legislative program was dictated by its perceptions of the needs of women workers rather than by the policies of the AFL, and it based its lobbying efforts on its identity as a women's organization concerned about the general welfare of American society. In sum, the British WTUL consolidated its identity as a women's labor organization, whereas the American WTUL became a social welfare organization focusing on the problems of women workers.

SIX

The Problems of a
Woman's Internationale:
The International
Federation of
Working Women

Although the International Federation of Working Women (IFWW) was an obscure and short-lived (1919-1925) organization, it is important to this study for two reasons: established by the combined efforts of the British and American Women's Trade Union Leagues, it is part of their shared history; and, more significant, it provides a fascinating and complex instance of the interaction between feminist and class attitudes.[1]

The idea that an international congress of women workers be held at the end of the war was first proposed at the 1917 convention of the American WTUL. During the war, trade union groups in various countries had decided that labor clauses standardizing and regulating wages, hours, and working conditions should be included in the future peace treaty, and by 1917 plans were underway for an international labor conference to be held in conjunction with the peace negotiations. The WTUL convention sent a formal request to the American Federation of Labor that it include women trade unionists among its delegates. WTUL members, however, felt there was also a need for a separate women's labor conference; they did not expect the international labor conference to include a significant number of female participants or to devote enough time to issues of particular concern to women workers.

The idea for a women's conference was supported by the WTUL Committee on Social and Industrial Reconstruction in its 1918 report. Increasingly confident of women's potential influence, the committee urged the calling of an International Congress of Working Women to facilitate "the exchange of thought and the concerted action required by the task before us."[2] Representing the WTUL, Rose Schneiderman and Mary Anderson went to Europe in early 1919 to present the reconstruction committee's recommendations to the Labor Commission, the body organizing the international labor conference, which was to be held under the auspices of the newly formed League of Nations. Schneiderman and Anderson met with leaders of the British WTUL and with a few women officers of French labor organizations to discuss the idea that a women's labor conference be held just prior to the League of Nations International Labor Conference. The positive response of both groups of labor women was conveyed to the June 1919 American WTUL convention when Schneiderman and Anderson reported on their European mission. Mary Macarthur and Margaret Bondfield attended the 1919 convention as fraternal delegates from the British WTUL and National Federation of Women Workers; they urged the American WTUL to call such a conference and pledged British support and cooperation.[3]

On the basis of this response, the 1919 WTUL convention voted to call an International Congress of Working Women to be held in the fall in Washington, D.C., a week prior to the International Labor Office (ILO) International Labor Conference, which would also be meeting in Washington. The American WTUL issued the official call to the women's congress in August, urging attendance at the congress and declaring that "women must now assume responsibilities in the affairs of the world" and that "fellowship and conference together can alone guarantee mutual faith and joint action which shall make for universal justice."[4] The call thus extended worldwide the values and approaches that characterized the WTUL's domestic efforts to improve the position of women workers.

Each country was entitled to ten delegates and ten votes, delegates must bring credentials signed by trade union organizations of their respective countries, and each delegation should designate one of its members to serve on the Executive Committee of the congress. Each delegation was asked to prepare material on the situation and views of working women in their country on the following issues, which were also to be discussed at the International Labor Conference: women's employment, especially in relation to childbirth, night work, and jobs involving dangerous substances such as lead, phosphorous, and arsenic; child labor; the eight-hour day; and the problem of unemployment. The conference was being planned by British and American labor women and in Washington, the delegates would be guests of the American Women's Trade Union League.[5] The American WTUL had begun a fund-raising drive shortly after its 1919 convention, and contributions from WTUL members and wealthy sympathizers enabled the league to subsidize this first International Congress of Working Women.

* * *

Representatives from nineteen countries attended the congress, which was held from October 28 to November 6, 1919.[6] (Ultimately, the women's congress coincided with, rather than preceded, the International Labor Conference, which met from October 29 to November 29.) Many of the delegates to the International Congress of Working Women (ICWW) were also technical advisers to their national delegations attending the labor conference. In addition, the women's conference was enriched by the informal attendance and participation of several female technical advisers to the ILO conference whose countries had not sent official delegates to the women's conference. As president of the American WTUL, Margaret Dreier Robins opened the conference with an address of welcome that stressed the special role of women. "What more fitting than that the women of the world should choose this hour to accept and assume their full responsibilities? Women are the builders of the race. To us is entrusted the protection of life. The social and industrial order must meet this challenge."[7]

This conference had three major objectives. First, to arrive at a set of recommendations expressing the views of organized working women on issues of particular concern to women that would be discussed at the International Labor Conference. Second, to begin developing an international sense of sisterhood and solidarity among women workers by providing a forum for personal contact and discussion of common problems. Third, to determine whether labor women were interested in creating an ongoing organization to deal with the special problems and needs of women workers throughout the world.

This first congress spent most of its time discussing the issues the delegates had been asked in advance to consider. The discussions were serious, substantive, and lively; conflicting points of view were dealt with openly and in a comradely manner. The problems of child labor, maternity benefits, and night work were discussed at the greatest length, the latter two causing the most controversy. On the issue of child labor, the conference agreed that sixteen should be the legal minimum age for the employment of children, that no one under eighteen should be allowed to work in a mine or quarry, that the legal workday for young people between the ages of sixteen and eighteen should be shorter than the legal workday for adults, and that no one under eighteen should be employed between 6:00 P.M. and 7:00 A.M.[8] Most existing or proposed legislation on child labor used fourteen and sixteen as the ages on which limitations were based, but the women at the conference unanimously agreed that they had a responsibility to the children of the world to attempt to raise the age limits to sixteen and eighteen.[9]

The question of maternity benefits also generated considerable controversy. All the delegates favored the principle of maternity insurance, but reflecting the different economic situations of their countries, the delegates disagreed over what forms such insurance should take. Should maternity aid mean access only to nursing and medical care or should it also include a cash benefit? If cash benefits were included, should they come from the state as a special grant or from a general health insurance fund under other control? Should maternity benefits be available to the wives of workers as well as to women wage earners? Should these benefits be available to all women, regardless of income, to remove any stigma of their being charity grants? Another question was whether the delegates were in favor of having nurseries attached to factories and giving mothers time off to nurse their infants or of payments to subsidize nursing mothers so they could stay home with their children.[10]

The delegates finally agreed on a majority resolution stating that it should be illegal to employ women six weeks before or six weeks after childbirth; that all women should be "entitled during maternity to free medical, surgical, and nursing care, either in a hospital or at home, and also to a monetary allowance"; and that this allowance should be "adequate for the full and healthy maintenance of mother and child" in this twelve-week period.[11] Feeling that this resolution was too idealistic and financially impractical, delegates from Belgium, Czechoslovakia, Poland, Italy, and Canada appended a minority report maintaining that maternity benefits should be available only to wage-earning women or the wives of wage-earning men and that cash payments should be based on the living wage in the region.

The Scandinavian delegates consistently opposed special laws for women regarding night work and hazardous occupations; they believed these problems should be fought in the name of all workers, and that from the point of view of labor solidarity, it was incorrect to define them as areas of special concern to women. The other delegates claimed that night work and dangerous substances did in fact particularly affect women because they involved their well-being as potential or actual mothers. The resolutions finally adopted by the congress took into account both points of view, calling for the exclusion of women "only in trades which cannot be made healthy for women as potential mothers" and the prohibition of night (9:00 P.M. to 6:00 A.M.) work for women and its elimination for men "except insofar as it may be absolutely necessary through the special nature of, or the continuity of, the occupation, or in the case of essential public service."[12]

On the basis of the available evidence, it is difficult to determine the extent to which the ICWW's recommendations influenced the conventions (the ILO term for resolutions) eventually adopted by the International Labor Conference. As resolutions were passed by the ICWW, they were conveyed to the ILO conference. Most of the women's recommendations were read to the assembled delegates at the ILO conference and were then referred to the committees charged with drafting conventions for formal considerations. According to *Life and Labor*, the presentation of the ICWW resolutions "undoubtedly exercised a considerable influence upon the views of the delegates, and . . . strengthened the hands of the women technical advisors in counsel there."[13] Since several of the conventions ultimately adopted by the International Labor Conference did embody the principles, if not the specific details, of the ICWW recommendations, *Life and Labor*'s assessment may well be accurate. Influence is of course difficult to verify, but available evidence suggests that, contrary to the claims of the *Life and Labor* article, the conference would have come to the same conclusions even if the ICWW had not met and expressed its collective point of view.

Although there are no records of the labor conference committee meetings, the verbatim proceedings of the general sessions contain no references to the ICWW recommendations during the discussions of issues on which it had expressed a position.[14] For example, the ICWW requested that the labor conference establish an international convention prohibiting night work for women in industrial jobs, defining night as the hours between 9:00 P.M. and 6:00 A.M. The ILO conference passed such a convention but defined night as the hours between 10:00 P.M. and 5:00 A.M.[15] There were similar kinds of discrepancies between the resolution on maternity benefits submitted by the ICWW and the one adopted by the ILO conference.[16] Whether these discrepancies and the rationale for them were discussed at the committee level cannot be known. The fact that they were not mentioned at all in the discussions of the plenary sessions seems to indicate that the recommendations of the ICWW were not taken as seriously as they might have been by the ILO conference delegates. If the delegates (all of whom were male) had seriously respected the labor women's views, then presumably they would either have fully adopted the ICWW recommendations or explained the ideological or pragmatic reasons for deviating from their details.

Another indication that the views of the labor women did not weigh heavily was the treatment accorded an ICWW resolution on the composition of the ILO conference delegations. The very first communication sent by the ICWW to the International Labor Conference was a request that the rules regarding the composition of national delegations to future conferences be revised so that of the six delegates from each country, two had to be women.[17] Several women were at the labor conference as technical advisers to their national delegations, but there were no women among the official, voting delegates. According to *Life and Labor*, "The power of the woman technical advisor in the sitting Conference is entirely dependent upon the good will of the man delegate whom she is appointed to assist. If he chooses, she may have the floor and exercise his vote upon any question involving women, and if he does not so choose, she must sit in unworthy suppression and silence."[18] The ILO conference ignored this proposal that women be guaranteed representation; unlike the other ICWW resolutions, this one was not read to the delegates in general session, was not referred to any committee, and did not come up for general discussion.

Considering that the agenda of the International Labor Conference was determined prior to the establishment of the ICWW and that there is very little evidence that once the ICWW was established, its views were given serious consideration, it is difficult to maintain that the ICWW recommendations significantly influenced the deliberations or outcome of the ILO conference. Despite the hopes of the ICWW, it seems that its views were adopted when they agreed with those of the labor conference delegates; otherwise they were ignored.[19] It was nonetheless a significant achievement for the women involved that the women's conference was organized and well attended and that it resulted in a set of resolutions expressing, for the first time, the collective views of an international group of trade union women.

In terms of its second objective—creating a sense of international solidarity among the labor women attending the congress—the ICWW was a success. Meeting together gave the participants a broadened perspective on their own nation's conditions and an increased understanding of the situation of women workers in other countries. Attending the congress made it clearer to the delegates what was unique about conditions in their own countries and in what respects the problems of working women were similar throughout the world. The realization that most problems should be dealt with at international, as well as national and local levels, dominated the congress. The ICWW delegates' awareness of the need to put aside national differences and the hostilities carried over from the war was illustrated during the discussion of the constitution when a French delegate urged that a place be left open among the vice presidents for a representative of the Central Powers, unrepresented at the congress. The suggestion was greeted with "spontaneous and unanimous applause."[20]

Numerous social activities added considerably to the spirit of warmth and sisterhood. The delegates were invited to a variety of luncheons, teas, and trips by different women's groups that wished to express their solidarity. Social activities included sightseeing trips arranged by a teachers' union and by women of the Federal Employees' Union, a tour of the Bureau of Printing and Engraving followed by a luncheon given by a women's local of bureau workers, an industrial pageant prepared by the War Work Council of the YWCA, and a luncheon held at the Women's Bureau of the Labor Department.[21] The general tone of the conference documents suggests that it was precisely this combination of formal and informal interaction that made the ICWW such an enriching experience. The conference served important educational and psychological functions for the participants, broadening their understanding of the problems discussed and renewing their commitment to continuing their work at home.

A third aspect of the ICWW was an extended discussion about forming a permanent organization. A provisional structure was created to provide for calling a second congress and transacting business until then, but disagreements over the basis of membership in the proposed organization made the delegates defer decisions on a permanent constitution until the next congress. The delegates unanimously favored establishing the ICWW as a permanent organization, but they did not feel ready to choose between two proposed structures for the new organization. One suggested constitution came from the group that served as the executive committee for the 1919 meeting (one delegate from each country represented), the other came from the English delegation, whose representative had not arrived in Washington in time to attend the executive committee meetings that worked out a suggested constitution.

The major difference between the two proposals was the basis for membership in the international organization. The executive committee suggested that membership be limited to trade union organizations, whereas the British proposed that organizations of nonworking working-class women as well as trade union women be included. The British argued that since a major function of the new organization was to monitor the legislative proposals of the International Labor Office, working-class wives and mothers, whose husbands and children would be affected by such legislation, were legitimately concerned. The British also argued that since an international trade union organization already existed (the International Federation of Trade Unions), there was less need for an international organization of trade union women than for an international organization of working-class women, be they workers or housewives.

For these reasons the British were proposing that the ICWW become a permanent organization with membership open to "all democratic organizations of women of the working class." Mary Macarthur, who explained the British position, made it clear that the plan did not envision the inclusion of philanthropic or charitable organizations. To be eligible for affiliation, an organization did not have to be a trade union, but it did have to be democratic, self-governing, and its membership predominantly working class. Thus, trade union women's auxiliaries and groups such as the English Women's Cooperative Guild, a working-class consumer cooperative, would be eligible for affiliation, as would women's political organizations, as long as they were "independent of the existing capitalistic parties."[22] Using their own newly formed Standing Joint Committee of Industrial Women's Organizations as a model, the British were proposing a broader, more politically innovative organization than the delegates to the ICWW were ready to accept. Although it was not explicitly presented as such, the British plan represented a sophisticated example of a strongly class-conscious feminism.

The discussion of the membership issue revealed that the majority of delegates was uncomfortable with the British proposals. Fears were expressed that adopting a broader basis for membership would open the ICWW to political factionalism and turn it away from work-related issues. There was, however, enough interest in the British plan for the delegates to decide to defer a vote on the constitution until the next congress.

Once this decision was made, the delegates elected a provisional group of officers consisting of Margaret Dreier Robins as president, Maud Swartz, who was also from the American WTUL, as secretary-treasurer, and Mary Macarthur of Britain, Jeanne Bouvier of France, Betzy Kjelsberg of Norway, and Louisa Landova-Stychova of Czechoslovakia as vice presidents. An additional vice presidency was left vacant, in the hope it would be filled by a representative of the Central Power countries. In recognition of the role the Americans had played in initiating the ICWW and as a reflection of the Europeans' preoccupation with domestic reconstruction in this immediate postwar period, the delegates decided that ICWW headquarters would be in Washington, D.C. They also agreed that the basis of representation at the next congress would be the same—women from various trade unions and women's organizations would be invited. Thus, recognizing that difficulties might lie ahead, the 1919 congress ended on a note of compromise and commitment—compromise in regard to some of the resolutions and to the deferred decision on the structure of a permanent organization and commitment to labor, feminist, and internationalist ideals.

* * *

Immediately following the congress, headquarters were established in Washington, D.C., and Miriam G. Shepherd, an American WTUL member, was hired as secretary to the executive committee. Her first task was publicizing the existence of the ICWW. She compiled a mailing list of about one thousand names covering forty-nine countries and sent these people copies of the resolutions passed at the congress with a letter urging that they be publicized as the goals of working women. Copies of the resolutions were also sent to the International Women's Suffrage Alliance, the International Council of Women, and the Women's International League for Peace and Freedom, as well as to the International Federation of Trade Unions, the Pan-American Federation of Labor, and the International Labor Organization.

One of the decisions made by the secretariat was to accept invitations to send fraternal delegates (a technical term used by men's and women's organizations) to the conventions of the three women's organizations mentioned above. ICWW officers were particularly anxious to have their organization represented at the 1920 meeting of the International Women's Suffrage Alliance, for the agenda for that convention included a proposal that the Alliance go on record opposing the protective legislation advocated by the

1919 International Labor Conference as inconsistent with the principle of equal rights of women. Jeanne Bouvier attended the suffrage convention; as a fraternal delegate she did not have the right to participate in convention discussions unless her views were solicited. When she realized that the alliance leadership did not intend to ask her to present the ICWW's position on protective legislation, she took the initiative in requesting the floor and was granted the right to speak. She chastised the suffrage delegates for believing themselves "entitled to decide on questions concerning economics without the advice of working women" and went on to say that since the International Labor Conference resolutions were supported by the ICWW, the International Women's Suffrage Alliance "would be making a great mistake" to oppose them. Its opposition "would create an antagonism between the suffrage women and the working women which would be prejudicial to suffrage," for "more and more the questions of economics are dominating politics, and there should not be any misunderstandings between workers and suffragists."[23] A few moments of surprised silence followed Bouvier's remarks, but the discussion that ensued indicated that her comments had had a significant impact on the delegates' views. In the end, the International Women's Suffrage Alliance did not go so far as to support the concept of protective legislation for women workers, but as a result of Bouvier's intervention, the alliance decided not to go on record opposing the International Labor Conference's resolutions on this issue.

In addition to establishing contact with potentially interested and supportive groups and individuals, early in 1920 the ICWW secretariat began to publish a periodic newsletter in English, French, and German editions. It contained accounts of the position of women workers in various countries and industries, allowed the delegates to keep in touch with one another, and provided a forum for discussion of the ICWW's eventual constitution.[24]

Marion Phillips, secretary of the British Standing Joint Committee of Industrial Women's Organizations, the organization through which British women were represented in the ICWW, wrote an article for the ICWW newsletter reiterating the British position at the 1919 congress. Phillips argued that it was essential "that the ICWW represent not only the women wage-earners, but the women in the homes."[25] The views of such women would be valuable on all industrial questions and it was especially important that their point of view be represented in ICWW discussions of legislation regarding maternity, child labor, and educational opportunities.

Phillips went on to point out how useful it had been to have an organization such as the Standing Joint Committee of Industrial Women's Organizations, which was composed of representatives from working-class political, cooperative, and labor groups. The organizations represented on the committee were unanimous "in believing that any step to confine representation of working women at the International Congress of Working Women to one section only, namely the Trade Union section, of women represented upon it would be disastrous." The committee felt strongly that "organizations of working women on the broader basis should be encouraged in all countries by the International Congress of Working Women as the most satisfactory method of getting a fully represented international body and should therefore be recognized as the method of representation recommended in its constitution." Phillips concluded her discussion of the British position:

> The Standing Joint Committee would be prepared to agree to some temporary method for such countries as were not willing or able to fall in immediately with this scheme, but the Trade Union women would with great regret feel themselves compelled to sever their connection with the Congress if a constitution was adopted which excluded representation of the Standing Joint Committee.[26]

Reaction to the British point of view varied. It was discussed at a series of WTUL regional conferences, and in general, American WTUL members supported the British proposal or some minor variation of it.[27] Some league members were quite excited and politically stimulated by the class-based feminism embodied in the British plan.[28] However, the Canadian and European groups affiliated to the ICWW felt strongly that the organization should be composed only of trade union women. They feared that an ICWW structured along the lines proposed by the British would be taken over by divisive political groups, and they also feared that trade union interests would be subordinated to political concerns. The Norwegians summed up this point of view:

> The Congress must abandon all political questions and abstain from all tasks and questions which may divide it into politics, whereby it should be divided into different views. The Congress ought to be strictly professional, only promoting questions which are of interest to the working woman as wage-earner, but not troubling itself about the many questions and problems which may be of interest to her as a member of society. In our opinion this will contribute to the inner

firmness of the Congress and the reliance in it, such homogeneousness being the very thing necessary for its international existence.[29]

Consensus on the membership question was not being reached through discussions in the newsletter. It loomed as the major issue to be dealt with at the 1921 ICWW meeting.

Planning and raising funds for the next congress, which was to be held in Geneva in October 1921, was a major project of the ICWW secretariat. Credential blanks were sent to labor organizations in forty-nine countries, along with copies of a questionnaire on working conditions prepared by the International Labor Office for use at the 1921 International Labor Conference. Once again the cost of the congress would be primarily met by American contributions, which were also responsible for maintaining the Washington office, whose expenses were greatly increased by the need to answer letters and publish materials in four languages. Margaret Dreier Robins and the office staff directed a major amount of their publicity efforts—letters, interviews, speeches, and articles—at Americans outside the labor movement, asking them for contributions to support the work and future meetings of the ICWW. In addition to gifts, the ICWW was sustained by contributions from trade union women and from a few labor unions, although the single most significant source of financial support was Robins herself, who turned what had initially been a loan into an outright gift and personally met many of the initial expenses of setting up and maintaining the headquarters.[30]

However, even though the Americans were financially better off than their European colleagues and were willing to take on a disproportionate share of financial responsibility to get the ICWW established and functioning, they were not willing to subsidize the ICWW permanently. The call for the second congress made it clear that each organization sending delegates would be responsible for the travel and living expenses of its delegation. The ICWW executive committee also requested all participating organizations to make whatever contributions they could toward the general cost of the congress. An item on the congress agenda would be formulating a plan for financing the permanent organization.[31]

The 1921 congress was to follow a format virtually identical to that of 1919; the topics for discussion were taken from the agenda to be followed by the International Labor Conference and dealt with similar issues of working conditions, insurance, and child labor.[32] An additional topic to be considered by both organizations was problems relating to agricultural work. The 1921

ICWW agenda also included reports on the status of resolutions adopted in 1919 and, of course, discussion of the permanent constitution.

Most of the points of view on the membership issue had already been expressed in the ICWW newsletter. An additional dimension to the problem, which came to the attention of Margaret Dreier Robins when she arrived in Europe a few weeks before the congress, was that several European groups were deeply concerned "that there be no misunderstanding regarding their orthodox position as trade unionists."[33] To counteract any such questions, they wanted the congress to make it clearly understood that the ICWW identified with the trade union movement represented by the International Federation of Trade Unions, whose headquarters were in Amsterdam. Thus, there were two aspects to the membership question facing the delegates: Was membership in the ICWW to be limited to trade union women or was it to include organized groups of working-class women outside the labor movement? What kind of connection would be established with the International Federation of Trade Unions?

* * *

Delegates from Belgium, Cuba, Czechoslovakia, France, Great Britain, Italy, Norway, Poland, South Africa, Switzerland, and the United States attended the ICWW; several other countries, including China, were represented unofficially by women visitors. The participants considered and passed resolutions on disarmament, unemployment, standards for agricultural workers, and precautions to protect textile workers from the spread of anthrax and workers in various other industries from lead poisoning. In addition to new resolutions, the delegates reported on the status of the conventions adopted by the 1919 International Labor Conference; they were assured by Albert Thomas, director of the International Labor Conference, that although the ratification process was slow, progress was being made in having the conventions approved in countries throughout the world.

A significant amount of time was devoted to a constitution for a permanent organization. After a series of tumultuous sessions, the constitution committee presented a document for consideration by the delegates. The first point, which was unanimously adopted, was that the name of the permanent organization would be the International Federation of Working Women (IFWW). The basis for membership proposed by the constitution committee was a compromise plan, which reflected majority sentiment but at the same time provided the possibility for organized groups of working-class women who were not trade unionists to be represented in the IFWW. The plan accepted by the delegates was that membership was to consist primarily of "national trade union organizations containing women members and affiliated to the International Federation of Trade Unions"; in addition, working-class women's organizations that accepted the "spirit, aims, and principles" of the International Federation of Trade Unions would be eligible for membership.[34] However, since the constitution also stipulated that each member country was to be represented by only one national organization, in practice non-trade-union women could be represented in the IFWW only when they were part of a national coalition, such as the British Standing Joint Committee of Industrial Women's Organizations.

This resolution satisfied the British to the extent that it allowed them to be represented in the IFWW through the Standing Joint Committee. However, they had hoped to win support for their idea that the IFWW should, rather than merely could, include representatives of non-trade-union working-class women's organizations. In the discussion on the constitution in the newsletter and at the 1919 and 1921 congresses, the British had argued that a political priority for all IFWW members should be establishing more broadly based organizations of working-class women at the national level. They hoped that the IFWW would eventually speak for working-class women as a whole, rather than just women wage earners. This idea of making it a priority to build an organization including representatives of working-class women in their roles as housewives and citizens, as well as workers, stemmed from a vision reflecting an integration of certain aspects of feminism and class consciousness.

Although British women had certainly not achieved anything resembling equality in labor or society, they were organizationally considerably more advanced than women in most other countries. As was noted, a 1920 reorganization of the Trades Union Congress had created a Women's Section, and indeed Britain was the only country where strong organizations of non-working-class women existed. Supporting the British proposal for a broader basis of membership in the IFWW was not a realistic option for women labor leaders from countries that lacked this level of structural development among working-class women. Most IFWW members felt that all their time was needed to work at their own jobs and to improve the status of wage-earning women. It would be a diversion of their energy and a less effective way of meeting the needs of women wage earners to accept the British proposal for expanding the scope and orientation of the IFWW.

Their decision makes sense from a tactical point of view, but it is to be regretted from a theoretical one. Had the IFWW been willing to adopt the British proposal and explore its implications, it seems likely that it would have led to fresh thinking and an expanded definition of workers to include the socially productive and vital work of the housewife, something the British themselves had not considered. As a result, the IFWW never fully faced the question of whether housewives should be seen as workers in their own right, in addition to their identity as the wives and mothers of workers.

In a similar vein, the decision to make adherence to the principles of the International Federation of Trade Unions a criterion for membership was a sensible tactical move for a new organization seeking support from the international labor movement. At the same time, however, the decision revealed how far the IFWW delegates were from seriously questioning accepted definitions of workers and how much they wanted the approval of their male colleagues. By the next IFWW congress, the relationship with the International Federation of Trade Unions would become a divisive issue within the IFWW; for the time being, it was accepted by most of the delegates without serious reservations.[35]

Other aspects of the constitution provide insight on the history of the IFWW. The opening section stated that the general object of the IFWW was "to unite organized women in order that they may resolve upon the means by which the standard of life of the workers throughout the world may best be raised." More specifically, the federation would promote trade union organization among women, develop "an international policy giving special consideration to the needs of women and children," examine all legislative projects proposed by the League of Nations International Labor Conference, and encourage "the appointment of women to represent organized working women on all organizations and committees dealing with questions affecting the welfare of the workers."[36]

In an article written shortly after the congress, Marion Phillips, the British delegate who was the IFWW's newly elected secretary, emphasized that the IFWW was not interested in establishing separate trade unions for women but rather was committed to women and men being in the same union. However, because the proportion of organized females was so much lower than that of males in virtually all industries, the IFWW held that the only way to get more women organized was to pay special attention to the "particular requirements of the woman worker," which could best be done by "bringing women concerned in these matters together and by developing the interest of the women within the Labour movement by directing special attention to their needs and desires." The IFWW existed because its members believed that "women are not yet 'pulling their weight' in the Labour world and that they must develop their powers of organisation and increase their knowledge of public life before the full strength of the workers' organisations can be attained."[37]

The rest of the IFWW constitution dealt with the election and duties of officers, the biennial congress, and the financial structure of the organization. Once the constitution was adopted, officers were elected to serve until the 1923 congress. (Margaret Dreier Robins was reelected president, Marion Phillips and Florence Harrison Bell of England were elected secretary and treasurer respectively, and vice presidents from each affiliated country were chosen; Maud Swartz was the American vice president and Margaret Bondfield the British.) It was also decided to move the headquarters from Washington, D.C., to London, given the European orientation of the organization. Thus, by the end of the 1921 congress, a permanent organization—the International Federation of Working Women—was established, a constitution adopted, a second set of resolutions passed, officers elected, and a London secretariat established.[38] As Margaret Dreier Robins noted, the American delegates left the congress "looking forward to a growing women's organization which should make for the training of women trade unionists and for the development of their leadership."[39]

Much to the disappointment of the Americans, the anticipated stability and permanence were not achieved; the IFWW remained in existence only another four years. A conflict, directly related to the issues of feminism and class consciousness, developed between the Americans and the Europeans, led by the British, over the direction of the organization. The debate focused on whether the IFWW should continue as an autonomous women's organization, seeking support from and interaction with other international women's organizations, such as the Women's International League for Peace and Freedom and the International Women's Suffrage Alliance, or whether the federation should dissolve itself to become the Women's Department of the International Federation of Trade Unions (IFTU). In order to understand the subsequent developments within the IFWW, it is necessary to turn to a discussion of the International Federation of Trade Unions and the relationship between that organization and the American Federation of Labor.[40]

* * *

The IFTU was an international (predominantly European) association of national labor federations. It was established in 1901 with affiliations from eight national trade union centers and a budget of around $200. By 1914 there were nineteen affiliated countries, a budget of close to $20,000, and a secretariat with a staff of twelve.[41] The British Trade Union Congress (then known as the General Federation of Trade Unions) was one of the original members; the American Federation of Labor joined in 1910.

Prior to World War I, the labor federations in the IFTU represented political attitudes and orientations toward trade unionism that fell into three categories: pragmatic, social reformist, and revolutionary. The first type was represented by the labor movement of Britain and the United States, where trade unions tended to be decentralized, organized on a craft rather than industrial basis interested primarily in collective bargaining, and "nonsocialist if not antisocialist in outlook."[42] The trade unions of Germany and Austria were models for the social reformist category. They were highly centralized, financially strong with large benefits programs, organized on an industrial basis, and had close ties to socialist parties. Thus, they were socialist in theory, but in practice they were oriented toward immediate reforms, believing that such changes would gradually lead to a socialist society. The revolutionary group was represented by French syndicalism, which advocated more or less violent class struggle as the only route to the abolition of capitalism. The dominant orientation within the IFTU was the social reformist position, although there were various internal struggles as IFTU policies and programs were developed.

Delegates to a 1907 IFTU conference decided that the federation would not deal with theoretical issues; its purpose would be the collection and distribution of information on trade union movements in different countries. In addition, the IFTU dealt with problems of international strikebreaking, and on various occasions it gave financial aid to striking workers. In general, the IFTU concerned itself with issues that affected labor on an international basis, such as the transferability of union membership when workers migrated from one country to another. The IFTU also considered the possibilities of an international campaign to achieve standardized legislation on problems such as the use of industrial poisons and the regulation of night and home work. From 1901 to the outbreak of World War I, the IFTU developed from a gathering of a few trade union officials into a permanent organization with its own staff and well-organized, regularly scheduled conferences. It developed the first pool of international labor statistics, and it facilitated contact among national labor leaders. The AFL was the first non-European federation to join the IFTU; by 1913 links had been established with the trade union centers of Argentina, South Africa, and Australia.

Despite this promising beginning, the IFTU fell apart during World War I, when most of its socialist and trade union members found that national loyalties overcame their ideological commitment to the concept of international working-class solidarity. However, a few weeks after the Versailles Peace Treaty was signed in the summer of 1919, an international trade union congress was held in Amsterdam. Representatives from thirteen European countries, including Germany and Austria, and from the United States, attended. The sessions were stormy ones, marked by many clashes over the labor conventions of the Versailles Treaty, the League of Nations, socialism, and the organizational and financial structure of a revived IFTU. Nevertheless, there was enough unity of purpose for the delegates to decide to reestablish the IFTU, adopt resolutions on the above issues, elect a new governing board, and relocate IFTU headquarters from Berlin to Amsterdam. The British rejoined the revived federation—in fact, an Englishman, W. A. Appleton, was elected president. But—and this is significant in terms of the split that later developed among the women—the Americans decided not to reaffiliate.

When the AFL had originally joined the IFTU in 1910, it had done so with serious reservations about its composition and procedures. Samuel Gompers had long been interested in maintaining contacts with European leaders, but he felt strongly that an international labor organization should be a pure trade union organization distinct from international socialist organizations. Representing the AFL, Gompers attended the 1909 IFTU conference in Paris, which he felt devoted too much time to general discussion and not enough to practical work; he was also displeased to find the French Confederation of Labor represented by people he considered anarchists and the Austrian and Dutch delegates men he characterized as "wholly socialistic."[43] However, the crucial issue for Gompers was that joining the IFTU not compromise the autonomy of the AFL. When this conference declared that IFTU policies would not be binding on member groups unless they were unanimously adopted, Gompers decided he could overlook his reservations about the politics of some IFTU members. On his return to the United States, he urged AFL affiliation with the IFTU as "in the best interests of the workers of America."[44] Once the AFL joined the IFTU, it played an active role in the organization, consistently promoting, and often gaining support for, proposals that increased the distinction between the IFTU and the Socialist Second

International and focused the IFTU on purely trade-union-oriented concerns. By the outbreak of World War I, the AFL, whose international orientation was very much the product of Gompers's interests and influence, had become an integral part of the international labor movement.

When for all practical purposes the IFTU disintegrated early in the war, there is evidence that Gompers began to think that he, as head of the labor movement of what was then a neutral country, might play a leading role in the reestablishment of the IFTU after the war.[45] This desire grew as Gompers played an increasingly prominent role in the American war effort as a member of the Council of National Defense. His appointment as chairman of the Commission on International Labor Legislation (the group responsible for framing the labor conventions for the Versailles Treaty and creating the International Labor Organization) strengthened Gompers's perception of himself as an international labor leader. However, his potential role in a revived IFTU was weakened by the conflicts between Gompers and the European members of the Commission on International Labor Legislation. Although Gompers's views prevailed in the end, there was considerable disagreement within the commission on the question of the powers and functions of the International Labor Organization. The entire Labor Commission was disappointed by the Peace Commission's modifications in the labor provisions finally adopted, but Gompers took a more accepting stance than did most of the other labor leaders, declaring that although the labor provisions were not perfect, they were "far in advance of any other of similar character." He regarded them as an important progressive move, because "for the first time in history, the rights, interests, and welfare of workers received specific recognition in an international treaty."[46]

By the end of the war, tensions had developed within the international labor movement over the peace treaty's labor clauses and the question of when, where, and under whose sponsorship an attempt to reconstruct the international trade union movement would be made. By the July 1919 conference in Amsterdam, there was little international support for Gompers's desire to become the leader of the international labor movement or for his plan to use the structure and philosophy of the AFL as a model for a revived IFTU. The meeting further confirmed the political differences between Gompers and the Europeans, for Gompers found himself in a minority position on virtually every important issue. The other delegates strongly criticized the Versailles labor conventions, which Gompers defended as an important first step in the recognition of the rights of workers. Gompers also opposed two other important resolutions adopted by the congress; one criticized the League of Nations as it was constituted, and the other declared that capitalism was inherently incapable of reorganizing production to bring about the well-being of the masses and called for "complete trade union organization as the necessary basis for the realization of the socialization of the means of production."[47] Gompers also disagreed with the dues schedule and was particularly upset by the decision that IFTU policy passed by a simple majority vote (rather than unanimously, as was previously the case) would be binding on the affiliated members.

Although an official decision on affiliation had to be made by an AFL convention, Gompers and the two other American delegates had come to Amsterdam feeling that it was important that the AFL be part of a revived IFTU. However, they returned with serious questions, and after discussion of the issue at the next AFL convention and further communication with IFTU officials, the AFL leadership decided that although it was "most anxious" to be part of the international labor movement, its objections to IFTU policies on dues, decision making, and socialism prevented it from rejoining the IFTU.[48] Relations between the AFL and the IFTU were extremely strained in the early 1920s. However, due to changes in the American labor movement and within the IFTU, the Americans did ultimately reaffiliate in 1937.

* * *

The foregoing is important background for understanding developments within the International Federation of Working Women, for by the 1923 convention, its main issue was the question of affiliation with the IFTU. As was noted, some connection with the IFTU or acceptance of its principles was required for membership in the IFWW. Between the 1921 and 1923 IFWW conventions, there were various indications from the British, whose role in the IFWW was considerably strengthened by the election of Marion Phillips as secretary and the relocation of IFWW headquarters from Washington to London, that they saw the 1921 decision on membership criteria as merely a first step in the direction of closer ties to the IFTU, rather than as a settled issue.

Two examples of this attitude are the report on the 1921 congress in *The Labour Woman*, the publication of British Labour Party women, and an exchange between Marion Phillips and Margaret Dreier Robins. Discussing the objects of the IFWW, *The Labour Woman* article stated:

> We aim at establishing an international organisation . . . which will in its turn be linked up with the international movement of working men and women. At present that connection will be sought through the International Federation of Trade Unions. . . . The two secretaries, as well as several members of its management centre, have given the congress their friendliest cooperation and interest, and we look forward to coming . . . into closer cooperation in the future.[49]

A possibility for closer cooperation with the IFTU presented itself in the form of an invitation from the IFTU to the IFWW to attend an IFTU conference in December 1922. The invitation was received by Marion Phillips in November 1922, and she immediately telegraphed Margaret Dreier Robins, urging her as president of the IFWW to attend.

Robins was firmly opposed to strengthening the ties between the IFWW and the IFTU and did not think it advisable that she attend the conference.[50] Robins had met with various IFTU officials prior to the 1921 IFWW congress, and those encounters left her with strong reservations about the IFTU and its attitude toward women. In addition, Robins was concerned about the relationship between the American WTUL and the AFL. In view of the AFL's attitudes toward the IFTU, it was not in the best interests of the American WTUL for its leaders to become too involved in IFTU-sponsored activities.[51] Presumably for the sake of harmony within the IFWW, Robins did not mention these reasons in her reply to Phillips and simply indicated that it would be impossible for her to arrange a trip to Europe at that time.

Later that same month, the possibility of IFWW affiliation with the IFTU was explicitly raised by Marion Phillips in a long letter to Robins. Phillips proposed that the IFWW dissolve itself as an independent organization and become a Women's Auxiliary of the IFTU:

> The proposition here with regard to the Federation and Europe generally is not satisfactory and I fear very much that there will be no substantial growth under our present constitution.
>
> In the first place there is great opposition in the Continental countries to the duplication of international organisation and especially to the formation of an independent women's organisation. For this I think there is a great deal of justification because they already feel themselves very burdened by the number of international bodies and they have also that very strong conviction that the women ought not to be having anything separate from the men. At the same time the International Federation of Trade Unions . . . have shown the very greatest desire to do something more to develop the women's side of the Movement and have throughout treated us in the friendliest fashion and given

us great help. . . . They accept entirely our point of view that leadership of women needs development. By undertaking the publication of our Monthly News Sheet and by many other helpful things which they have done they have shown the readiness to spend money freely on our behalf. The national trade union centres have shown no readiness to give us anything at all as an independent organisation but they have made no complaint about the International Federation of Trade Unions doing it itself from the funds supplied by the national centres which constitute of course the whole of their income.

I think we might build a very strong women's movement if we built on a somewhat different basis. I need not repeat to you the constitution of the Standing Joint Committee of Industrial Women's Organisations in this country. . . . If we do agree on a plan of this kind I think the IFTU would pay the whole of the expenses and provide the necessary secretariat. It would be in the nature of an auxiliary movement to the general movement. Quite clearly it cannot be regarded as an independent body with executive power. I am not sure whether this is a disadvantage but if we hold it a disadvantage at least we must reflect on the fact that at the present time we have not got more than the name of an organisation and there seems to be no clear prospect of gaining more. . . . I think under my suggestion we might get a wider and more powerful movement of women than we can under our own scheme without losing any of the essentials.[52]

Phillips's views, which were shared by her British colleagues, indicate a consistent emphasis on class solidarity rather than feminist concerns. The British basic insistence on having the IFWW be a class-based organization initially led them to propose the inclusion of nonworking working-class women; it now led them to propose this closer affiliation with the IFTU. In both cases the British vision for the IFWW did not encompass the Americans' concern for female autonomy or general interest in feminist groups or causes.

Robins responded to Phillips's letter saying that she would defer a full reply to the proposal until she had had a chance to discuss it with the WTUL Executive Board. However, she did comment:

Personally I find it very difficult to see an organization of women of today becoming an auxiliary to a men's organization. I know that the first reaction of the Working Women of America will be in opposition of it, but it may be necessary and wise for us to accept such a plan because of the conditions in Europe and Great Britain.[53]

The series of meetings Robins had had with IFTU officials prior to the 1921 IFWW congress had left her suspicious and resentful of their attitude toward women in the labor movement. They insisted that European workers, in contrast to Americans, believed men and women should be organized into the same unions. They would not believe her claims that the American labor movement, including the WTUL, did think men and women workers should be organized together. Further, IFTU officers maintained that women were not interested in the labor movement and that "the International Federation of Trade Unions will of course wish to control the Congress."[54] During the 1921 IFWW congress Robins had written angrily to Elisabeth Christman, secretary of the American WTUL:

> The latest plan is, as worked out by the Amsterdam Federation, that we are to become a section of the International Federation of Trade Unions. Do you suppose that I have fought and bled and nearly died for the cause to give the Congress of Working Women into the keeping of Messrs. Oudegeest, Fimmen and Jouhaux?[55]

Such remarks about control had apparently not been made to Marion Phillips, and she did not share Robins's concern about organizational autonomy. However, Robins may have taken too seriously some passing remarks, for the IFTU's behavior toward the IFWW between 1921 and 1923 was cooperative and supportive, and there was no indication that it objected to the existence of the IFWW as a separate organization. Early in 1922 the IFTU Bureau told Phillips that it was going to propose that all women members of IFTU-affiliated organizations also be considered members of the IFWW and that the IFTU pay the appropriate affiliation fees to the IFWW out of its treasury (which consisted of dues paid by constituent members). The idea was rejected by the IFTU's member organizations, which were skeptical about the need for a separate women's organization, but the fact that it was proposed indicated support for the IFWW on the part of the IFTU's leadership. Despite the decision by its membership, the IFTU Bureau continued to support the IFWW in small but significant ways by publishing its newsletter and a major study done by IFWW members on the working conditions of women and children in the textile industry. In connection with the 1923 IFWW convention, IFTU officials planned to invite members of the IFWW and representatives of IFTU-affiliated trade union centers to a meeting to discuss the best ways of promoting the organization of women. Phillips mentioned this plan to Margaret Dreier Robins and Maud Swartz:

> They are very hopeful that this will be the means of clearing up all misunderstandings and getting the countries which have not yet adhered

definitely into the Federation [IFWW], and in sending out the invitations they will ask the centres which have not yet adhered to us to send their delegations in time to be present on the first day and to take part on the second. Anyhow, they will be able to mix with the other women there and talk things over in a friendly kind of way.[56]

A major reason for the refusal of organized women in some countries to affiliate with the IFWW, despite their membership in the IFTU, was their opposition to a separate organization for women and especially to one that was in various ways in touch with the middle-class women's movement. Dutch women perceived the IFWW as representing the suffrage movement, rather than as a serious labor organization.[57] German women, the most important of the IFWW's opponents, claimed there was no need for a separate women's labor organization, and they were extremely wary of what they perceived to be a strong feminist orientation within the IFWW. Speaking for German women workers at the 1922 IFTU convention, Gertrud Hanna explained that women workers did face special problems, but they firmly believed such problems were best solved by men and women together in class-based organizations. German women workers opposed the IFWW because:

> The first idea was to form an organisation solely to champion the rights of women. This is evident from the resolutions adopted at Washington. From the opening address of the President . . . and from numerous documents I have received since the Congress, it is obvious that the intention of the officers of the International Federation of Working Women was to induce women to organise as a separate movement, with the object of taking action solely from the women's standpoint. This view is extremely naive. . . . Our experience of the countries where women have the vote is that the women do not and cannot unite independently of existing parties for the furtherance of their own interests, but that their resolutions are influenced by their political outlook, and that men and women both vote for the party to which they belong, without regard to sex.[58]

Hanna's perceptions of the separatist tendencies of the IFWW were somewhat exaggerated, but by the 1923 convention, the British IFWW leaders had come to share her feeling that there was no reason for the federation to continue as a separate women's labor organization. The 1921 convention had made it clear to the British that there was little support among IFWW members for their idea of an organization that would represent working-class women as a whole. Once it was established that the IFWW would be composed primarily of women trade unionists, the British felt it was tactically and ideologically wiser for the IFWW to become part of the IFTU.

This issue was discussed at a meeting of British and American IFWW leaders in London just prior to the August 1923 convention. Speaking for the American WTUL, Margaret Dreier Robins announced that "the organized working women of America did not object to a women's department in the International Federation of Trade Unions . . . provided it were under wise and capable leadership," but they felt "the International Federation of Working Women could function better as a Federation of Working Women than as a Women's Department of the International Federation of Trade Unions."[59] In other words, as far as the Americans were concerned, if the IFTU wanted to establish a women's department, it should reinforce rather than replace the IFWW. Robins also told the British women that the consensus of the Executive Board of the American WTUL was that there was a definite need for an independent organization such as the IFWW and that the British were making a judgment on the IFWW's effectiveness before it had had a fair chance to prove itself.[60] Shortly after this meeting, Robins wrote to an American colleague that the British response had been that it was pointless, impossible, and inappropriate for the IFWW to continue as constituted, for "both British and European women, as well as men, do not see the value of such a federation, in view of the fact that there are in existence other international federations with men and women members." Robins went on to say:

> It was quite impossible for me to have our British fellow members understand the possibilities of work and responsibility and development we see in the IFWW. Of course it is quite self-evident that if neither the British nor the European working women want an International Federation of Working Women, we cannot establish one. As a substitute for the word "Federation" I suggested "Committee" or "Congress" so that there might be some chance of the trade union women coming together internationally to compare notes and exchange thought and opinion. These conferences however, our British colleagues thought, could be held very simply under the Women's Department of the IFTU.[61]

Although Robins spoke for the majority of the WTUL Executive Board, which considered itself the voice of organized American working women, the British proposal had in fact generated a considerable amount of controversy within the American league. Robins was warm and well meaning, but she was also a forceful and domineering woman accustomed to having things go her way, especially on matters related to American involvement in the IFWW, which she considered her special project. For both ideological and pragmatic reasons, she felt strongly that the IFWW should not become the women's division of the IFTU, and she expected that other American labor women would agree. However, Maud Swartz, a member of the Typographical Union, the current president of the American WTUL (Robins had retired after sixteen years in office in 1922), and the American vice president of the IFWW, was strongly in favor of the merger and conducted a vigorous campaign to gain support among members of the American WTUL.[62]

* * *

The 1923 congress of the IFWW was held in Vienna from August 14 to 18, and it was attended by official delegates from Belgium, France, Great Britain, Italy, Sweden, and the United States. Labor organizations in Argentina, Chile, China, Cuba, Hungary, Japan, and Romania sent fraternal delegates, and although the German and Austrian trade union centers had refused to send official representatives because of their opposition to an independent women's trade union organization, women from those two countries attended as visitors.

One of the first items on the agenda was the Report of the Secretariat, covering the work of the IFWW since the 1921 convention. It was presented by Marion Phillips, whose introductory remarks on the goals of the IFWW reflected the prevailing ideological consensus. The aims of the IFWW were to get women workers in all countries "to join the general Trade Union Movement of men and women," to have women "take their place beside the men in the fight against the evils of capitalism and bear their share in reconstructing society on an economic basis of justice and right," and to develop a sense of responsibility in women "not only in obtaining better hours and wages, but in the work of the wider Trade Union Movement." Phillips went on to say:

> The greatest need was for an intellectual and moral solidarity between the workers—men and women. They [the IFWW] wanted them [women workers] not only to take part in the war against war which the Trade Union Movement was waging, but to take part in the war against civil war—the war of poverty—that went on in every country and which was waged between people who pursued industry for their private profit and those they employed to make

and to increase those profits. They wanted the women in the different countries to realize that in the war to be carried on for better social and economic conditions, there would never be success until men and women, boys and girls stood together the whole time. It should also be realized that until the mothers of the boys and girls also understood the problem of industrial and national life, the boys and girls would not enter the Trade Union Movement as they grew up.[63]

Phillips also mentioned that the resolutions of the 1921 IFWW convention had been sent to the International Labor Office and they had been read to the International Labor Conference and included in its report. Throughout the past two years the International Labor Office had been helpful to the IFWW in various ways, especially its cooperation in the preparation of a pamphlet on "International Labor Legislation and the Woman Worker." In addition, Signora Cabrini Casartelli, an Italian IFWW member, had represented the federation at the 1923 International Women's Suffrage Alliance Congress, where she expressed the IFWW point of view on equal pay for equal work and protective legislation for women. Cabrini Casartelli had taken part in a "very active struggle" at the convention, and she "succeeded in getting resolutions adopted which were not opposed to our aims in regard to these subjects."[64]

Phillips had begun her report with a description of the extensive interaction and cooperation of the IFWW and the IFTU between 1921 and 1923; she concluded it by noting that there was much work to be done "stimulating and increasing Trade Union activity amongst women and bringing into the unions an ever greater proportion of women workers to act in cooperation with their men comrades." Her final sentences stressed the value of the IFWW becoming an official part of the IFTU:

> Our two years work has shown how greatly our activity must depend upon cooperation with the IFTU. This body forms the international centre for the larger part of the Trade Unions throughout the world and must necessarily bear a great part in shaping the progress of industrial organisation. We look forward to a continually increasing cooperation by means of which the International Federation of Working Women shall carry on its special work within a great International organisation of the workers of the world.[65]

The question of the IFWW's relationship with the IFTU was the most serious issue dealt with at the 1923 convention, but it was not the only topic on the agenda. The delegates also discussed methods for organizing working women, the regulation of wages of home workers, and the payment of family allowances in addition to wages. Many of the delegates had prepared written reports on these practices in their countries, and information of considerable interest and value was exchanged. One of the most potentially useful results of the congress was the set of guidelines established for the organization of women workers. The recommendations finally agreed upon reflect the views of IFWW members based on their experiences as workers and labor activists.

1. That where men and women are employed in the same industry, they should be organized into the same union.

2. That each country shall through its national body, endeavor to secure an intensive campaign amongst women and girl workers, giving particular attention to the lowest paid workers. The campaign should be carried on with the assistance of women speakers and organisers having a practical knowledge of conditions in the trade or industry.

3. The issue of special leaflets setting out the aims and objects of the unions, concentrating upon improvements achieved by organized labour in the respective trades.

4. That attention be directed towards the need for encouraging the development of the recreation of the workers through their respective organisations. Trade unions can best develop this side of the Union's activity by appointing recreation or social committees which shall be responsible for arranging social entertainments and sports.

5. The encouragement of the educational side under the following headings:
   A. General education
   B. Craft or specialized education
   C. Trade union organisation

6. That particular attention should be given to the fact that a large number of women workers are in industry for a comparatively short period and therefore no opportunity should be lost to awaken the social consciousness or these young workers, so that when they leave industry for marriage, their moral support of the labour movement may be retained.[66]

The basis for considering the IFWW's relationship to the IFTU was the concluding statement of Marion Phillips's report, which was supplemented by a specific proposal from the British members of the IFWW Secretariat. They urged that the IFWW "endeavor to secure within the IFTU the development of a Women's Section and that if we succeed in getting the IFTU to adopt a satisfactory scheme that the IFWW should carry on its work through that

Section instead of in its present form."[67] As reasons for proposing this change, the British cited the financial problems of the IFWW, the lack of support of Central European trade union women for a separate women's labor organization, and the increased interest on the part of the international labor movement in organizing women workers.

Financially the IFWW had been almost totally supported by the Americans and the British, with the Americans contributing by far the larger share. The British claimed that in view of the reluctance of the British Trades Union Congress and other European trade union centers to pay affiliation fees for their women members to both the IFTU and the IFWW, it did not appear that the IFWW could "develop successfully as an organization which is independent in form and must raise separate funds." Although British women had originally hoped the IFWW would include women in the political and cooperative movements, given the situation in other countries, such an organization was not a realistic possibility, and "we therefore think that the line of development must be on a Trade Union basis." However, they considered the effectiveness of the IFWW as a trade union organization severely compromised by the failure of Germany and Austria to join, and it seemed unlikely that German and Austrian opposition to the IFWW existing as an independent organization would change. In addition to these negative factors, the British cited as a positive reason, "the great change" that had taken place in the European trade union movement as a result of the creation of the IFWW:

> The question of the organisation of working women is becoming an infinitely more important question receiving a great deal more public attention from the International Movement than it was before and that encourages us in the belief that the time is now ripe for a greater development which would relieve us from financial difficulties and from the difficulties arising from the non-adhesion of the Central European countries.[68]

The proposal concluded with an assessment of what might be gained and lost by turning the IFWW into the Women's Department of the IFTU. American IFWW members felt the British were proposing the replacement of an independent body by a dependent one. The British did not see it this way; "at the present time we are bound to accept only those who agree with the principles and spirit of the IFTU and we would seek our representative through the very same bodies from whom we are now seeking them." Since these representatives were also bound by the decisions of their national trade union centers, the British felt that it was illusory to regard the IFWW as a genuinely independent organization. Thus, they did not see significant losses coming from the change they proposed, and they did feel there was much to be gained from it.

> In our opinion the gain would be very great because we would have behind us . . . the support of the whole Trade Union Movement. . . . Moreover, it appears to us the natural line of development probably because it is the line of development which we have pursued in our own country where in both the Trade Union and the Political Movements we have men and women working side by side but in both we have groups or committees specially devoted to women's concerns. . . . We think that internationally as well as nationally this line of development is one which meets the needs of the times and would be far more satisfactory than the present constitution where we lack the whole-hearted support of the international movement.[69]

This proposal, along with the concluding sentences of the Report of the Secretariat, was referred to the constitution commission. After due consideration, the commission recommended to the congress that negotiations be opened with the IFTU leading to the development of a Women's Department with a woman head secretary; the creation of an internationally representative Women's Committee, which would meet at least once a year, to work with the Women's Department and the IFTU executive in furthering trade unionism among women workers; and the holding of a Congress of Working Women prior to the Biennial Congress of the IFTU. The committee also recommended that the result of these negotiations with the IFTU be communicated to all IFWW members. After receiving their responses, the IFWW Executive Board would decide the future of the organization.[70]

These recommendations were accepted by all the delegations except the American one, which abstained from voting and issued the following statement to explain its position:

> The American Delegation represented in this Congress is not authorized to vote for a change in the form of the International Federation of Working Women as proposed and recommended in the report of the Commission on the Constitution.
>
> The American Delegation wishes to point out further to this Congress that America is in a different position from other countries in regard to the International Federation of Trade Unions at Amsterdam. Your national trade unions are already a part of the International Federation of Trade Unions, while

our American Federation of Labor is not affiliated with it. We therefore do not record our vote on this report.[71]

Final action on this matter would be taken by the June 1924 WTUL convention, which would consider the decisions of the 1924 IFTU congress regarding the IFWW proposal.

This response was generally interpreted (and intended) as negative rather than neutral, and it came as a surprise and disappointment to many IFWW members. It had been clear in the discussions of this issue that the IFWW delegates felt the American WTUL could, and hoped that it would, continue its involvement in the international women's labor movement, despite the American Federation of Labor's lack of affiliation to the IFTU. Taken at face value, the statement raises valid points and seems to be an appropriate reflection of the American situation. However, viewed critically, it becomes more interesting for what it does not say than for what it does. Two serious questions are why the American delegation, unlike every other delegation, came to the congress unauthorized to vote on the proposal, and why the Americans' only reservation about the plan was the problem with the AFL.

It was true that the possibility of the IFWW becoming part of the IFTU had not been considered by an American WTUL convention (the WTUL met biennially—the last convention had been in June 1922, and the next one would be in June 1924), but that still does not fully explain why the WTUL Executive Board, which was aware of British interest in changing the structure of the IFWW, did not raise the issue with its membership in its communications to local leagues. One possibility is that the WTUL leaders simply assumed that league members would share their opposition to the British plan, but it is also possible that the lack of discussion reflected a certain reluctance on the part of WTUL leaders to consult others—a feeling that they were the ones who were most involved in the IFWW and best understood the dimensions of this problem. However, it seems most probable that the Americans underestimated the importance of the British proposal. It is likely that, based on negative reports of Phillips's behavior in the British labor movement and as IFWW secretary, the American WTUL leaders erroneously assumed that Phillips's ideas about the future of the IFWW were more the product of her own thinking than a reflection of the views held by the majority of European members. It is also probable that the Americans were assuming that because of their key role in the IFWW, their opposition to the proposal would keep it from being presented to the IFWW congress.[72] Thus, the American delegation went off to the 1923 IFWW congress without an explicit mandate on the affiliation issue, but with the knowledge that the Executive Board was opposed to the British proposal. Apparently the Americans hoped or assumed that somehow a compromise could be reached that would keep a formal decision on affiliation with the IFTU from having to be made at this convention.

The other question raised by the statement is why the burden of American uneasiness with the affiliation decision was placed on the relations between the AFL and IFTU and nothing was said about the feminist reservations of the Americans. The AFL's hostility toward the IFTU, more than the simple fact of its nonaffiliation, did put the WTUL in a considerably different position from other IFWW members; for them the proposed change would presumably improve their relationship with their national trade union center, whereas for the Americans it would only complicate the relationship between the AFL and the WTUL.

However, self-interest aside, the Americans genuinely felt it was in the best interest of the IFWW to maintain itself as an autonomous women's labor organization. They argued with other IFWW members that belonging to the IFTU would mean that women could not take independent stands on various issues; that the proposed structural relationship, which did not provide for a representative of the Women's Department on the IFTU Executive Board, would mean that women's issues would be put in a subordinate position; that women's labor groups would get involved in general IFTU activities and would have less time to focus on specifically women's issues; and that the proposed plan would provide fewer opportunities for the development of women labor leaders.[73] In effect, the Americans were arguing that primacy be given to issues relevant to women workers as women, whereas the Europeans wanted to emphasize women workers' identity as workers.

It is curious that none of these more feminist points was even alluded to in the public statement. Since there are no records of the discussion that took place during the drafting of the American statement, the reason(s) they were omitted can only be speculative. The statement was drafted to explain the American position, but it might also have been presented in the hope that it would influence the IFWW delegates to reconsider their decision. If that were the case, then the statement might be seen to reflect the Americans' awareness that there was little support for their feminist arguments but that the AFL issue was a problem to which IFWW members would be sympathetic. The Americans may also have felt that if women in the IFWW were having difficulties justifying the need for a separate organization of women workers to their own labor movements, it might be easier for them to use the AFL issue as a public justification, keeping feminist reasons as a private understanding. A third and very real possibility is that the Americans intended the statement to mean no more and no less than it said—that ideologically and tactically they gave primacy to their relationship with the American Federation of Labor.

This last possibility raises the final question related to the statement, and that is how the Americans would have responded to the idea of the IFWW becoming the Women's Department of the IFTU if the AFL *had* been a member of the IFTU. It seems reasonable to assume they still would initially have opposed the idea. They then would have tried to convince IFWW members to ask for more than an advisory role. But, in the end, they would have given priority to their commitment to an international approach to the problem of women workers and would have gone along with the majority decision. They would have had serious reservations about the direction the IFWW was taking, but probably they would not have withdrawn from the organization, as they officially did in 1924.

The Americans had assumed the IFWW would be an international version of the American WTUL—it would exist to educate the international labor and feminist movements regarding the problems and needs of women workers and it would work *with* but not *under* the leadership of both those movements.[74] The Europeans, on the other hand, assumed the IFWW would be much more oriented to the international labor movement, and they did not share the Americans' tactical and ideological concerns with the issue of female autonomy. There is evidence that by the 1921 convention, the Americans were aware that the relationship of the IFWW to other international women's organizations was a sensitive issue within the IFWW and that they held back from injecting as much mention of suffrage and related issues into IFWW correspondence and meetings as they would have liked.[75] In other words, the Americans, recognizing the Europeans' reluctance to identify more closely with purely feminist issues, were tactically reduced to stressing the AFL problem, rather than being able to present forcefully the more profound issue of feminist principles. Thus, in answer to the hypothetical question posed above, it seems quite probable that the Americans would have been reasonably content to have the IFWW function as a women's labor organization relating primarily to other labor organizations, but AFL membership in the IFTU notwithstanding, they would have been most uncomfortable with the decision that the IFWW become the Women's Department of the IFTU.[76]

While all the American delegates at the 1923 convention opposed the proposed change in the IFWW, it seems likely that their opposition reflected in part their loyalty to Margaret Dreier Robins and her influence over them. She was strongly opposed to the British plan and was extremely upset by the decision of the convention. Robins had given time and money to help create and sustain the IFWW, and she regarded the 1923 decision a violation of the integrity of the IFWW, a rejection of her leadership (which to some extent it was), and a crushing blow to her hopes that women could achieve sisterly solidarity despite class differences. She recognized that "European delegates could not quite understand the American point of view. They were unaccustomed to women who were not industrial workers being interested in them and trying to help them better their industrial conditions and establish fellowship among women generally." However, she could not understand why, "When there were differences of opinion as there inevitably were, they wrote it down to the 'middle class' point of view and to the women who simply could not comprehend the workers' viewpoint."[77]

The 1923 IFWW convention decision was discussed extensively at the fall meeting of the WTUL Executive Board. It was assumed that the IFTU would accept the IFWW proposal that it become part of that organization; the Executive Board also assumed that the 1924 WTUL convention would vote to withdraw from further participation in the IFWW when it became the IFTU Women's Department. Reflecting this reasoning, the Executive Board drafted a statement for *Life and Labor* explaining the actions of the 1923 convention.

> Underlying the different points of view of the American and the European working women on this proposal, are their different conceptions of economics and social structure. American women have recognized the necessity for a woman movement within the labor movement; hence, the existence of the National Women's Trade Union League of America, an autonomous body working in co-operation with the American Federation of Labor, but specializing upon the problems of working women, which are admittedly different in many vital aspects from the problems of working men, and need to be emphasized by women in women's own way. The European labor movements, on the other hand, emphasize class-consciousness and deprecate a woman movement within their class. European working women agree with European working men in this.[78]

It is of course impossible to know what the IFWW would have accomplished had it remained autonomous. British women were aware that women "must fight all the time to get attention focused on women's affairs within a general organization of workers," but for just that reason, they felt it was important to concentrate women's energies on such organizations, rather than dividing them between separate women's organizations, such as the IFWW, and more established labor organizations, such as the IFTU.[79] British IFWW members realized that, if the IFWW joined the IFTU, getting the IFTU to deal seriously with the problems of women workers would involve a certain amount of struggle, but they were prepared to wage that struggle and were hopeful of success. However, it is clear in retrospect that the American women were in fact correct in their perceptions of what would happen to women within the IFTU. The relationship between women and the IFTU from 1923 to the beginning of World War II does not suggest that dissolving the IFWW and working within the IFTU significantly advanced the cause of women workers.

* * *

Shortly after the 1923 IFWW convention, the Executive Board sent a memo to the IFTU, proposing the incorporation of the IFWW into the IFTU. Consistent with the decision of the convention, the memo proposed the development of a Women's Department with a woman secretary, the establishment of a Women's Committee to work with the Women's Department and the IFTU Bureau in developing a trade union movement among women, and the holding of a Congress of Working Women at least every two years, preferably prior to the IFTU Biennial Congress. The memo cited the urgent need for trade union organization among women, pointing out that union membership among European women was declining. The memo went on to say:

> As it is always the women who form the greater part of the cheapest labor in the industrial work, it is from them that the greatest danger comes, and we are convinced that the Trade Union Movement must give more attention to these lower ranks and build from the bottom rather than from the top. Moreover, our special study of women's problems in the industrial world has we believe been of real value in spreading knowledge and preparing the way for better international labour legislation and has shown us that an educational movement

among women workers is necessary before their problems can be given adequate attention.

The Trade Union Movement developed out of the need felt by the workers to regulate their own lives. Up to the present the women workers have not taken their full share in this task and we are convinced that they never will do so until their problems are given special place in the workers' organisation and until attention is concentrated upon propaganda amongst them.[80]

The IFTU responded by setting aside a day just prior to its 1924 convention for a conference of women trade unionists, IFTU officials, and representatives of national trade union centers to discuss problems and methods of organizing women workers, the attitudes of national trade union centers to the IFWW, and the IFTU Bureau's response to the IFWW memo. Johann Sassenbach, IFTU secretary, presided over the meeting, and he announced at the beginning of the conference that the IFTU Secretariat was prepared to urge the IFTU Congress to support the proposals that separate women's conferences be held periodically and that an International Women's Committee be appointed. He added that "in view of the general financial position, it would not be possible at the moment to appoint a woman secretary for a separate women's department of the IFTU." Sassenbach assured the assembled women that the IFTU would nonetheless "do its best to take into account the wishes of the Conference for the strengthening of the working women's organization."[81]

The participants were united in the view (which had been a basic tenet of the IFWW) that women should not be organized into separate unions. They agreed that working-class solidarity and strength were ultimately dependent on having women and men operate out of the same structural base, but they contended that "at the present time special propaganda was still necessary among women" and that "new and different means must be developed to reach women than those which were effective with men workers." The women considered it extremely important that special conferences be held to discuss these problems in order to share information about methods being tried in various countries to bring women into the trade union movement. Therefore, they were pleased that the IFWW was prepared to call such conferences and create an International Women's Committee. It is interesting to note that they accepted without question Sassenbach's explanation that the IFTU was not in a position to create a Women's Department with a paid secretary. At the last session of the conference, a statement was adopted endorsing the IFTU Bureau's willingness to convene women's conferences, create an International

Women's Committee, and consider "the subsequent appointment of a special woman secretary for propaganda among women." The statement also declared that it was the duty of the women at the conference "to give the most energetic support to propaganda among the working women in their respective countries."[82]

As expected, the IFTU Congress accepted the recommendation of the IFTU Bureau, and this action was immediately communicated to the American WTUL, which was meeting in New York for its 1924 convention. After a full report by Margaret Dreier Robins on the five-year history of the IFWW, and with virtually no discussion of the issue, the WTUL delegates voted to withdraw from the IFWW and not participte in women's activities of the IFTU.[83] Like the American statement to the 1923 IFWW convention, the letter communicating this decision to the IFWW Executive Board cited the AFL's lack of membership in the IFTU as the primary reason for the decision. However, this time the Americans insisted the major problem was that because the AFL did not belong to the IFTU, American women would be without voting representatives in the IFTU; in other words, they were opposed to participating in an advisory group to an organization in which neither they nor their national trade union center were voting members.[84]

By early 1925 the IFTU had appointed the International Women's Committee, and once that was done, the IFWW Executive Board, which had not wanted to disband the IFWW until "the right kind of machinery was established in the IFTU," dissolved itself and the IFWW.[85] The IFTU fulfilled its promise to sponsor conferences on women workers and create an International Women's Committee, but it never created a Women's Department, and it does not appear that the committee or conferences had much impact on the organization as a whole. The committee rarely met with the IFTU leadership, although its advice was "always available to the IFTU by correspondence."[86] Women's conferences were held in conjunction with three of the five IFTU congresses between 1925 and 1939; at these conferences, which were presided over by a male officer, valuable discussions took place and resolutions were passed on problems such as home work, protective legislation, and women's right to work, but nothing more than verbal support was ever forthcoming from the IFTU Bureau or general membership. Virtually no funds were allocated to support work leading toward the implementation of any of the women's resolutions, and the IFTU never made the problems of women workers a significant part of its programs. The history of the Women's Committee thus reveals a familiar pattern in the treatment of women: the

IFTU acknowledged the existence of women workers and their problems through the creation of the Women's Committee and the sponsorship of periodic conferences, but ultimately it refused to pay serious attention to the needs of its female members.

The most interesting aspect of all this is the apparent lack of struggle waged by women in the IFTU to change the situation. The only evidence of discontent comes from a comment by Mary Anderson. As head of the Women's Bureau in the United States Department of Labor, she had gone to Geneva for the 1931 meeting of the International Labor Organization. While she was there she attended an IFTU women's conference.

> It was pathetic. . . . Some of the younger women . . . told the presiding officer what they thought of the situation. They protested that the committee was useless and they suspected that they had been appointed just as figureheads. They said that the problem was to organize women, but that this committee had no way of doing the work, that all they did was make recommendations and have discussions but there was no action and no funds to enable them to take action. The man who was presiding acted as if what they were talking about did not mean a thing. The meeting was really only a gesture. It was the same old idea of putting women on the side, forming a committee at which they could talk and then not paying more attention to them.[87]

It is easy to be critical of the men in the IFTU for such attitudes and behavior. But explanations for the women's relative acceptance of this situation must also be sought. Perhaps the women did not consider feminine influence in the IFTU important; perhaps they in effect abandoned the effort on discovering that it required a longer and harder struggle than they had anticipated. Although the women were committed in principle to developing a strong women's department, in practice they were so involved in their national labor movements that they simply did not have the time or energy necessary for increasing the role of women in the IFTU. After all, there were very few working-class women in any country with the skills, sophistication, and motivation to put them in positions of leadership at the national or international level.

* * *

Concerned feminists are constantly faced with having to decide whether their cause's best chance lies in autonomous structures of their creation or through cooperation with male-dominated institutions. The history of the IFWW reveals that European and American women took their different positions for both ideological and pragmatic reasons. The Europeans were ideologically committed to class struggle, whereas the Americans were inclined to give precedence to the special problems of women. Each group's views were reinforced by tactical considerations based on its experience with its national labor movement. European labor organizations had been much more receptive than the American Federation of Labor to dealing with the problems of women workers; in addition, the European national trade union centers were committed members of the IFTU, while the American women feared that becoming part of the IFTU would antagonize the AFL and cause further strain on the already tenuous relationship between the WTUL and the AFL.

Thus, the positions taken by both groups of women can be understood as logical responses, given their ideological views and their own societies. There is certainly no basis for predicting that the IFWW would have become an effective vehicle for improving the conditions of women workers had it maintained itself as an autonomous women's labor organization. What can be stated with certainty is that, although the decision to affiliate with the IFTU was in many respects logical, becoming part of the IFTU did not significantly advance the cause of women workers. The problems of women and this concomitant structural dilemma of affiliation or autonomy are so deep that either approach leads only to limited gains. A study of the International Federation of Working Women illustrates in general terms the complexity of this structural problem and suggests that, between the wars at least, it had no solution.

Notes

EDITOR'S INTRODUCTION

1. Edward T. James, Janet Wilson James, and Paul S. Boyer. eds. *Notable American Women, 1607-1950: A Biographical Dictionary*, 3 vols. (Cambridge: Harvard University Press, 1971); Barbara Sicherman and Carol Hurd Green, eds., *Notable American Women, the Modern Period: A Biographical Dictionary* (Cambridge: Harvard University Press, 1980).
2. New York: R.R. Bowker, 1979.

INTRODUCTION

1. Although these dates do not encompass the total history of both leagues, this time span covers the years when the leagues were most active and had the greatest impact.

   The British league was actually established in 1874 as the Women's Protective and Provident League. The name was changed to the Women's Trade Union League in 1890, and the change reflected a shift in the leadership and in the orientation of the league. As the original name indicates, the league was initially more concerned with the establishment of organizations among women workers that were closer to the model of a friendly society than a trade union. After 1890 the WTUL placed greater emphasis on the trade union model, urging women to unionize so they could use their collective strength to gain improvements in their working conditions and wages. The WTUL remained in existence until 1921, when it was absorbed into the newly created Women's Department of the Trades Union Congress.

   Modeled on the British league, the American WTUL was formed in 1903. Although its membership base and financial resources were declining by the mid-1920s, the WTUL limped along through the 1930s and 1940s, finally dissolving itself in 1950.
2. Between 1940 and 1970 there were no scholarly secondary accounts written about the British WTUL, and the American league was discussed in only three publications: Gladys Boone, *The Women's Trade Union Leagues of Great Britain and the United States of America* (New York, 1942); Allen Davis, "The Women's Trade Union League: Origins and Organization," *Labor History* 5

(Winter 1964), 3-17; and William O'Neill, *Everyone Was Brave: The Rise and Fall of Feminism in America* (Chicago, 1969), 98-102.

3. See Nancy Schrom Dye, "The Women's Trade Union League of New York, 1903-1920," Ph.D. dissertation, University of Wisconsin, 1974. Dye has published portions of her dissertation in "Sisterhood and Class Conflict in the New York Women's Trade Union League," *Feminist Studies* 2, no. 2/3 (1975), 24-38 and "Feminism or Unionism: The New York Women's Trade Union League and the Labor Movement," *Feminist Studies* 3 (Fall 1975), 111-25. See also William Chafe, *The American Woman: Her Changing Social, Economic, and Political Roles, 1920-1970* (New York, 1972); Alice Kessler-Harris, " 'Where Are the Unorganized Women Workers?'," *Feminist Studies* 3 (Fall 1975), 92-110 and "Organizing the Unorganizable: Three Jewish Women and Their Union," *Labor History* 17 (Winter 1976), 5-23; J. Stanley Lemons, *The Woman Citizen: Social Feminism in the 1920s* (Urbana, 1973); and William O'Neill, *The Woman Movement: Feminism in the United States and England* (Chicago, 1971).

4. The works by Dye and Kessler-Harris address this problem more extensively than the others, but Dye's discussion is limited to the New York league and Kessler-Harris's work is not focused on the WTUL. Nonetheless, both authors make important contributions to the field of women's history.

CHAPTER ONE

1. They were primarily in agricultural, clerical, manufacturing, and service jobs. See P. Bairoch, *The Working Population and Its Structure* (Brussels, 1968), 189, 158-59 for a more detailed statistical breakdown of female employment patterns in Britain and the United States.

2. Although the number of local leagues fluctuated over the years, they were consistently concentrated in the East and Midwest. For example, in 1916 local branches of the WTUL existed in Chicago, New York, Boston, St. Louis, Kansas City, Baltimore, Denver, Philadelphia, Worcester, and Springfield, Illinois.

3. See the review essay by Elizabeth Pleck, "Two Worlds in One: Work and Family," *Journal of Social History* 10 (Winter 1976), 178-95 for a stimulating discussion of the relationship between industrialization, work roles, and family patterns.

4. The percentage of females in the British labor force actually declined slightly between 1891 and 1921. In 1891 females constituted 31 percent of the total labor force and in 1921 29 percent. The percentage increased in the United States from 17 percent in 1890 to 20 percent in 1920. These percentages were calculated on the basis of statistics in Bairoch, *Working Population*, 183, 153.

5. See Mabel H. Willet, *The Employment of Women in the Clothing Trade*, Columbia University Studies in History, Economics, and Public Law, vol. 16, no. 2 (New York, 1902), chap. 3.
6. "The Girls' Own Stories," *Life and Labor*, 1 February 1911, 51, 52.
7. National Women's Trade Union League, *Some Facts Regarding Unorganized Working Women in the Sweated Industries* (Chicago, 1914), 4-6. A typical weekly budget of a single woman living away from her family was:

    one half of furnished room = $1.50
    7 breakfasts, rolls and coffee, at 10¢ = 70¢
    7 luncheons, coffee and sandwich, at 10¢ = 70¢
    7 dinners, at 20¢ = $1.40
    carfare = 60¢
    clothes at $52 a year, weekly = $1.00
        Total = $5.90

    The remaining 10¢ had to cover laundry, doctor bills, newspapers, recreation, savings.
8. Mary R. Macarthur, "Trade Unions," in *Women in Industry*, ed. Gertrude Tuckwell (London, 1908), 66.
9. Ibid., 67.
10. Rose Schneiderman with Lucy Goldthwaite, *All for One* (New York, 1967), 50.
11. Theresa Malkiel, *The Diary of a Shirtwaist Striker* (New York, 1910), 12.
12. See, for example, Dorothy Richardson's account of her work experiences in New York around the turn of the century, in *The Long Day: The Story of a New York Working Girl* (New York, 1905).
13. For further discussion on the impact of industrialization on women, see Edith Abbott, *Women in Industry: A Study in American Economic History* (New York, 1910); Alice Henry, *Women and the Labor Movement* (New York, 1923); B. L. Hutchins, *Women in Modern Industry* (London, 1915); Ivy Pinchbeck, *Women Workers and the Industrial Revolution, 1750-1850* (London, 1930); U.S. Congress, Senate, *Report on Condition of Women and Child Wage-Earners*, "History of Women in Industry," by Helen L. Sumner, v. 9, S. Doc. 645, 61st Cong., 2nd sess., 1910; and Tuckwell, *Women in Industry*.

    See Barbara Welter, "The Cult of True Womanhood: 1820-1860," *American Quarterly* 18 (Summer 1966), 151-74 for a fuller discussion of this ideology.
14. See O'Neill, *Everyone Was Brave* and *The Woman Movement*.
15. For further discussion on this point, see Gerda Lerner, "The Lady and the Mill Girl: Changes in the Status of Women in the Age of Jackson," *Mid-Continent American Studies Journal* 10 (Spring 1969), 15.
16. The classic nineteenth-century works on this subject are August Bebel, *Woman under Socialism*, Daniel De Leon, trans. (New York, 1904) and Frederick Engels, *The Origin of the Family, Private Property, and the State* (London, 1940). The most important contemporary discussions are Juliet Mitchell, *Woman's Estate* (New York, 1973) and Sheila Rowbotham, *Women,*

Resistance, and Revolution: A History of Women and Revolution in the Modern World (New York, 1972).

17.   Engels, *The Origin of the Family*, 184; quoted in Mitchell, *Woman's Estate*, 104-5.

18.   Ibid., 81.

19.   Ibid., 100-101.

20.   Harold Goldman, *Emma Paterson* (London, 1974), 23.

21.   Ibid., 121.

22.   Ibid., 29.

23.   This article, which was originally published in *The Labour News*, April 1874, is reprinted in ibid., 117-24.

24.   Ibid., 119.

25.   Ibid.

26.   Ibid., 119, 124.

27.   Legislation in 1871 legally recognized trade unions and protected their funds, but it left trade unionists open to criminal prosecution for all forms of picketing, and laws against conspiracy could still be applied to strikers. The legal situation was improved by new legislation in 1875, but British trade unionists were concerned about the security of their legal rights through the end of the nineteenth century and into the early years of the twentieth. The position of trade unions was not legally secure until 1906, when a Liberal government with a large number of Labour M.P.'s came to power. See Henry Pelling, *A History of British Trade Unionism* (London, 1963), chapters 5-7.

28.   Women's Protective and Provident League, *First Annual Report* (London, 1875), 15, 8.

29.   Goldman, *Emma Paterson*, 121.

30.   Women's Protective and Provident League, *Report*, 4.

31.   Ibid., 7.

32.   Barbara Drake, *Women in Trade Unions* (London, 1920), 22.

33.   "The League Conference," *Women's Union Journal*, October 1886, 97.

34.   See William English Walling to Margaret Dreier Robins, November 1, 1904, National Women's Trade Union League (NWTUL) papers, Box 25, Library of Congress (LC).

35.   For a complete profile of O'Sullivan, see *Notable American Women*, s.v. "O'Sullivan, Mary Kenney," by Eleanor Flexner and Janet Wilson James.

36.   Mary Kenney O'Sullivan to Alice Henry, n.d. [c. 1914], NWTUL papers, Box 28, LC.

37.   William English Walling to Mary McDowell, November 25, 1903, NWTUL papers, Box 25, LC. For further information on Kehew, see *Notable American Women*, s.v. "Kehew, Mary Morton," by Robert Sklar.

38.   Walling to McDowell, November 25, 1903, NWTUL papers, Box 25, LC.

39.   See "Reports of meetings held for the purpose of organizing the WTUL," November 14, 17, and 19, 1903, NWTUL papers, Box 1, v. 1, LC. For further information on McDowell, Wald, and O'Reilly, See *Notable American*

Women, s.v. "McDowell, Mary," by Louise C. Wade; "Wald, Lillian," by Robert Bremner; and "O'Reilly, Leonora," by Charles Shivley.

40. "Constitution of the WTUL, adopted in Faneuil Hall, Boston, November 17-19, 1903," NWTUL papers, Box 1, v. 1, LC.

41. The work of Mary McDowell and Lillian Wald mentioned above and the activities of the working girls' club movement, the National Consumers' League, and the Working Women's Society were all concerned with the problems of women workers. See Dye, "The Women's Trade Union League of New York," 39-43 for a discussion of these efforts.

42. "Constitution," NWTUL papers, Box 1, v. 1, LC.

43. Mary E. Dreier, *Margaret Dreier Robins: Her Life, Letters, and Work* (New York, 1950), 9-10, 12, 18-20.

44. See "Minutes of the Second Meeting of the National Board," October 7, 1904, NWTUL papers, Box 1, f. 2, Schlesinger Library (SL).

CHAPTER TWO

1. Macarthur, "Trade Unions," 65.

2. See for example, "Women's Trade Union Provident League," *Fifteenth Annual Report* (London, 1889), 4; "New Year's Prospects," *Women's Union Journal*, January 15, 1890, 1; and Mary E. Dreier, "Expansion Through Agitation and Education," *Life and Labor* 11 (June 1921), 163.

3. For Britain, see B. R. Mitchell and Phyllis Deane, *Abstract of British Historical Statistics*, University of Cambridge, Department of Applied Economics, Monographs, no. 17 (Cambridge, 1971), 68, and Bairoch, *Working Population*, 183. For the United States, see Leo Wolman, *The Growth of American Trade Unions 1880-1923* (New York, 1924), 99, and Bairoch, *Working Population*, 153.

4. See Wolman, *American Trade Unions*, 97-108.

5. For the distribution patterns, see Bairoch, *Working Population*, 189 for British data and 158-59 for the American figures.

6. The 4,751,000 women in the British labor force in 1901 represented 24.9 percent of the total female population over the age of ten; in 1911 there were 5,413,000 gainfully employed women, accounting for 25.7 percent of the female population; and in 1921 the number was 5,699,000, which was 25.5 percent of the female population over the age of twelve. (The age base was raised in the 1921 census.) Ibid., 183.

7. There were 5,319,400 women in the U.S. labor force in 1900, representing 14.3 percent of the total female population over the age of ten. In 1910 the number was 7,444,800 (16.7 percent) and in 1920, 8,636,500 (16.7 percent). Ibid., 153.

8. See Mitchell and Deane, *British Historical Statistics*, 68, for a breakdown of trade union membership by sex.

Female trade union membership from 1889 to 1921 was greatest in the textile trades. For details on membership by trade union, see Great Britain, Parliament, *Parliamentary Papers* (Commons), *1914-1916*, v. 61 (Accounts and Papers), Cmnd. 7733, "Seventeenth Abstract of Labour Statistics of the United Kingdom," 202-3; *Parliamentary Papers* (Commons), *1926*, v. 29 (Accounts and Papers), Cmnd. 2740, "Eighteenth Abstract of Labour Statistics of the United Kingdom," 178-79; and Drake, *Women in Trade Unions*, table 1.

9. In the United States female trade union membership was concentrated in the garment industry, with textiles a distant second. For details on the female membership of individual unions, see Wolman, *American Trade Unions*, 98-99.

10. Comparing the extent of organization among women to men, rough calculations (again excluding workers in agriculture and domestic service) indicate that in Britain 19.1 percent of the male labor force was organized in 1901, compared to 5.7 percent of the female. In 1911 the percentage of organized workers was 25.5 percent for men and 10.6 percent for women, and in 1921, 47.3 percent for men and 26.8 percent for women. In the United States 11.7 percent of the male labor force was organized in 1910, compared to 2.2 percent of the female, and in 1920 the figures were 21.4 percent for men and 7.5 percent for women. These calculations are based on data in Mitchell and Deane, *British Historical Statistics*, 68, Bairoch, *Working Population*, 158, 189, and in Wolman, *American Trade Unions*, 33, 99.

Another measurement of the greater success of the British comes from calculating the rate of growth, which in Britain was 561.2 percent for 1901 to 1921 and 417.2 percent for 1910 to 1920 in the U.S. Assuming hypothetically that there were no women in trade unions in the U.S. in 1900, the greatest growth rate possible for the U.S. from 1900 to 1920 would be 396.9 percent (compared to the actual figure of 561.2 percent for the British).

11. For a biography of Macarthur, see Mary Agnes Hamilton, *Mary Macarthur: A Biographical Sketch* (London, 1925).

12. This characterization of Robins is based on Dreier, *Margaret Dreier Robins* and on her papers at the University of Florida and the WTUL papers in the Schlesinger Library and the Library of Congress.

13. See *Women's Union Journal*, June 30, 1876, 28.

14. See Drake, *Women in Trade Unions*, chapter 3 for detailed information on this trend.

15. Women's Trade Union League, *Sixteenth Annual Report* (London, 1890), 5.

16. Women's Protective and Provident League, *Fourteenth Annual Report* (London, 1888), 4, 5.

17. Mary Macarthur, "Can Men Be Free?: The Woman's Cause is Man's," *Woman Worker*, June 12, 1908, 2.

18. Macarthur, "Trade Unions," 72.

19. Hamilton, *Mary Macarthur*, 197.

20. Macarthur, "Trade Unions," 83.

21. *Women's Trades Union Review*, October 1911, 4.
22. Macarthur, "Trade Unions," 83.
23. A copy of her essay is reprinted in her autobiography, Agnes Nestor, *Woman's Labor Leader* (Rockford, Ill., 1954), 115-17.
24. National Women's Trade Union League, "Proceedings of the 1909 Convention," Morning session, September 27, 1909, printed insert following p. 5 of typescript, NWTUL papers, LC.
25. Mary Anderson, "The Trade Agreement," *Life and Labor* 1 (July 1911), 195; Nestor, *Woman's Labor Leader*, 117.
26. Nestor, *Woman's Labor Leader*, 117.
27. Margaret Dreier Robins, "Self-Government in the Workshop," *Life and Labor* 2 (April 1912), 109. The article was reprinted as a pamphlet and was part of the WTUL literature list through the 1920s.
28. Nestor, *Woman's Labor Leader*, 117.
29. Schneiderman, *All for One*, 67-68.
30. Robins, "Self-Government in the Workshop," 109, 110.
31. Dreier, "Expansion Through Agitation and Education," 163.
32. Macarthur, "Trade Unions," 74.
33. See for example, Richardson, *The Long Day*.
34. "The Chicago Conference," *Union Labor Advocate* 7 (August 1907), 21.
35. Ibid., 22.
36. Isabella O. Ford, "Women as Trade Unionists," *Women's Trades Union Review*, January 1900, 12.
37. Macarthur, "Trade Unions," 67.
38. Dreier, "Expansion Through Agitation and Education," 163.
39. See "Women as Trade Unionists," *Women's Trades Union Review*, January 1900, 3-15, and Malkiel, *Diary of a Shirtwaist Striker*.
40. U.S. Department of Commerce and Labor, Bureau of Labor, *The Women's Trade Union Movement in Great Britain* by Katherine Graves Busbey, Bulletin no. 83 (Washington, D.C., 1909), 10.
41. Ibid.
42. Ibid.
43. National Women's Trade Union League, *Proceedings of the 1909 Convention* (Chicago, 1910), 31.
44. Schneiderman, *All for One*, 110-11.
45. Ibid., 111.
46. Hamilton, *Mary Macarthur*, 50.
47. Ibid.
48. Ibid., 52.
49. Ibid., 51-53.
50. Ibid., 54. Information on this strike and organizing campaign can also be found in the WTUL's *Annual Report* for 1906 and in that year's issues of the *Women's Trades Union Review*.

51. An incomplete set of reports from NFWW annual meetings can be found in the WTUL papers in the Trades Union Congress Library. More specific information on NFWW local branches is contained in *Woman Worker*, a sporadic publication of the WTUL and NFWW.
52. Hamilton, *Mary Macarthur*, 57.

CHAPTER THREE

1. *Women's Union Journal* 15 (December 15, 1890), 91. As the Women's Protective and Provident League, the WTUL published the *Women's Union Journal* monthly from 1875 to 1890. Although it always contained news of league activities, its primary function was to provide information on the conditions of women workers in Britain. Aimed at both the general public and at women workers, it never had a very wide circulation among the latter group. In the fall of 1890, league officials decided it would be more useful to issue a quarterly publication emphasizing the work of the WTUL, rather than continuing the more generally oriented *Journal*.
2. Hamilton, *Mary Macarthur*, 69.
3. "The Last Word," *Woman Worker*, December 30, 1908, 765.
4. Neither WTUL nor NFWW records indicate why another member of either organization did not take over the editorship. Presumably it was because there was no one either qualified or available to assume the position.
5. "Editorial," *Woman Worker*, September 1907, 1.
6. "Editorial," ibid., December 1907, 61.
7. "Editorial," ibid., November 1907, 41.
8. Constance Smith, "Put to the Proof," ibid., September 1907, 10.
9. "The Last Word," ibid., July 24, 1908, 214.
10. Keighly Snowden, "To Ladies in Revolt," ibid., September 11, 1908, 372; September 13, 1908, 395.
11. "Letters to the Editor," ibid. September 25, 1908, 430.
12. "Correspondence," ibid., November 1907, 54.
13. It was superseded by *Life and Labor Bulletin*, a four-page newsletter published from August 1922 to June 1949. Reflecting the WTUL's deteriorating financial status, publication of the bulletin was suspended in the summer of 1925, from February 1932 to April 1933, and from March 1935 to October 1939.
14. National Women's Trade Union League, "Proceedings of the 1909 Convention," 7, WTUL papers, LC.
15. "Editorial," *Life and Labor* 1 (January 1911), 1.
16. These articles, which were heavily concentrated in 1919, dealt primarily but not exclusively with the situation of black women who had entered the industrial labor force during World War I. An interesting exception was an article in the September 1914 issue reporting on a convention of the National

Association of Colored Women, the black equivalent of the General Federation of Women's Clubs.

17. These dual-language editorials appeared only in the February, March, and April 1913 issues.
18. "Mail Bag," *Life and Labor*, 1 (December 1911), 384.
19. Octavia Roberts, "The White Satin Gown," ibid., 4 (December 1914), 369.
20. Ibid., 370.
21. See National Women's Trade Union League, "Proceedings of the 1913 Convention," 98, NWTUL papers, LC.
22. In a fund-raising letter written in January 1914, Robins indicated that circulation ran five to six thousand copies a month. See Margaret Dreier Robins to George W. Perkins, January 23, 1914, Margaret Dreier Robins papers, University of Florida.
23. Margaret Dreier Robins to James Mullenbach, March 4, 1913, Robins papers.
24. Ibid. By early 1916, Robins had contributed almost $11,000. See Alice Henry to Executive Board Members, December 19, 1914, Rose Schneiderman papers, Box D119, f. NWTUL, Tamiment Library; and Margaret Dreier Robins to Emma Steghagen, February 11, 1916; NWTUL papers, Box 1, v. 3, LC.
25. See Margaret Dreier Robins to Mary E. Dreier, April 26, 1917, Robins papers.
26. Alice Henry to Margaret Dreier Robins, March 24, 1914, NWTUL papers, Box 1, v. 1, LC.
27. Stella Franklin to Melinda Scott, November 16, 1914, NWTUL papers, Box 1, v. 1, LC.
28. Stella Franklin to Agnes Nestor, May 26, 1916, Agnes Nestor papers, f. 4, Chicago Historical Society.
29. Ibid.
30. "The New York Conference," *Union Labor Advocate* 9 (October 1908), 21.
31. See Margaret Dreier Robins, "How to Take Part in Meetings," *Life and Labor* 1 (June 1911), 170-71; (July 1911), 202-3; (September 1911), 272-73; (October 1911), 297-99; (November 1911), 336-37; and Elvira D. Cabell, "How to Write Letters," ibid., 2 (January 1912), 23-24.
32. See "Report of the National Women's Trade Union League," *Union Labor Advocate* 9 (December 1908), 52; National Women's Trade Union League, "Proceedings of the 1911 Convention," 356; NWTUL papers, LC.
33. Mary E. Dreier, "Expansion Through Agitation and Education," ibid., 11 (June 1921), 164.
34. See "Annual Report for 1909-1910 of the Women's Trade Union League of New York," 18, NWTUL papers, Box 1, f. 4, SL.
35. "A Report from the New York League," *Union Labor Advocate* 8 (July 1908), 29.
36. Violet Pike, *New World Lessons for Old World Peoples* (Chicago, n.d.), 4. A copy of the primer is in the NWTUL papers, Box f. 4, SL.
37. Ibid., 8-9.
38. Ibid., 10.
39. Ibid., 15.

40. Ibid., 11.
41. See Agnes Nestor, "Ushering in the New Day," *Life and Labor* 11 (June 1921), 170.
42. By the time the WTUL school closed in 1926, the resident worker education programs included summer schools for women workers at Bryn Mawr, Barnard, and Sweet Briar; a summer program for women and men at the University of Wisconsin; and year-round sessions at Brookwood Labor College in Katonah, N.Y., and at Commonwealth College in Mena, Arkansas. For brief surveys of workers' education programs, see Spencer Miller, "Summer Schools for Workers," *American Federationist* 32 (July 1925), 569-71, and Mark Starr, *Workers' Education Today* (New York, 1941).
43. "The Fourth Biennial Convention," *Life and Labor* 3 (July 1913), 210.
44. Louisa Mittelstadt to Stella Franklin, December 6, 1913, NWTUL papers, Box 1, v. 1, LC.
45. Stella Franklin to Executive Board Members, February 27, 1914, Schneiderman papers, Box D119, f. NWTUL.
46. Margaret Dreier Robins to Mrs. Willard Straight, February 15, 1916, NWTUL papers, Box 2, f. 12, SL.
47. See Kessler-Harris, "Organizing the Unorganizable," 14.
48. "Staff Meeting Held March 12 (1914) to discuss work of National League and especially plans for the National Training School," Schneiderman papers, Box D119, f. NWTUL.
49. Margaret Dreier Robins to Mrs. Willard Straight, February 22, 1918, NWTUL papers, Box 2, f. 12, SL.
50. Stella Franklin to Executive Board Members, February 22, 1918, NWTUL papers, Box 2., f. 12, SL.
51. Ibid.
52. "Report from Secretary of Educational Department," February 11, 1921, NWTUL papers, Box 2, v. 1, LC.
53. Olive Sullivan to Margaret Dreier Robins, October 27, 1916, Robins papers.
54. "Extracts from Reports of Professor Douglas and Professor Nelson," NWTUL papers, Box 2, f. 12, SL.
55. Elisabeth Christman and Penn Shelton Burke to Members of the Executive Board, November 30, 1923; NWTUL papers, Box 2, v. 3, LC.
56. Ibid.
57. Alice Henry, "Report of the Education Department," June 5, 1922, 3, NWTUL papers, Box 2, f. 12, SL.
58. This estimate is based on reports indicating that by 1920 the WTUL had spent slightly over $28,000 on the school and over $35,000 by early 1923. Untitled, undated documents in NWTUL papers, Box 2, f. 12, SL. Since twelve more students attended the school between 1923 and 1926, and taking into account overhead costs as well as scholarships, $50,000 is probably a conservative estimate.
59. Margaret Dreier Robins to Mrs. William Cochran, August 31, 1916, Robins papers.

60. Margaret Dreier Robins to Mrs. Willard Straight, October 5, 1916, Robins papers.

61. "Distribution of the Scholarship Fund," NWTUL papers, Box 2, f. 12, SL.

62. Elisabeth Christman to Maud Swartz, April 12, 1923, NWTUL papers, Box 2, v. 3, LC.

63. Ibid.; Elisabeth Christman to Members of the Executive Board, July 5, 1923, NWTUL papers, Box 2, f. 12, SL.

64. Emma Steghagen to Members of the Executive Board, January 9 and 11, 1917, NWTUL papers, Box 1, v. 3, LC.

65. Elisabeth Christman to Members of the Executive Board, July 12, 1922, NWTUL papers, Box 2, v. 3, LC.

66. Elisabeth Christman to members of the Executive Board, May 23, 1927, Robins papers.

67. Agnes Burns, Dora Lipschitz, Lilly Brzostek, Mary Thompson, Florence Adesska, and Julia O'Connor to the Executive Board of the National Women's Trade Union League, November 1916; NWTUL papers, Box 1, v. 3, LC.

68. The minutes of the executive board meeting simply state that a "full discussion" of the memo took place and that it was decided to appoint Mary Anderson as head of the fieldwork program. "Minutes of the Executive Board Meeting," November 4-5, 1916, NWTUL papers, Box 1, v. 3, LC.

69. Margaret Dreier Robins to Mrs. Willard Straight, February 22, 1918, NWTUL papers, Box 2, f. 12, SL.

70. Helen Hill, "Report on Training School," n.d. [summer 1925], NWTUL papers, Box 2, f. 12, SL.

71. Burns et al., to Executive Board, November 1916, NWTUL papers, Box 1, v. 3, LC.

72. The associate director, however, was an ally who had formerly served as head resident of a settlement house in Baltimore, and it may well be that she was the primary target of the students' criticisms, even though they do not explicitly say so in their memo.

73. National Women's Trade Union League, *Twenty-Fifth Anniversary Program* (Chicago, 1929), 15. This summary indicates that by 1928, three of the forty-four students who had attended the school had died and that thirty-two (or 78 percent) of the remaining forty-one had been active in the labor movement. Of the three deceased students, I can only identify Myrtle Whitehead, but since she worked as an organizer for a period prior to her death, I am counting her in the total of activists. Discounting the other two who died, this means that 79 percent of the students went on to serve the labor movement.

74. There were especially close ties between the WTUL and the Summer School for Women Workers established at Bryn Mawr College in 1921. The program was run by a Joint Administrative Board consisting of an equal number of college and industrial women, and most of the latter were trade union members of the WTUL. At different times in the 1920s, Alice Henry and Helen Hill served as instructors at the school, and Agnes Nestor and Matilda

Lindsay (an active, working-class member of the WTUL) were associate directors. The school ran for eight weeks and accepted about one hundred students each summer. It offered an academic program similar to that of the WTUL's school, but it did not include fieldwork, and it was not nearly as trade union oriented. The Bryn Mawr Summer School remained in existence until 1938, when it moved to New York to become the Hudson Shore Labor School, a coeducational institution with year-round programs.

For further information see Helen D. Hill, *The Effect of the Bryn Mawr Summer School as Measured in Activities of its Students* (New York, 1929); U.S. Department of Labor, Women's Bureau, *The Industrial Experience of Women Workers at the Summer Schools, 1928-1930* by Gladys L. Palmer, Bulletin no. 89 (Washington, D.C., 1931); and Hilda W. Smith, *Women Workers at the Bryn Mawr Summer School* (New York, 1929).

75. Gertrude Tuckwell papers, f. Trade Unions for Women, Trades Union Congress Library.

76. See entry for June 18, 1908 in the 1905-10 Minute Book and for May 11, 1911 in the 1911 Minute Book, Women's Trade Union League (WTUL) papers, Trades Union Congress Library.

77. "The Congress of 1895," *Women's Trades Union Review*, October 1895, 5.

78. "Trades Union Congress," *Woman Worker*, October 1917, 1.

79. Interview with Nora Jones, London, June 20, 1972.

80. Schneiderman, *All for One*, 77, 78.

81. Ibid., 159.

82. Mary Dreier to Margaret Dreier Robins, June 15, 1912, Robins papers.

83. "How We Play," *Woman Worker*, July 1918, 10.

84. This incident was noted with great approval by Gertrude Tuckwell, Lady Dilke's niece, in her unpublished autobiography. See Gertrude Tuckwell, "Memoir," 195, Tuckwell papers.

85. Mary McDowell, "The National Women's Trade Union League," *Survey* 23 (October 16, 1909), 104. (Macarthur made this remark in a speech at a public meeting held in conjunction with the American WTUL's 1909 convention.)

86. "Minutes of the Meeting of the National Executive Board of the Women's Trade Union League," June 18, 1909, Leonora O'Reilly papers, Box 16, f. 374, SL.

87. Schneiderman, *All for One*, 153.

88. Nestor, *Woman's Labor Leader*, 232.

89. MacDowell, "The National Women's Trade Union League," 106.

90. Elisabeth Christman, "Foreword," Dreier, *Margaret Dreier Robins*, vii, ix.

91. The minutes of these meetings contain useful information on the unions that showed an interest in the organization of women, for they generally list the trades represented. The minutes, however, provide only terse summaries of the topics raised for discussion each year. See "Minute Book of WTUL-TUC Conferences," WTUL papers.

92. See for example, the WTUL's report of its involvement in the 1908 Illinois State Federation of Labor Convention, "The State Federation of Labor at Peoria," *Union Labor Advocate* 9 (December 1908), 18.

93. See Trades Union Congress, *Proceedings of the 1908 Trades Union Congress* (London 1908), 54.

94. Beginning in 1907, WTUL conventions were held biennially through 1919. Financial problems caused the convention scheduled for 1921 to be deferred until 1922, but the regular schedule was followed for the next two conventions in 1924 and 1926. After 1926 the WTUL held only three more national meetings—in 1929, 1936, and 1947. Typescripts of the proceedings of these conventions are included in the WTUL papers at the Library of Congress; shorter reports can be found in *Life and Labor* and *Life and Labor Bulletin* for the relevant years.

95. For a complete discussion of the WTUL's involvement in the suffrage movement, see Robin Miller Jacoby, "The Women's Trade Union League and American Feminism," *Feminist Studies* 3 (Fall 1975), 126-40.

96. "Labor Joins the Suffragists," *Life and Labor* 7 (October 1917), 163.

97. A set of these letters is in Schneiderman papers, Box D119, f. New York WTUL.

98. Letter 15, ibid.

99. See for example, Emilia F. S. Dilke, "Trades Unionism among Women," *Fortnightly Review*, May 1891, 741-46; Dilke, "Preface," Agnes Bulley and Margaret Whitley, *Women's Work* (London, 1894), v-xiii; and Tuckwell, *Woman in Industry*.

100. Tuckwell, "Memoir," B, Tuckwell papers.

101. Dilke, "Trades Unionism among Women," 744.

102. "Lady Dilke's Notebook," WTUL papers.

103. "The Portrait Gallery: Miss Gertrude Tuckwell," *Woman Worker*, June 26, 1908, 95.

104. See Hamilton, *Mary Macarthur*, 62.

105. See Tuckwell, "Memoir," 207, 275, Tuckwell papers.

106. This incident was recounted in *Woman Worker*, January 6, 1909, 12.

107. Women's Trade Union League, *Thirty-First Annual Report* (London, 1906), 16.

108. Rose Schneiderman, "The Woman Movement and the Working Woman," *Life and Labor* 5 (April 1915), 65.

109. See Jacoby, "The Women's Trade Union League." Although the British WTUL supported woman suffrage in principle, it was more closely linked to the adult suffrage movement than to the woman suffrage movement. The former was lobbying for universal adult suffrage (i.e., the removal of existing property qualifications), whereas the latter was demanding that the franchise be extended to women "on the same ground as it is or may be granted to men." For further discussion of the British league's relationship to the British suffrage movement, see Robin Miller Jacoby, "Feminism and Class Consciousness in the British and American Women's Trade Union Leagues,"

in Berenice Carroll, ed., *Liberating Women's History: Theoretical and Critical Essays* (Urbana, 1976), 144-46.

110. See Nestor, *Woman's Labor Leader*, 65; "Minutes of the First National Executive Board Meeting," March 20, 1904, NWTUL papers, Box 25, f. WTUL Historical Data, LC; and Henry, *Women and the Labor Movement*, 119, for accounts of this incident.
111. Nestor, *Woman's Labor Leader*, 66.
112. See "Club Programs of 1905-1906," NWTUL papers, Box 1, v. 1, LC.
113. A copy of this advertisement appears on the back cover of *Life and Labor*, September 1912.
114. Nestor, *Woman's Labor Leader*, 66-68.
115. Ibid., 74.
116. See "1909-1910 Annual Report of the Women's Trade Union League of New York," 21-22, NWTUL papers, Box 1, f. 4, SL.
117. "Report of Mrs. Robins' Trip," NWTUL papers, Box 2, v. 1, LC.
118. Schneiderman, *All for One*, 8.
119. Malkiel, *Diary of a Shirtwaist Striker*, 40-41.
120. Margaret Dreier Robins to a Mr. Roberts, April 3, 1925, Robins papers.
121. "Votes for Women," *Life and Labor* 1 (February 1911), 62.
122. Pauline Newman to Margaret Dreier Robins, August 5, 1911, Robins papers.

CHAPTER FOUR

1. Emma Paterson, "The Position of Working Women and How to Improve It," *Labour News*, April 1874, reprinted in Goldman, *Emma Paterson*, 118-19.
2. Drake, *Women in Trade Unions*, 16.
3. See ibid., 19-21, for a discussion of these conflicts.
4. Ibid., 19.
5. Ibid.
6. Ibid.
7. Although the WTUL responded to this request, attempts to organize the Cradley Heath chainmakers proved futile until legislation establishing minimum wage rates was passed in 1909.
8. Drake, *Women in Trade Unions*, 18.
9. The woman was May Abraham, a WTUL activist, who had been one of the four women appointed by the 1891 Royal Commission on Labour to prepare a report on the condition of women workers in Britain. In addition to being competent and comprehensive, the report is noteworthy as the first investigation of women's work carried out by women. For further information on May Abraham [Tennant], see Violet Markham, *May Tennant: A Portrait* (London, 1949).
10. "The League Conference," *Women's Union Journal*, October 1886, 97.

11. See *Women's Trade Union Review*, April 1891, 9-10; July 1891, 1-4; Drake, *Women in Trade Unions*, 27-28; Tuckwell, *Women in Industry*, 121-25.
12. This campaign included sending a deputation of laundry workers to the Home Secretary and organizing a demonstration of several thousand laundry workers in Hyde Park. Drake, *Women in Trade Unions*, 28; Women's Trade Union League, *Seventeenth Annual Report* (London, 1891), 3.
13. The WTUL's campaign achieved partial success in 1895, when some provisions covering laundry workers were included in the Factory and Workshops Bill. It took, however, another six years of WTUL agitation before legislation was passed that effected significant improvements in the situation of laundry workers.
14. *Women's Trade Union Review*, April 1891, 1.
15. Emilia F. S. Dilke, "Trades Unionism for Women," *New Review*, January 1890, 45-46.
16. Women's Trade Union League, *Eighteenth Annual Report* (London, 1892), 2.
17. Clementina Black, "The Coming Factory Act," *Contemporary Review* 59 (May 1891), 710.
18. Women's Trade Union League, *Twenty-Third Annual Report* (London, 1897), 3.
19. See B. L. Hutchins and A. Harrison, *A History of Factory Legislation* (London, 1903), chap. 9.
20. Committee of the Society for Promoting the Employment of Women, *Factory and Workshops Bill* (London, 1894), 1.
21. Freedom of Labour Defense League, *First Annual Report* (London, 1895), 1.
22. E. J. Boucherett, *The Fall in Women's Wages* (London, 1898), 6.
23. Beatrice Webb, "Diary," v. 21, entry for January 2, 1901; Webb papers, London School of Economics.
24. In Bulley and Whitley, *Women's Work*, vi.
25. Tuckwell, *Women in Industry*, 101.
26. Women's Trade Union League, *Thirty-Seventh Annual Report* (London, 1911), 3.
27. See for example, Women's Trade Union League and Women's Labour League, *Women's Labour Day Souvenir Booklet* (London, 1909), 11.
28. The following discussion is based on information in WTUL records for 1906 to 1910; Drake, *Women in Trade Unions*, 47-49, 57-58; Hamilton, *Mary Macarthur*, 64-69, 76-92; and Gertrude Tuckwell, "The Regulation of Women's Work," Constance Smith, "The Minimum Wage," and Clementina Black, "Legislative Proposals," in Tuckwell, *Women in Industry*.
29. See Roy Jenkins, *Sir Charles Dilke: A Victorian Tragedy* (London, 1965), 395-97.
30. See Constance Smith, "The Sweated Industries Exhibition," *Women's Trade Union Review*, July 1906, 7-10.
31. Hamilton, *Mary Macarthur*, 68.

32. Great Britain, Parliament, *Parliamentary Papers* (Commons), *1907*, v. 6 (Reports), "Report of the Select Committee on Home Work," ii.
33. Ibid., 178-208, 203.
34. Tuckwell, "Memoir," 211.
35. "Report of the Select Committee on Home Work," 207.
36. See Tuckwell, "Memoir," 212, and Hamilton, *Mary Macarthur*, 79-80.
37. National Women's Trade Union League, "Proceedings of the 1909 Convention," 11, WTUL papers, LC.
38. Smith, "The Minimum Wage," 41.
39. Hamilton, *Mary Macarthur*, 83.
40. Women's Trade Union League, *Thirty-Sixth Annual Report* (London, 1910), 5.
41. Hamilton, *Mary Macarthur*, 86-87.
42. Women's Trade Union League, *Thirty-Sixth Annual Report*, 6.
43. See the WTUL's annual reports, the *Women's Trade Union Review*, and the minutes of the WTUL's annual conference for TUC delegates, available in the WTUL papers.
44. See the *Women's Trade Union Review* for 1911-1913; Hamilton, *Mary Macarthur*, 108-20.
45. Drake, *Women in Trade Unions*, 63.
46. See Tuckwell papers, f. 452a.
47. *Daily Herald*, August 15, 1914 (clipping in ibid).
48. Among its members were Margaret Bondfield, Susan Lawrence, and Marion Phillips from the women's labor movement and Lady Crewe, May Abraham Tennant, and Lady Askwith. For information on this committee, see the set of newspaper clippings in ibid. and Hamilton, *Mary Macarthur*, 137-42.
49. Hamilton, *Mary Macarthur*, 139.
50. *Reynold's Newspaper*, August 23, 1914, in Tuckwell papers, f. 462.
51. *Daily Sketch*, August 20, 1914, in ibid.
52. Drake, *Women in Trade Unions*, 69.
53. War Emergency Workers' National Committee, *National Conference on War Service for Women* (London, 1915), 3. (A copy of this pamphlet can be found in Women's Labour League papers, Labour Party Library.)
54. The following discussion is based on information in the *Women's Trade Union Review* and WTUL annual reports for these years, newspaper clippings in the Tuckwell papers, Drake, *Women in Trade Unions*, 68-110, and Hamilton, *Mary Macarthur*, 129-66.
55. Hamilton, *Mary Macarthur*, 150-51.
56. Ibid., 155.
57. Mary Macarthur, "Women in Munition Work, " *Woman Worker*, January 1916, 6-7.
58. Quoted in Hamilton, *Mary Macarthur*, 158.
59. The *Times*, January 5, 1917, 5.

60. This calculation takes into account the 150 percent increase in the cost of living that occurred during the war. For further information on the wage rates of women in other industries, see Hamilton, *Mary Macarthur*, 161, and Drake, *Women in Trade Unions*, 83-96.
61. Hamilton, *Mary Macarthur*, 162.
62. A reasonably complete collection of documents pertaining to the Standing Joint Committee can be found in the WTUL papers.
63. Standing Joint Committee, "Constitution," WTUL papers.
64. Standing Joint Committee, "Annual Report for the year ending February 28, 1917," WTUL papers.
65. See Standing Joint Committee, "Minute Book," WTUL papers.
66. "The Working Women of Great Britain," *Labour Woman* 13 (December 1, 1925), 196.
67. For a summary of the property qualifications determining the eligibility of male voters at the beginning of the twentieth century, see Constance Rover, *Women's Suffrage and Party Politics in Britain 1866-1914* (London, 1967), 27. For statistical information on the composition of the British electorate in the twentieth century, see David Butler and Jennie Freeman, *British Political Facts, 1900-1968*, 3rd ed. (London 1969), 155.
68. See Jacoby, "Feminism and Class Consciousness," 144-46.
69. Margaret Bondfield, who later became the first woman cabinet member when she was made Minister of Labour in 1924, was the most active WTUL member in the adult suffrage movement. See Women's Freedom League, *Verbatim Report of Debate on December 3, 1907: Sex Equality (Teresa Billington-Grieg) Versus Adult Suffrage Margaret Bondfield* (Manchester, 1908).
70. Minutes for July 21, 1904, "1904 Minute Book," WTUL papers.
71. Unidentified newspaper clipping (1909), Tuckwell papers, f. 321.
72. See Rover, *Women's Suffrage*, 146-67, and Marian Ramelson, *The Petticoat Rebellion: A Century of Struggle for Women's Rights* (London, 1967), chap. 14.
73. "Report of the Delegates to Labour Party Conference: Proceedings of the 1912 Women's Labour League Conference," 55-56, Women's Labour League papers.
74. Ramelson, *Petticoat Rebellion*, 158.
75. Ibid., 158-59, and "Proceedings of the 1912 Women's Labour League Conference," 56, Women's Labour League papers.
76. Women's Labour League, *Annual Report for 1918* (London, 1918), 21.
77. *Labour Leader*, October 21, 1918, quoted in Hamilton, *Mary Macarthur*, 170.
78. In response to this ruling, Macarthur's campaign literature simply used her first name. For a detailed account of the campaign, see ibid., 172-80.

CHAPTER FIVE

1. "National Women's Trade Union League," 2, NWTUL papers, Box 25, LC.
2. National Women's Trade Union League, *Twenty-Fifth Anniversary Program* (Chicago, 1929), 19.
3. *New York Call*, June 15, 1915, 1, quoted in Dye, "Women's Trade Union League," 396.
4. See David Thelen, *The New Citizenship* (Columbia, Missouri, 1972); James Weinstein, *The Corporate Ideal in the Liberal State* (Boston, 1968); and Robert Wiebe, *The Search for Order, 1877-1920* (New York, 1967). See also Dye, "Women's Trade Union League," chapter 9 for a discussion of how the history of the New York WTUL reflects this broader trend.
5. A law prohibiting the employment of women for more than ten hours a day "in any mechanical establishment or factory or laundry" had been passed in Oregon in 1903. Curt Muller, the owner of a laundry in Portland, was arrested for violating this law. The National Consumers' League undertook the defense and Louis D. Brandeis volunteered his services as counsel. The case came before the Supreme Court in the fall of 1907. The complete text of Brandeis's brief and of the court's decision, which was announced on February 24, 1909, has been published as Louis D. Brandeis, *Women in Industry* (New York, 1908; reprint ed., New York, 1969).
6. Ibid., 6.
7. "Statement of Miss Elisabeth Christman," NWTUL papers, Box 4, f. 45, SL.
8. "Minutes of the October 4, 1904 Meeting of the Executive Board of the National Women's Trade Union League," 3, NWTUL papers, Box 1, v. 1, LC.
9. Alice Henry, "Convention of the National Women's Trade Union League," *Union Labor Advocate* 10 (November 1909), 22.
10. "The Woman's Department," *Union Labor Advocate* 8 (June 1908), 15 and (July 1908), 23; Nestor, *Woman's Labor Leader*, 90-91.
11. Nestor, *Women's Labor Leader*, 91, 92.
12. See ibid., 118-19.
13. Margaret Dreier Robins to Irene [Lewisohn?], June 2, 1909, Robins papers.
14. Although the WTUL started out relying primarily on the health and welfare arguments elaborated in the Brandeis brief, over the years it developed a more comprehensive rationale for limiting the hours of women's work. For example, the back cover of a pamphlet issued by the WTUL in 1915 declared:
    Since modern industry with its machine process, specialization, speeding up, etc., has increased the strain upon the worker—
    Since legislation restricting the hours of work for women exists and has proved a benefit to other states, and has been declared constitutional—
    Since the principle of the short work-day has been recognized by the United States Government and by more than half the states through the provision of an eight-hour day for the men in their employ—

Since women stand in greater need of restriction of hours than do men because of their physical constitution and because their health affects more directly that of the coming generation—

Since shorter hours increase the efficiency of the worker, and do not result in diminished output—

Since shorter hours do not mean lower wages—

Since shorter hours increase regularity of employment—

Since it is possible for business to be arranged to conform with such legislation—

THEREFORE AN EIGHT-HOUR BILL SHOULD BE PASSED!

National Women's Trade Union League, *The Eight-Hour Day for Women* (Chicago, 1915).

15. Nestor, *Women's Labor Leader*, 277.

16. This discussion is largely based on Leon Stein, *The Triangle Fire* (Philadelphia, 1967).

17. Ibid., 14.

18. Schneiderman, *All for One*, 100-101.

19. For a detailed discussion of the ILGWU's organizing efforts among women garment workers after the fire and of the New York WTUL's growing disillusionment with this union, see Dye, "Women's Trade Union League," chapter 4.

20. Stein, *Triangle Fire*, 210.

21. See ibid. for further information on legislation sponsored by the Factory Investigation Commission.

22. Samuel Gompers, "The American Labor Movement," *American Federationist* 21 (July 1914), 544.

23. Samuel Gompers, "Woman's Work, Rights and Progress," ibid., 20 (August 1913), 627.

24. Gompers, "The American Labor Movement," 544.

25. Gompers, "Woman's Work," 626, 627.

26. Gompers, "Coming Into Her Own," *American Federationist* 22 (July 1915), 518.

27. Margaret Dreier Robins, "The Minimum Wage," *Life and Labor* 3 (June 1913), 168, 170, 172.

28. National Women's Trade Union League, "Proceedings of the 1915 Convention," 236, NWTUL papers, LC.

29. See Dye, "Women's Trade Union League," 419-20.

30. Mary Dreier to Melinda Scott, August 14, 1914, O'Reilly papers.

31. "Proceedings of the 1915 Convention," 231, 262, 253.

32. Ibid., 254.

33. Ibid., 267-68.

34. Mary Anderson with Mary Winslow, *Woman at Work* (Minneapolis, 1951), 115.

35. See U.S. Senate, *Report on Condition of Woman and Child Wage-Earners*.

36. This statement appears at the beginning of each volume of the Senate study.

37. See Lemons, *The Woman Citizen*, 27 and Henry, *Women and the Labor Movement*, 169-71.
38. See Anderson, *Woman at Work*, 92-93, for a full account of the WTUL's efforts at the 1916 AFL convention.
39. For further information on the creation and work of this agency, see ibid., 86-90, and Henry, *Women and the Labor Movement*, 173-75.
40. See Henry, *Women and the Labor Movement*, 175-80; Anderson, *Women at Work*, 94-107; Lemons, *Woman Citizen*, 29-30; "League Member Called to Larger Service" and "At Last—A National Woman's Labor Bureau," *Life and Labor* 7 (August 1918), 158-61.
41. This extension did not come without a struggle. See Ethel M. Smith to Margaret Dreier Robins, March 4, 1919, Robins papers.
42. Henry, *Women and the Labor Movement*, 178.
43. This discussion is based on Marjorie Shuler, "Women and the New Administration," *Woman Citizen* 5 (June 19, 1920), 71, quoted in Lemons, *Woman Citizen*, 30-31.
44. Ibid., 30.
45. Ibid., 30-31.
46. See U.S. Department of Labor, Women's Bureau, *Bulletin of the Women's Bureau*, a publication beginning in 1921 and continuing to the present.
47. The following discussion of the WJCC is based on the WTUL papers and Lemons, *Woman Citizen*.
48. In addition to the WTUL, the League of Women voters invited representatives of the following organizations to this meeting: National Consumers' League; National Council of Women; General Federation of Women's Clubs; Association of Collegiate Alumnae; Women's Christian Temperance Union; National Federation of Business and Professional Women's Clubs; Parent and Teachers' Association; American Home Economics Association; Council of Jewish Women; Young Women's Christian Association; Daughters of the American Revolution; United Daughters of the Confederacy; and Federation of College Women's Clubs. See Ethel Smith to "Chairman and Members of the Legislative Committee," November 29, 1920, WTUL papers, Box 2, v. 1, LC.
49. See ibid.
50. The allies were Margaret Dreier Robins and Alice Henry and the trade unionists were Agnes Nestor, Elisabeth Christman, and Emma Steghagen. See Agnes Nestor to Ethel Smith, December 4, 1920, NWTUL papers, Box 2, v. 1, LC.
51. Ethel Smith to Agnes Nestor, December 8, 1920, NWTUL papers, Box 2, v. 1, LC.
52. Ibid.
53. Although there is no direct evidence that the WTUL executive committee took the following issues into consideration, it seems reasonable to assume that in addition to the arguments put forward by Ethel Smith, the board's decision to join the WJCC was motivated by its realization that it was unrealistic to rely on AFL support for WTUL lobbying efforts and that the organizational base

did not exist in the United States to allow the creation of a coalition more precisely analogous to the British Standing Joint Committee of Women's Industrial Organizations.

The other charter members were: National League of Women Voters; General Federation of Women's Clubs; Women's Christian Temperance Union; Parent and Teachers' Association; National Federation of Business and Professional Women's Clubs; National Consumers' League; Association of Collegiate Alumnae (which became the American Association of University Women); National Council of Jewish Women; and American Home Economics Association.

54. Lemons, *Woman Citizen*, 153.
55. The new members were: American Nurses Association; American Federation of Teachers; Council of Women for Home Missions; Girls' Friendly Society of America; Medical Women's National Association; National Association of Colored Women; National Council of Women; National Educational Association; Young Women's Christian Association; Service Star Legion; and National Committee for a Department of Education.
56. See Lemons, *Woman Citizen*, 56-57.
57. See "Report of the Legislative Secretary, 1922-1924," NWTUL papers, Box 25, LC.
58. This article appeared in 1915 in *Woman's Protest*, an antisuffrage publication. See Women's Joint Congressional Committee, "Summary of Report of Special Committee," [1927], 2, NWTUL papers, Box 25, LC.
59. See the file "Attacks on the WTUL" in the NWTUL papers, Box 25, LC, and Lemons, *Woman Citizen*, chapter 8.
60. See "Summary of Report of Special Committee," 3.
61. Josephine Goldmark, *Impatient Crusader: Florence Kelley's Life Story* (Urbana, 1953), 205.
62. Marguerite Mooers Marshall, *Life and Labor* 10 (March 1920), 84.
63. Ibid.
64. Ibid.
65. Pauline Newman, ibid. (May 1920), 153.
66. Rose Schneiderman, ibid., 152.
67. Margaret Dreier Robins, ibid. (March 1920), 96.
68. Newman, 154.
69. Lemons, *Woman Citizen*, 183.
70. Cornelia Bryce Pinchot to Alice Paul, October 7, 1920; Cornelia Bryce Pinchot papers, Box 11, LC, quoted in ibid., 186.
71. Ibid., 183.
72. Anderson, *Women at Work*, 161.
73. Maud Younger to Ethel Smith, October 8, 1921, WTUL papers, Box 22, LC.
74. George Sutherland to Ethel Smith, December 24, 1921, Pinchot papers, Box 19, quoted in Lemons, *Woman Citizen*, 185-86.
75. Felix Frankfurter to Ethel Smith, September 8, 1921, NWTUL papers, Box 22, LC.

76. Ibid.
77. Lemons, *Woman Citizen*, 191.
78. Anderson, *Woman at Work*, 172.
79. There was considerable controversy over the form this investigation should take. Mary Anderson appointed a six-member advisory committee consisting of three representatives of the NWP and three representatives of groups opposing the ERA. The former argued vehemently for open hearings rather than the standard Women's Bureau approach of sending investigators into the field, and the latter group eventually resigned from the committee, impatient with the NWP's unwillingness to compromise. At this point, Anderson dissolved the committee, since it was no longer bipartisan, and the investigation proceeded without further conflicts. (The primary objection to the idea of open hearings was that women workers would not feel free to testify against their employers, who tended to oppose protective legislation.)
80. The 500-page report still stands as one of the most extensive studies published by the Women's Bureau. See U.S., Department of Labor, Women's Bureau, *The Effects of Labor Legislation on the Employment Opportunities of Women*, Bulletin no. 65 (Washington, D.C., 1928).
81. Anderson, *Women at Work*, 171. See also ibid., 43-54.
82. Elisabeth Christman to Maud Wood Park, April 12, 1923, Robins papers.

CHAPTER SIX

1. The International Federation of Working Women was initially (1919-1921) known as the International Congress of Working Women, so for the sake of accuracy, it will be referred to as the ICWW in discussions of its early history.
    The only manuscript sources are the IFWW papers in the Schlesinger Library of Radcliffe College and materials in the WTUL papers in the Library of Congress. The IFWW is briefly mentioned in the following books: Anderson, *Woman at Work*; Dreier, *Margaret Dreier Robins*; Henry, *Women and the Labor Movement*; and Schneiderman, *All for One*.
2. National Women's Trade Union League, *Women and Reconstruction: Report of the Committee on Social and Industrial Reconstruction* (Chicago, 1918), 6.
3. National Women's Trade Union League, "Proceedings of the 1919 Convention," 12, NWTUL papers, LC.
4. National Women's Trade Union League, "The First International Congress of Working Women," August 5, 1919, 1, IFWW papers, f. 2.
5. Ibid., 1-6.
6. Argentina, Belgium, Canada, Czechoslovakia, France, Great Britain, India, Italy, Norway, Poland, Sweden, and the United States sent official delegations. Women from Cuba, Denmark, Japan, the Netherlands, Serbia, Spain, and Switzerland attended as interested visitors.
7. Margaret Dreier Robins, "Address of Welcome," 1, IFWW papers, f. 2.

8. National Women's Trade Union League, *Resolutions Adopted by the First International Congress of Working Women* (Chicago, 1919), 3-4, IFWW papers, f. 2.

9. See "Proceedings of the First International Congress of Working Women," 17, IFWW papers, f. 3.

10. See ibid., 18-30; "With the First International Congress of Working Women," *Life and Labor* 9 (December 1919), 310; and "Our Women Delegates in Washington," *The Labour Woman* 8 (February 1920), 24.

11. National Women's Trade Union League, *Resolutions*, 4; IFWW papers, f. 2.

12. Ibid., 6, 8.

13. "With the First International Congress of Working Women," 312.

14. See League of Nations, *International Labor Conference: First Annual Meeting, October 29-November 29, 1919* (Washington, D.C., 1920).

15. Ibid., 245-46.

16. Ibid., 259-60.

17. See National Women's Trade Union League, *Resolutions*, 2, IFWW papers, f. 2.

18. "With the First International Congress of Working Women," 311.

19. Since the ICWW had adjourned before the ILO conference adopted its conventions, the ICWW was not in a position to pressure the International Labor Conference through formal or informal means to adopt conventions more precisely in accordance with the ICWW recommendations. The only people who could argue the ICWW's point of view were the women technical advisers who had also attended the ICWW conference. Since the dynamics of the ILO conference committee meetings are not known, the role played by these women can be assessed only at the speculative level. While it seems clear that the influence of the women advisers was limited, it does seem logical to assume that their position was enhanced to some degree by their having attended the ICWW conference. Participating in ICWW discussions presumably strengthened and clarified their views on women's issues and gave them intangible but significant psychological support in dealing with their delegations. Thus, their influence may have been partially responsible for the ILO conference adopting conventions as close to the ICWW recommendations as some of them were.

20. "Our Women Delegates in Washington," 24.

21. For a complete list of the social activities and a delegate's response to them, see "General Information on the 1919 Congress" and the fragment from Jeanne Bouvier, "Mes Memoires," June 1950, NWTUL papers, Boxes 11 and 21, LC.

22. "Proceedings of the 1919 International Congress of Working Women," November 6, 1919, morning sessions, 5, 6, IFWW papers, f. 3.

23. Jeanne Bouvier to Margaret Dreier Robins, June 23, 1920, NWTUL papers, Box 2, vol. 3, LC.

24. An incomplete set of newsletters can be found in the NWTUL papers, Box 21, LC.

25. "Constitution of the International Congress of Working Women," 1-2, n.d., NWTUL papers, Box 21, LC.
26. Ibid.
27. International Congress of Working Women, *Newsletter*, July 7, 1920, 8, NWTUL papers, Box 21, LC.
28. "Summary of views on proposed constitution from WTUL regional conferences," NWTUL papers, Box 21, LC.
29. "Constitution," 2-3, NWTUL papers, Box 21, LC.
30. See "Report of Secretary to Executive Committee," January 1, 1920-August 31, 1921, NWTUL papers, Box 18, LC.
31. International Congress of Working Women, "Call to the Second Meeting of the International Congress of Working Women," IFWW papers, f. 5.
32. The ICWW again planned its conference to precede the International Labor Conference; the ICWW met from October 17 to 25, while the ILO conference met from October 25 to November 19. Thus, once again the ICWW defined its task as preparing resolutions on topics to be considered by the International Labor Conference, but it was not prepared to influence that conference's deliberations beyond the written presentation of ICWW recommendations. There was virtually no discussion at the 1921 ICWW conference regarding its impact on the ILO conference.
33. National Women's Trade Union League, "Proceedings of the 1924 Convention," 23, NWTUL papers, LC.
34. "The Constitution recommended to the Congress by the Constitution Commission, October 22, 1921," 1, IFWW papers, f. 4.
35. The point of this policy decision was to exclude trade unions organized on a religious basis and those affiliated with the Moscow International but to include groups, such as the American WTUL, that were sympathetic to the goals and policies of the IFTU but whose national trade union centers did not belong to the IFTU. The only protests came from delegates from trade unions associated with the Catholic union movement.

    This membership decision was strongly supported by the IFTU. The account of the 1921 congress in the IFTU journal lauded the IFWW for "definitely and fully" declaring its primary identification with the international labor movement. The IFTU assessed the outcome of the congress as follows:

    > The resolutions of the Congress mean a radical repudiation of the old error of the bourgeois women's movement, namely that the rights of women must be wrested from men. The resolutions of the Congress mean an unqualified recognition of the basis of the Labour Movement. Labour holds that divergent interests in the economic struggle have as little to do with the sexes as with nations or races; and that there is only one real demarcation in this struggle: the demarcation between Worker and Exploiter of Labour. The resolutions also signify a repudiation of the belief that working women can attain their object by collaboration with bourgeois or neutral organizations which are outside the trade union movement.

"The International Congress of Working Women at Geneva," *The International Trade Union Movement* 1 (1921), 14.

36. "Constitution," 1, IFWW papers, f. 4.
37. Marion Phillips, "The Aims and Constitution of the International Federation of Working Women," *Canadian Congress Journal* 1 (August 1922), 436.
38. For a summary of resolutions passed at the 1921 congress, see International Congress of Working Women, "Second International Congress of Working Women: Summary of Proceedings," October 24, 1921, NWTUL papers, Box 18, LC.
39. National Women's Trade Union League, "Proceedings of the 1924 Convention," 94, NWTUL papers, LC.
40. The following account of the IFTU and its relationship to the AFL is based on American Federation of Labor, *Report of the Proceedings of the Convention of the American Federation of Labor* (Washington, D.C., 1919-1924); Lewis L. Lorwin, *The International Labor Movement: History, Politics, Outlook* (New York, 1953); Lorwin, *Labor and Internationalism* (New York, 1929); and Louis A. Reed, *The Labor Philosophy of Samuel Gompers* (New York, 1930; reprint ed., Port Washington, N.Y., 1966).
41. Lorwin, *International Labor Movement*, 34.
42. Ibid., 33.
43. Ibid., 40.
44. American Federation of Labor, *Report of Proceedings* (1909), 39.
45. See Lorwin, *Labor and Internationalism*, 185-88; Lorwin, *International Labor Movement*, 56-57; Reed, *Philosophy of Gompers*, 150-69.
46. Samuel Gompers, *Why the Peace Treaty Should be Ratified* (Washington, 1919), quoted in Reed, *Philosophy of Gompers*, 160.
47. Lorwin, *International Labor Movement*, 60.
48. See ibid., 78-83, and Reed, *Philosophy of Gompers*, 166-69, for further discussion on this point.
49. "Working Women at Geneva," *The Labour Woman* 9 (November 1921), 176.
50. This is reconstructed on the basis of Alice Henry to Margaret Dreier Robins, November 4, 1922, and Marion Phillips to Robins, November 24, 1922, Robins papers.
51. The IFTU did in fact see the support of American women for the IFTU (through the IFWW) as a potential opening wedge for renewed American identification with the IFTU. The IFTU account of the 1921 IFWW congress declared:

It is a very welcome sign that although the American trade unions are still undecided in regard to affiliation with Amsterdam, the working women of America are strongly convinced of the necessity of international cooperation and have identified themselves with the International Federation of Trade Unions.

"The International Congress of Working Women at Geneva," 14.
52. Phillips to Robins, November 24, 1922, Robins papers.

53. Robins to Phillips, December 21, 1922, Robins papers.
54. Robins to Elisabeth Christman, September 30, 1921, NWTUL papers, Box 2, v. 2, LC.
55. Robins to Christman, October 21, 1921, NWTUL papers, Box 2, v. 2, LC. (Oudegeest, Fimmen, and Jouhaux were IFTU officers.)
56. Phillips to Maud Swartz and Robins, April 24, 1923, Robins papers.
57. Robins to Christman, October 12, 1921, NWTUL papers, Box 2, v. 2. LC.
58. International Federation of Trade Unions, *Report of the IFTU Congress* (Amsterdam, 1922), 45-46.
59. Robins to Miss Mellen, July 24, 1923, Robins papers.
60. "Minutes of the NWTUL Executive Board," January 14-15, 1923, 9-10, NWTUL papers, Box 2, v. 3, LC.
61. Robins to Mellen, July 24, 1923.
62. There is no way of piecing together a full account of this internal conflict. It is referred to in Anderson, *Woman at Work*, 131; Robins to Anderson, March 21, 1924, and Anderson to Robins, March 24, 1924, Mary Anderson papers, f. 8, SL. None of these sources goes into very much detail about the extent of support for Swartz's position.
63. "Proceedings of the 1923 IFWW Congress," 27; NWTUL papers, Box 18, LC.
64. International Federation of Working Women, "Report of the Secretariat to the 1923 IFWW Congress," 5, NWTUL papers, Box 13, LC.
65. Ibid.
66. International Federation of Working Women, *Working Women in Many Countries: Report of Congress Held at Vienna, August 1923* (Amsterdam, 1923), 7.
67. "Statement Made by Marion Phillips on the Proposals Submitted by the British Members of the Secretariat to the Congress at Vienna," 1, NWTUL papers, Box 2, v. 3, LC.
68. Ibid., 2.
69. Ibid., 3.
70. See "Recommendations to the 1923 Congress by the Commission on the Constitution," NWTUL papers, Box 21, LC. There are no records of the commission's meetings, although it is known that the American members of the commission, Agnes Nestor and Maud Swartz, opposed the report. Swartz's opposition is interesting in light of her support for the British proposal prior to the congress. One can only speculate whether her vote on the commission reflected a genuine change in her position or a feeling that internal organizational struggles should not be exposed and that a display of external WTUL solidarity was necessary.
71. International Federation of Working Women, *Working Women in Many Countries*, 12.
72. These hypotheses are based on comments in Alice Henry to Robins, October 23, 1922, NWTUL papers, Box 2, v. 2, LC; Anderson to Robins, January 3, 1923, Robins papers; Miriam Shepherd to Robins, March 6, 1923, Robins

papers; Robins's report on the IFWW to the 1924 WTUL convention, NWTUL, "Proceedings of the 1924 Convention," 97, NWTUL papers, LC.

73. See Robins's report to the 1924 WTUL convention; Anderson, *Woman at Work*, 131-33; Dreier, *Margaret Dreier Robins*, 184-85; and Schneiderman, *All for One*, 170-71.

74. The clearest statement of this position is found in a press release written by Ethel Smith, an American WTUL member, just prior to the 1923 IFWW congress:

> The IFWW combines the impulses of the two greatest democratic movements of the world, the labor movement and the woman movement. It has, consequently, to make its way through the complexities of both; through misunderstanding by men in the labor movement and by women in the woman movement.
>
> We find on the part of some labor men a neglect of women's interests, a disposition to regulate the competition of women workers by arbitrarily limiting their occupational opportunities—a resistance to women's efforts to free themselves from the old order and the old economic subjection of women to men.
>
> We find on the part of some feminists a disposition to enforce upon the working women the individualism of the old economic order and the old subjection of the working people to the non-workers—a harking back to the outworn economic philosophy of laissez faire.
>
> As women we have to contend with remnants of sex prejudice within the labor movement.
>
> As workers, we find ourselves forced to contend with a tendency to class opposition within the woman movement.
>
> The labor movement has advanced economic justice but moves slowly toward sex equality.
>
> These facts we believe are due to the failure of men to understand women's problems, and the failure of non-working women to understand labor problems.
>
> The third biennial Congress of the International Federation of Women Workers therefore addresses to the labor men of the world and to the feminists of the world the following declaration and asks for their support in carrying out its principles.

Ethel Smith, "Statement," July 1923, NWTUL papers, Box 21, LC.

75. See Shepherd to Robins, March 6, 1923, Robins papers.

76. There is no evidence to contradict this assumption, but the only explicit evidence supporting it is found in a copy of a letter from Ethel Smith to Elisabeth Christman sent to Mary Anderson. See Smith to Christman, October 24, 1923, Anderson papers, f. 5.

77. Dreier, *Margaret Dreier Robins*, 165.

78. "International Federation of Working Women," *Life and Labor Bulletin* 2 (November 1923), 2.

79. Edith McDonald to Maud Swartz, April 29, 1924, NWTUL papers, Box 21, LC.
80. International Federation of Working Women, "Memorandum from the International Federation of Working Women to the International Federation of Trade Unions," n.d., IFWW papers, f. 6.
81. International Federation of Trade Unions, "International Conference of Women Trade Unionists," *Report of IFTU Activities* (Amsterdam, 1924), 175.
82. Ibid., 174, 178.
83. National Women's Trade Union League, "Proceedings of the 1924 Convention," 92-98, NWTUL papers, LC.
84. See Elisabeth Christman to Edith McDonald, July 12, 1924, NWTUL papers, Box 3, LC.
85. McDonald to Christman, June 8, 1924, NWTUL papers, Box 3, LC.
86. John Price, *The International Labor Movement* (London, 1945), 67.
87. Anderson, *Woman at Work*, 133.

Bibliography

PRIMARY SOURCES

Manuscript Collections—American

Anderson, Mary. Collected papers. Schlesinger Library, Radcliffe College, Cambridge, Massachusetts.

Catt, Carrie Chapman. Collected papers. Manuscripts Division, Library of Congress, Washington, D.C.

International Federation of Working Women. Official Records. Schlesinger Library, Radcliffe College, Cambridge, Massachusetts.

National American Woman Suffrage Association. Collected papers. Manuscripts Division, Library of Congress, Washington, D.C.

National Women's Trade Union League. Collected papers (includes official records, correspondence, convention proceedings, and papers of the International Federation of Working Women). Manuscripts Division, Library of Congress, Washington, D.C.

_____. Collected papers. Schlesinger Library, Radcliffe College, Cambridge, Massachusetts.

Nestor, Agnes. Collected papers. Chicago Historical Society, Chicago, Illinois.

O'Reilly, Leonora. Collected papers. Schlesinger Library, Radcliffe College, Cambridge, Massachusetts.

Robins, Margaret Dreier. Collected papers. University of Florida, Gainesville, Florida.

Schneiderman, Rose. Collected papers. Tamiment Institute Library, New York University, New York, New York.

Manuscript Collections—British

Autograph Collection: Suffrage and Women in Industry. The Fawcett Library, London.
Macdonald, Margaret. Collected papers. London School of Economics, London.
Tuckwell, Gertrude. Collected papers. Trades Union Congress Library, London.
Webb, Beatrice. Collected papers. London School of Economics, London.
Women's Labour League. Collected papers. Labour Party Library, London.
Women's Social and Political Union. Collected papers. London Museum Library, London.
Women's Trade Union League. Collected papers. Trades Union Congress Library, London.

Publications of the Women's Trade Union Leagues— American Serials

National Women's Trade Union League. *Life and Labor*, 1911-1921.
_____. *Life and Labor Bulletin*, 1922-1932.
_____. "Woman's Department." In *Union Labor Advocate*, 1904-1910.

Pamphlets

Boston Women's Trade Union League. *The Case for Trades Unions*. Boston, 1920.
Dalzell, Ruth. *The Early History of Women Trade Unionists of America*. Chicago, 1914.
National Women's Trade Union League. *Convention Handbook*. Chicago, 1909.
_____. *The Eight-Hour Day for Women*. Chicago, 1915.
_____. *English Women in the Labor and Co-operative Movements*. Chicago, 1919.
_____. *The Forty-Eight-Hour Week for Women*. Chicago, 1917.
_____. *How to Organize: A Problem*. Chicago, 1929.
_____. *The International Federation of Working Women*. Chicago, 1921.

_____. *Protective Legislation in Danger: Trade Union Women Oppose Blanket Amendment*. Chicago, 1922.

_____. *Resolutions Adopted by First International Congress of Working Women*. Chicago, 1919.

_____. *Some Facts Regarding Unorganized Working Women in the Sweated Industries*. Chicago, 1914.

_____. *Twenty-Fifth Anniversary Program*. Chicago, 1929.

_____. *The Voice of Labor*. Chicago, 1919.

_____. *Why Labor Laws for Women?* Chicago, 1923.

_____. *Women and Reconstruction*. Chicago, 1918.

_____. *Women in Trade Unions in the United States*. Chicago, 1920.

Nestor, Agnes. *The Trend of Legislation Affecting Women's Hours of Labor*. Chicago, 1917.

Pike, Violet. *New World Lessons for Old World People*. Chicago, n.d.

Robins, Margaret Dreier. *Margaret Dreier Robins to the Enfranchised Women of the United States*. Chicago, 1916.

Smith, Ethel M. *Equal Rights and "Equal Rights": What is Wrong with the Woman's Party Amendment*. Chicago, 1924.

Publications of the Women's Trade Union Leagues— British Serials

National Federation of Women Workers. *Woman Worker*, 1907-1910; 1916-1921 (ceased publication 1911-1915).

Women's Protective and Provident League. *Women's Union Journal*, 1876-1890.

Women's Trade Union League. *Annual Reports*. London, 1875-1921.

_____. *Women's Trades Union Review*, 1891-1919.

Pamphlets

Dilke, Emilia F.S. *The Industrial Position of Women*. London, n.d.

Women's Trade Union League. *Factory and Workshop Legislation*. London, 1901.

Women's Trade Union League and Women's Labour League. *Women's Labour Day Souvenir Booklet*. London, 1909.

Government Publications—United States

U.S. Congress. Senate. *Report on Condition of Woman and Child Wage-Earners.* "History of Women in Industry in the United States" by Helen L. Sumner. Vol. 9. S. Doc. 645, 61st Cong., 2nd sess., 1910.

——. *Report on Condition of Woman and Child Wage-Earners.* "History of Women in Trade Unions" by John B. Andrews and W. D. P. Bliss. Vol. 10. S. Doc. 645, 61st Cong., 2nd sess., 1911.

U.S. Department of Labor. Women's Bureau. *Chronological Development of Labor Legislation for Women in the United States* by Florence P. Smith. Bulletin no. 66-II. Washington, D.C., 1932.

——. *The Development of Minimum-Wage Laws in the United States, 1912-1927.* Bulletin no. 61. Washington, D.C., 1928.

——. *The Effects of Labor Legislation on the Employment Opportunities of Women.* Bulletin no. 65. Washington, D.C., 1928.

——. *The Industrial Experience of Women Workers at the Summer Schools, 1928-1930* by Gladys L. Palmer. Bulletin no. 89. Washington, D.C., 1931.

——. *Proceedings of the Women's Industrial Conference.* Bulletin no. 33. Washington, D.C., 1923.

Government Publications—Great Britain

Great Britain. Parliament. *Parliamentary Papers* (Commons), *1907.* Vol. 6 (Reports). "Report of the Select Committee on Home Work."

——. *Parliamentary Papers* (Commons), *1914-1916.* Vol. 61 (Accounts and Papers). Cmnd. 7733, "Seventeenth Abstract of Labour Statistics of the United Kingdom."

——. *Parliamentary Papers* (Commons), *1926.* Vol. 29 (Accounts and Papers). Cmnd. 2740, "Eighteenth Abstract of Labour Statistics of the United Kingdom."

Works by Participants—American

Anderson, Mary, with Mary Winslow. *Woman at Work: The Autobiography of Mary Anderson.* Minneapolis, 1951.

Barnum, Gertrude. "Women in the American Labor Movement." *American Federationist* 22 (September 1915): 731-33.

Christman, Elisabeth. Interview, July 27, 1971, Washington, D.C.

Dreier, Mary E. *Margaret Dreier Robins: Her Life, Letters, and Work.* New York, 1950.

Henry, Alice. *The Trade Union Woman.* New York, 1915.

_____. *Women and the Labor Movement.* New York, 1923.

Hill, Helen D. *The Effect of the Bryn Mawr Summer School as Measured in Activities of its Students.* New York, 1929.

Leslie, Mabel. "An Adventure in Education." *American Federationist* 34 (April 1927): 436-38.

McDowell, Mary. "The National Women's Trade Union League." *Survey* 23 (October 16, 1909): 101-7.

Nestor, Agnes. *Woman's Labor Leader: An Autobiography.* Rockford, Ill., 1954.

O'Reilly, Leonora. "To All Organized Working Men." *American Federationist* 22 (October 1915): 848-49.

Robins, Margaret Dreier. "Freedom Through Organization." *American Federationist* 22 (September 1915): 727-29.

Schneiderman, Rose, with Lucy Goldthwaite. *All for One.* New York, 1967.

Scott, Melinda. "The Way to Freedom." *American Federationist* 22 (September 1915): 729-31.

Works by Participants—British

Black, Clementina. "The Coming Factory Act." *Contemporary Review* 59 (May 1891): 710-17.

Dilke, Emilia F. S. *The Book of the Spiritual Life with a Memoir of the Author by the Right Honorable Sir Charles Dilke.* New York, 1905.

_____. "Trades Unionism among Women." *Fortnightly Review* (May 1891): 741-46.

_____. "Trades-Unions for Women." *North American Review* (August 1891): 227-39.

Jones, Nora. Interview, June 20, 1972, London.

Phillips, Marion. "The Aims and Constitution of the International Federation of Working Women." *Canadian Congress Journal* 1 (August 1922): 436-38.

_____. *Women and the Labour Party*. New York, 1918.

Tuckwell, Gertrude, ed. *Women in Industry from Seven Points of View*. London, 1908.

Related Contemporary Publications—American

Abbott, Edith. *Women in Industry: A Study in American Economic History*. New York, 1910.

American Federation of Labor. *Report of the Proceedings of the Convention of the American Federation of Labor*. Washington, D.C., 1909, 1919-1925.

Brandeis, Louis D. *Women in Industry*. New York, 1908; reprint ed., New York, 1969.

Dorr, Rheta Childe. *What Eight Million Women Want*. Boston, 1910.

Gompers, Samuel. "The American Labor Movement." *American Federationist* 21 (July 1914): 537-48.

_____. "Coming Into Her Own." *American Federationist* 22 (July 1915): 517-19.

_____. *Seventy Years of Life and Labor*. New York, 1925.

_____. "Woman's Work, Rights and Progress." *American Federationist* 20 (August 1913): 624-27.

Hasanovitz, Elizabeth. *One of Them: Chapters from a Passionate Autobiography*. Boston, 1917.

Herron, Belva Mary. *The Progress of Labor Organization Among Women, Together with Some Considerations Concerning Their Place in Industry*. Urbana, 1905.

Kelley, Florence. *Modern Industry in Relation to the Family Health, Education, Morality*. New York, 1914.

Malkiel, Theresa. *The Diary of a Shirtwaist Striker*. New York, 1910.

Marot, Helen. *American Labor Unions*. New York, 1914.

Miller, Spencer. "Summer Schools for Workers." *American Federationist* 32 (July 1925): 569-71.

Richardson, Dorothy. *The Long Day: The Story of a New York Working Girl*. New York, 1905.

Smith, Hilda W. *Women Workers at the Bryn Mawr Summer School*. New York, 1929.

Willett, Mabel H. *The Employment of Women in the Clothing Trade.* Columbia University Studies in History, Economics, and Public Law, Vol. 16, No. 2. New York, 1902.

Related Contemporary Publications—British

Boucherett, E. J. *The Fall in Women's Wages.* London, 1898.
Bulley, Agnes, and Margaret Whitley. *Women's Work.* Preface by Emilia F. S. Dilke. London, 1894.
Collier, D. J. *The Girl in Industry.* London, 1918.
Committee of the Society for Promoting the Employment of Women. *Factory and Workshops Bill.* London, 1894.
Drake, Barbara. *Women in Trade Unions.* London, 1920.
Freedom of Labour Defense League. *First Annual Report.* London, 1895.
Hall, Leonard. *The Old and New Unionism.* Manchester, 1894.
Trades Union Congress. *Proceedings of the 1908 Trades Union Congress.* London, 1908.
Webb, Beatrice. *Beatrice Webb's Diaries, 1912-1924.* Edited by Margaret Cole. London, 1952.
_____. *Beatrice Webb's Diaries, 1924-1932.* London, 1956.
Webb, Beatrice, ed., *The Case for the Factory Acts.* London, 1902.
Women's Co-operative Guild. *Votes for Which Women?* London, n.d.
_____. *Why Women Should Have the Vote.* Kirkby Lonsdale, Westmoreland, n.d.
Women's Freedom League. *Verbatim Report of Debate on December 3, 1907: Sex Equality (Teresa Billington-Grieg) Versus Adult Suffrage (Margaret Bondfield).* Manchester, 1908.
Women's Labour League. *Annual Reports.* London, 1911-1925.
_____. *The Labour Woman,* 1913-1936.

Related Contemporary Publications—International

International Federation of Trade Unions. *The Activities of the International Federation of Trade Unions, 1933-1935 and Minutes of the London Congress, 1936.* Paris, 1937.

_____. "International Conference of Women Trade Unionists." In *Report of IFTU Activities*, 173-78. Amsterdam, 1924.

_____. *The International Trade Union Movement, 1921-1939.*

_____. *Report of the International Federation of Trade Unions Congress.* Amsterdam, 1922.

_____. *Yearbook.* Amsterdam, 1922, 1924-1927, 1930; Paris, 1934, 1938.

International Federation of Working Women. *Working Women in Many Countries: Report of Congress Held at Vienna, August 1923.* Amsterdam, 1923.

League of Nations. *International Labor Conference: First Annual Meeting, October 29-November 29, 1919.* Washington, D.C., 1920.

Oudegeest, J. "The International Trade Union Movement and the Labour Office." *International Labour Review* 1 (January 1921): 41-44.

SECONDARY SOURCES

Women and Labor in the United States

Baker, Elizabeth Faulkner. *Protective Labor Legislation.* Columbia University Studies in History, Economics, and Public Law. Vol. 116, No. 2. New York, 1925.

_____. *Technology and Woman's Work.* New York, 1964.

Boone, Gladys. *The Women's Trade Union Leagues of Great Britain and the United States of America.* New York, 1942.

Bullard, Arthur [Albert Edward]. *Comrade Yetta.* New York, 1913.

Carroll, Mollie Ray. *Labor and Politics: The Attitude of the American Federation of Labor Toward Legislation and Politics.* Boston, 1923.

Chafe, William H. *The American Woman: Her Changing Social, Economic, and Political Roles, 1920-1970.* New York, 1972.

Conway, Jill. "Women Reformers and American Culture, 1870-1930." *Journal of Social History* 5 (Winter 1971-72): 164-78.

Davis, Allen. *Spearheads for Reform: The Social Settlements and the Progressive Movement, 1890-1914.* New York, 1967.

_____. "The Women's Trade Union League: Origins and Organization." *Labor History* 5 (Winter 1964): 3-17.

Dick, William M. *Labor and Socialism in America: The Gompers Era.* Port Washington, N.Y., 1972.

Dye, Nancy Schrom. "Feminism or Unionism: The New York Women's Trade Union League and the Labor Movement." *Feminist Studies* 3 (Fall 1975): 111-25.

_____. "Sisterhood and Class Conflict in the New York Women's Trade Union League." *Feminist Studies* 2, no. 2/3 (1975): 24-38.

_____. "The Women's Trade Union League of New York, 1903-1920." Ph.D. dissertation, University of Wisconsin, 1974.

Encyclopedia of the Social Sciences, 1935. S.v. "Women's Organizations," by Gladys Meyerand.

Goldmark, Josephine. *Impatient Crusader: Florence Kelley's Life Story*. Urbana, 1953.

Greenbaum, Fred. "The Social Ideas of Samuel Gompers." *Labor History* 7 (Winter 1966): 35-61.

Jacoby, Robin Miller. "Elisabeth Christman." In *Notable American Women: The Modern Period*, 148-50. Edited by Barbara Sicherman and Carol H. Green. Cambridge, 1980.

_____. "Feminism and Class Consciousness in the British and American Women's Trade Union Leagues, 1890-1925." In *Liberating Women's History: Theoretical and Critical Essays*, 137-60. Edited by Berenice A. Carroll. Urbana, 1976.

_____. "The Women's Trade Union League" and "An Annotated Bibliography of the Women's Trade Union League." In *Papers of the Women's Trade Union League and Its Principal Leaders: Guide to the Microfilm Edition*, 19-58. Edited by Edward James. Woodbridge, Conn., 1981.

_____. "The Women's Trade Union League and American Feminism." *Feminist Studies* 3 (Fall 1975): 126-40. Reprinted in *Sex, Class, and the Woman Worker*, 203-24. Edited by Milton Cantor and Bruce Laurie. Westport, Conn., 1976.

_____. "The Women's Trade Union League Training School for Women Organizers." In *Sisterhood and Solidarity: Education Programs for Women Workers, 1914-1984*, 3-35. Edited by Joyce Kornbluh and Mary Frederickson. Philadelphia, 1984.

Kenneally, James. "Women and Trade Unions, 1870-1920." *Labor History* 14 (Winter 1973): 42-55.

Kessler-Harris, Alice. "Organizing the Unorganizable: Three Jewish Women and Their Union." *Labor History* 17 (Winter 1976): 5-23.

_____. " 'Where Are the Unorganized Women Workers?' " *Feminist Studies* 3 (Fall 1975): 92-110.

Kraditor, Aileen S. *The Ideas of the Woman Suffrage Movement, 1890-1920.* New York, 1965.

Kraditor, Aileen S., ed. *Up from the Pedestal: Selected Writings in the History of American Feminism.* Chicago, 1968.

Laslett, John. *Labor and the Left.* New York, 1970.

Lemons, J. Stanley. "Social Feminism in the 1920s: Progressive Women and Industrial Legislation." *Labor History* 14 (Winter 1973): 83-91.

_____. *The Woman Citizen: Social Feminism in the 1920s.* Urbana, 1973.

Lerner, Gerda. "The Lady and the Mill Girl: Changes in the Status of Women in the Age of Jackson." *Mid-Continent American Studies Journal* 10 (Spring 1969) 5-15.

Levine, Louis. *The Woman Garment Workers: A History of the International Ladies' Garment Workers' Union.* New York, 1924.

Nathan, Maud. *Once Upon a Time and Today.* New York, 1933.

_____. *The Story of an Epoch-Making Movement.* New York, 1926.

Notable American Women. S.v. "Henry, Alice," by Frederick D. Kershner, Jr.

_____. S.v. "Kehew, Mary Morton," by Robert Sklar.

_____. S.v. "McDowell, Mary," by Louise C. Wade.

_____. S.v. "Nestor, Agnes," by Clarke A. Chambers.

_____. S.v. "O'Reilly, Leonora," by Charles Shively.

_____. S.v. "O'Sullivan, Mary Kenney," by Eleanor Flexner and Janet Wilson James.

_____. S.v. "Robins, Margaret Dreier," by Allen Davis.

_____. S.v. "Wald, Lillian," by Robert Bremner.

O'Neill, William L. *Everyone Was Brave: The Rise and Fall of Feminism in America.* Chicago, 1969.

O'Neill, William L., ed. *The Woman Movement: Feminism in the United States and England.* Chicago, 1971.

Pleck, Elizabeth. "Two Worlds in One: Work and Family." *Journal of Social History* 10 (Winter 1976): 178-95.

Reed, Louis A. *The Labor Philosophy of Samuel Gompers.* New York, 1930; reprint ed., Port Washington, N.Y., 1966.

Starr, Mark. *Workers' Education Today.* New York, 1941.

Stein, Leon. *The Triangle Fire.* Philadelphia, 1967.

U.S. Department of Commerce. Bureau of the Census. *Women in Gainful Occupations, 1870-1920* by Joseph A. Hill. Census Monographs IX. Washington, D.C., 1929.

U.S. Department of Labor. Women's Bureau. *Toward Better Working Conditions for Women: Methods and Policies of the National Women's Trade Union League*. Bulletin no. 252. Washington, D.C., 1953.

_____. *Women's Occupations Through Seven Decades* by Janet M. Hooks. Bulletin no. 218. Washington, D.C., 1947.

Welter, Barbara. "The Cult of True Womanhood, 1820-1860." *American Quarterly* 18 (Summer 1966): 151-74.

Wolfson, Theresa. *The Woman Worker and the Trade Unions*. New York, 1926.

Wolman, Leo. *The Growth of American Trade Unions 1880-1923*. New York, 1924.

Yans-McLaughlin, Virginia. "Italian Women and Work: Experience and Perception." Unpublished paper, 1974.

_____. "Patterns of Work and Family Organization: Buffalo's Italians." *Journal of Interdisciplinary History* 2 (Autumn 1971): 299-314.

Women and Labor in Great Britain

Askwith, Betty. *Lady Dilke: A Biography*. London, 1969.

Citrine, Walter M. *The Trade Union Movement of Great Britain*. Amsterdam, 1926.

Cole, Margaret. *Beatrice Webb*. London, 1945.

Goldman, Harold. *Emma Paterson*. London, 1974.

Gwynn, Stephen, with Gertrude Tuckwell. *The Life of the Right Honorable Sir Charles Dilke*. London, 1917.

Hamilton, Mary Agnes. *Margaret Bondfield*. London, 1924.

_____. *Mary Macarthur: A Biographical Sketch*. London, 1925.

Hewitt, Margaret. *Wives and Mothers in Victorian Industry*. London, 1958.

Hutchins, B.L. *Women in Modern Industry*. London, 1915.

Hutchins, B.L., and A. Harrison. *A History of Factory Legislation*. London, 1903.

Jenkins, Roy. *Sir Charles Dilke: A Victorian Tragedy*. London, 1965.

Lewenhak, Sheila T. "Trade Union Membership among Women and Girls in the United Kingdom, 1920-1965." Ph.D. dissertation, London School of Economics, 1971.

Markham, Violet R. *May Tennant: A Portrait*. London, 1949.

Neale, R. S. "Working-Class Women and Women's Suffrage." In *Class and Ideology in the Nineteenth Century*, 143-68. London, 1972.

Pankhurst, E. Syliva. *The Suffragette Movement: An Intimate Account of Persons and Ideals*. London, 1931.

Pelling, Henry. *A History of British Trade Unionism*. London, 1963.

Pinchbeck, Ivy. *Women Workers and the Industrial Revolution, 1750-1850*. London, 1930.

Ramelson, Marian. *The Petticoat Rebellion: A Century of Struggle for Women's Rights*. London, 1967.

Roberts, B. C. *The Trades Union Congress, 1868-1921*. London, 1958.

Rover, Constance. *Women's Suffrage and Party Politics in Britain, 1866-1914*. London, 1967.

Strachey, Ray. *"The Cause": A Short History of the Women's Movement in Great Britain*. London, 1928.

_____. *Millicent Garrett Fawcett*. London, 1931.

Trades Union Congress. *The History of the Trades Union Congress, 1868-1968*. London, 1968.

U.S. Department of Commerce and Labor. Bureau of Labor. *The Women's Trade Union Movement in Great Britain* by Katherine Graves Busbey. Bulletin no. 83. Washington, D.C., 1909.

General Works

Bairoch, P. *The Working Population and Its Structure*. Brussels, 1968.

Bebel, August. *Woman under Socialism*. Translated by Daniel De Leon. New York, 1904.

Butler, David, and Jennie Freeman. *British Political Facts, 1900-1968*. 3rd ed. London, 1969.

Engels, Frederick. *The Origin of the Family, Private Property, and the State*. London, 1940.

Lorwin, Lewis L. *The International Labor Movement: History, Politics, Outlook*. New York, 1953.

_____. *Labor and Internationalism*. New York, 1929.

Mitchell, B. R., and Phyllis Deane. *Abstract of British Historical Statistics*. University of Cambridge, Department of Applied Economics, Monographs, no. 17. Cambridge, 1971.

Mitchell, Juliet. *Woman's Estate*. New York, 1973.

Price, John. *The International Labor Movement*. London, 1945.

Rowbotham, Shelia. *Women, Resistance, and Revolution: A History of Women and Revolution in the Modern World*. New York, 1972.

Schevenels, Walter. *Forty-Five Years: A Historical Precis of the International Federation of Trade Unions*. Brussels, 1956.

Thelan, David. *The New Citizenship*. Columbia, Mo., 1972.

Weinstein, James. *The Corporate Ideal in the Liberal State*. Boston, 1968.

Wiebe, Robert. *The Search for Order, 1877-1920*. New York, 1967.

Index

Pike, Violet
  and American WTUL, 51-55
Pinchot, Cornelia Bryce
  and American WTUL, 142
"The Position of Women and How to
    Improve It" (Emma Smith Paterson), 10
Potter, Francis Squire
  and American WTUL, 83
Pratt, Hodgson
  and Women's Protective and Provident
    League, 10
*Private Woman, Public Person: An Account of
    the Life of Julia Ward Howe from 1819 to
    1868* (Mary Grant), xvi
"Put to the Proof" (*Woman Worker*), 40-41

Robins, Margaret Dreier
  and American WTUL, 16, 21, 25-27, 46-
    49, 71, 73-74, 79, 84, 86, 123, 128,
    130, 138, 141-42, 151, 157
  and international labor, 157, 160-61, 164,
    168-74, 182, 185
  marriage of, 16
  and Training School for Women
    Organizers, 55-67
Roosevelt, Eleanor
  as member of American WTUL, 72-73
Roosevelt, Franklin
  and New Deal, 138
Roosevelt, Theodore
  and labor legislation, 131
Roth, Darlene, xv

Sassenbach, Johann
  and international labor, 184
Schneiderman, Rose
  and American WTUL, 5, 26, 30, 31-32,
    71, 73, 83, 85, 119, 125, 141-42, 150
Scott, Anne Firor, xii, xiv
Scott, Melinda
  and American WTUL, 56, 59
Scudder, Vida
  and AFL, 14-15
Settlement house movement
  and influence on women's labor move-
    ment, 13-14
  and publications, 51
Shipton, George
  and Women's Protective and Provident
    League, 10

Shirtwaist strike (New York)
  and American WTUL, 85
Sitch, C. H.
  as labor negotiator, 103
Sklar, Kathryn Kish, xi
Slavery, xiv-xv
Smith, Alexia
  and American WTUL, 64
Smith, Constance
  and British WTUL, 101
Smith, Emma
  See Peterson, Emma Smith
Smith, Ethel
  and American WTUL, 135-37, 143
Social Democratic Federation, 98
Society for Promoting the Employment of
    Women
  and British legislation, 94
Sources for Women's History, xi-xiii
Spider Web Chart
  as device to attack womens' groups, 137-
    38
Spruill, Julia, xv
Standing Joint Committee of Women's
    Industrial Organizations
  as coalition for working-class women,
    112-14, 114-17, 134-35, 156, 158-59,
    162
Status of Women in Georgia, 1783-1860
    (Eleanor Miot Boatwright), xiv-xv
Steinschneider, Janice, xviii
Sullivan, Rose
  and Training School for Women
    Organizers, 60
Sutherland, George, 143
Swartz, Maud
  and labor organizations, 157, 164, 171,
    174

Tarbell, Ida, xvi
Thomas, Albert
  and IFWW, 161
Times (London)
  issues of women in, 111
Trades Union Congresses (TUC)
  discussion of women's involvement in, 10,
    21, 33, 69-70, 74-75, 78, 90-92, 104,
    117-18, 162
  integration of British WTUL into, 118